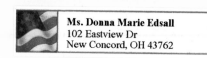

Ms. Donna Marie Edsall
102 Eastview Dr
New Concord, OH 43762

D1111384

HATING AMERICA

HOST OF FOX NEW CHANNEL'S *THE BIG STORY*

JOHN GIBSON

HATING AMERICA
THE NEW WORLD SPORT

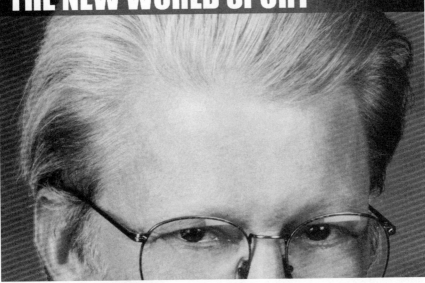

Regan Books
Celebrating Ten Bestselling Years

An Imprint of HarperCollins*Publishers*

FIRST EDITION

Designed by Publications Development Company of Texas.

Printed on acid-free paper

Library of Congress Cataloging-in-Publication Data has been applied for.

ISBN 0-06-058010-0

04 05 06 07 08   PDC/RRD   10 9 8 7 6 5 4 3 2 1

To the two people most important—
my wife, Susan, and my son, Jake.

CONTENTS

HATING AMERICA

INTRODUCTION

MOHAMMED ATTA VS. MY FRIEND ROY

MY FRIEND ROY BOUGHT me a drink tonight. He promised to call a friend and help me to get an upgrade at a hotel where I had reservations—the kind of small, thoughtful gesture friends often make toward friends. My friend Roy is in the prime of life. He and his wife Alison are a beautiful couple. They live in Jersey City; he works in lower Manhattan as an IT guy in the Wall Street/Lower Manhattan financial district.

On the night of September 10, 2001, Roy and another friend J.R. were drinking at a Jersey City bar and restaurant two blocks west of the Hudson River. They stayed out late, maybe drank a bit too much, but they promised each other they would meet on the 8 A.M. ferry from Colgate dock the next morning, crossing the Hudson River to the World Financial Center.

Though he was hung over, J.R. made it to the 8 A.M. boat. Roy did not. J.R. remembers thinking, "The guy said he was going to be here. He must've got more sideways than I thought."

1

Roy also missed the 8:15 A.M. ferry, but caught the 8:30. He was crossing the Hudson for an appointment on the 101st floor of the World Trade Center, North Tower, at Windows on the World. His appointment was for a breakfast meeting at 8:30 A.M., and he was late.

Roy hurried off the boat, crossed West Street, and entered the building. He took the elevator to the sky lobby on the seventy-eighth floor, where he transferred to the next bank of elevators that would carry him to the 101st.

At 8:46 A.M. Roy was sixteen minutes late, but only twenty-three floors away. At almost the instant the elevator doors closed to take him up to the top of the World Trade Center, the first hijacked airliner, American Airlines Flight 11 from Boston, struck the North Tower sixteen floors above. The elevator shuddered and lurched, then stopped; then the doors opened—no more than eighteen inches, in Roy's estimation—and he jumped out, his clothes soaked in jet fuel, and on fire. One woman in the crowded elevator saw him jump, and she darted through the door right behind him. Later she told friends, "He ran like a deer, and I followed." She hesitated no more than a second, or a fraction of one, yet she wasn't quick enough to avoid the flames shooting down the elevator shaft from the impact zone above. A blast of flame followed her through the small opening of the door, and she suffered severe burns. The doors remained open, and the people left inside were incinerated.

Roy and the woman who followed him then dashed through the elevator lobby, the so-called Sky Lobby on the seventy-eighth floor, as flames shot through the cracks of the doors in the huge bank of elevators. Roy stumbled through an open door, his clothes still burning. A Port Authority security man patted out the flames, but Roy suffered second- and third-degree burns on his arms and face.

Roy made it down the stairwell quicker than he might have expected: he and the woman who had followed him through the elevator doors were both visibly burned, and the uninjured evacuees, calmly but urgently walking down the stairs from the floors below the impact, let them pass.

In the time it took to walk down seventy-eight floors, the South Tower was struck by the second hijacked airliner—United Airlines Flight 175 from Boston—at 9:03 A.M.

In the tumult and chaos of the ground floor, Roy and the woman were triaged by emergency medical workers and sent in different ambulances to nearby hospitals. Thousands of people were on the streets running from the two burning towers.

Roy wound up in an ambulance awaiting orders a few blocks away, where he was given treatment. The ambulance driver received a call to turn around and go pick up some seriously injured people in the plaza in front of the South Tower.

Roy said to the driver, "One of the firemen told me the building isn't sound."

The driver said he was going. Roy got out of the ambulance, to make his own way north from the towers. The ambulance turned back south on West Street—and disappeared into a cascade of concrete as the South Tower collapsed, fifty-six minutes after it had been struck.

The North Tower was hit first, but stood a little longer. One hour and forty-two minutes after the first airliner knifed into the building between the ninety-fourth and ninety-eighth floors, it collapsed.

Roy made his way to St. Vincent's Hospital, where he was treated for his burns. His face had been torched as if by an atomizer of flame: the first layer of skin on his face was fried to a crisp, but the lower layers were unharmed. He was the first patient to be released from St. Vincent's from the attack of September 11.

My friend Roy was almost killed, twice, by Mohammed Atta.

After a few weeks, he recovered with no visible scars. Today Roy is still alive, buying me a drink, having dinner with a client, hanging out with friends in Jersey City and New York, enjoying life.

As far as Atta and his fellow terrorists were concerned, things weren't supposed to turn out that way. My friend Roy was supposed to be dead—twice.

SEE ROY FAIRLY OFTEN, and I am constantly reminded that the attacks of September 11 were designed to kill him—or almost anyone else, including me and you.

I take the New York Waterways ferry from Colgate in Jersey City to the World Financial Center with some frequency. At the foot of Grand Street, in view of where the towers stood for thirty years, is a monument of a few feet of twisted steel, bearing the engraved names of the people who died from Jersey City. They were commuters who crossed the river each morning on an easy and convenient ferry. They walked a block to the Trade Center towers, rode elevators to their offices, did their work. If they were lucky or successful or both, their offices might have had a sliver of a view out the towers' narrow windows.

Their crime—Roy's crime, too, though he avoided punishment— was going to work that morning.

Roy's salvation was that he stayed out late, overslept fifteen minutes, missed two ferries, and when the first plane hit was still far enough away to escape with his life. His story is like that of many other survivors: Theirs were the closest of close calls.

The terrorists' intention was that those survivors should all die. Many thousands escaped, but 2,752 died, including some two hundred who plummeted from the upper stories of the first tower hit (according to *USA Today*), having confronted the instant and wrenching decision to stay and face the flames, or jump one hundred stories. Either way, death was certain. The choice involved a calculation of pain.

The pictures of people falling to the streets were some of the most devastating images of that entire horrific hour. They were in their business clothes; they had planned ordinary days. One picture the *New York Times* published of a falling person was of a black man, falling upside down, his business suit in tatters, appearing strangely calm and accepting. Ric Burns's three-hour documentary *The Center of the World* showed a startling number of those freefall victims: ordinary people, tried and convicted in absentia by theocratic plotters in far-off lands, who died in the most horrifying of ways. As Tom Brokaw noted shortly after 9/11, the television networks were reluctant to show precisely how awful the attack was; rather than sensationalize the attack, they "sanitized" the day in deference to the perceived sensibilities of the families and the American public.

When I arrive on the Manhattan side of the river, I walk east on Vesey Street, along a narrow path that has taken the name World Trade Center Walk. It crosses the distance from West Street to Church Street, along the north side of what was the Trade Center. Now that the cleanup is long over, workmen are preparing the site for whatever will be built to take the Center's place.

People come from around the world to linger on the World Trade Center Walk. They stand on Church Street in front of the centuries-old stone church (which improbably survived its proximity to the cataclysm), looking at something that is no longer there. They gaze upward at towers that are gone, staring through the construction fence at a deep hole in the ground. They stand and marvel.

I got into the city just after noon on September 11, making a mad dash from western New Jersey to get to work at the Fox News Channel. I crossed the Hudson by ferry. The Weehawken line was evacuating people from the city, and the captains were ordered to refuse passengers going into New York: The city was closed, and they didn't want to waste time loading passengers for a return trip. Everybody out, nobody in.

I wheedled my way onto the boat, nonetheless, and hid in the ladies' room until we shoved off, in case the man who waved me on was countermanded by someone with superior authority.

When we were underway, I came on deck. Four hours after the collapse of both towers, lower Manhattan was a towering thundercloud of smoke, boiling and rolling into the sky. The stunned crewmen were gazing into the smoke. I asked one what he had seen. He said they were crossing over to Jersey when the first plane hit, and they were coming back to New York when the buildings came down.

He felt attacked. So did I, as did thousands and thousands of New Yorkers and Washingtonians. This was a war waged on civilians: the fulfillment of Osama bin Laden's 1998 *fatwa,* which proclaimed American civilians legitimate targets of his Islamist war on the United States. In early September 2003, that same *fatwa* was re-issued under bin Laden's name.

As an attack on the U.S. government, as we soon realized this was, 9/11 was only partially successful. The real intention was to execute a decapitation attack on America's leaders in the nation's capitol. They hit Donald Rumsfeld's building, but weren't lucky enough to strike precisely the right spot, and he survived. The president was in Florida, but it's questionable whether the hijackers paid much attention to his schedule. They wanted to hit him, and for that they evidently targeted the White House. They also wanted to hit the Capitol dome, to rain fire down upon the houses of Congress. We know that one plane destined for either the White House or the Capitol was brought down short, in Pennsylvania, and some experts think that yet another hijacking plan, destined for the second of the primary targets in Washington, D.C., was aborted when the plane was late in taking off.

This potential five-airliner attack succeeded in hitting three targets, failing to accomplish attacks on two others. A 60 percent success that left nearly three thousand dead, the Pentagon on fire, smoldering bodies strewn over America's dual capitals—al Qaeda had a good day.

I did not, and no one else who works and lives in America did either.

Unquestionably, the continued threat of terrorism is felt most strongly by people in the Northeast, which has been a continuing terrorist target. People in Los Angeles or San Francisco may feel less threatened, but all Americans recognized that their country was under attack on September 11, and that their lives were at risk. Every single commercial airliner was grounded instantly, on the quite reasonable fear that more hijackers may have been waiting for the right moment to take over more airliners. The airliners that were actually hijacked had been destined for San Francisco and Los Angeles. The impact was felt from coast to coast.

I am from the West. I spent my first five decades in California, a native-born, state-educated, Los Angeles- and San Francisco-employed Californian through and through. I came to the East just before my fiftieth birthday, and by September 11, 2001, I had spent a total of six years living on the East Coast.

I had fewer anguished connections to the victims than all those New York families whose husbands, wives, brothers, sons, sisters, daughters, and grandkids worked in the Towers, or were firefighters, emergency workers, or cops who rushed to help, and didn't come home. The attacks in New York reminded us of the city's generations-long connections to the Irish and Italians and Puerto Ricans and African Americans who made up the New York Fire Department, the men who were still marching up the staircases to save people when the buildings came down. In those families, the attacks drove a stake through generations, and the grief and damage was unfathomably deep and raw.

I was just a guy who'd moved East. Had a few friends. Learned my way around. Had no particular New York loyalties (*Go Yanks!*). I just happened to be in the area because New York is the headquarters of my industry, the news business. But even newcomers and late arrivals felt the threat. They tried to kill us all. And they got a substantial number.

MY FRIEND ROY BUYS me a drink. I buy him a drink. We say, "See ya later." I will see him tomorrow. He's supposed to be dead; they came close to making him number 2,753. Roy and the woman who followed him out of the elevator would have increased the total by two. But they got away.

That day—and the days that followed, which saw the arrests of hundreds of suspected al Qaeda supporters—shaped my attitude about the president's policy of preemptive war, and the Justice Department sweeps here at home. I am not a supporter of Bush; I am a *driver* of Bush. *Do more,* I think. *Do it soon.*

Likewise, nobody had to stir the pot for me on Saddam Hussein. He was always a threat to America, every bit as determined as al Qaeda and considerably more clever and sly. The mud-hut war of Afghanistan had to happen, but no one I know thought the end of the Taliban was the end of the War on Terror. I have believed for years that a man like Saddam, who ran a state where terrorists could get money, weapons, state protection, travel documents, and training centers to attack America, would ultimately have to go.

To me, and many Americans, it was as obvious as the hole in the ground in lower Manhattan.

The 2004 Democratic presidential candidates and their supporters, with their allies in anti-American Europe, have shouted themselves hoarse that there was no connection between Saddam Hussein and al Qaeda and the September 11 attacks.

The American who knew al Qaeda best—and who held the position of chief federal agent specializing in Osama bin Laden and al Qaeda—has spoken from the grave saying otherwise. John P. O'Neill had left his job as head of the FBI's counter terrorism office, and was two weeks into his new position as head of security at New York's World Trade Center, when he died in the collapse of the North Tower, killed by the very terrorists and al Qaeda plotters he had pursued for a decade with the FBI.

Two weeks before the second anniversary of the attack, the family of John O'Neill filed a lawsuit in the U.S. District Court, District of Columbia, seeking a billion dollars in damages from the frozen assets of the government of Iraq, al Qaeda, Osama bin Laden, Saddam Hussein, and dozens of other entities associated with various terrorist groups that have declared war on the United States.

The lawsuit alleged a clear connection between al Qaeda, Iraq, Osama bin Laden, and Saddam Hussein, and cites evidence and arguments drawing on both fresh and previously known information.

Taken at least in part from John O'Neill's personal files, the lawsuit carries the weight of the dead man's voice. And it asserts that "al Qaeda was Iraq's favorite partner in terror."

Bush administration officials have taken pains to emphasize that they have made no connection between Saddam Hussein and the 9/11 attacks. And yet, as late as the second anniversary of the attacks, 69 percent of Americans believed Saddam had a hand in the atrocity.

I'm with the 69 percent. Most Americans apply the simple logic of what they know to be true about human nature, even if the human involved speaks a different language, worships differently, and lives halfway around the globe. And they know this: Revenge has been Saddam Hussein's driving force since he was humiliated in the 1991 Gulf War.

Though it has taken a long time to become clear, it's now possible to see that in bombing the World Trade Center in 1993, Ramzi Yousef—who was most likely an Iraqi intelligence agent—was firing the opening shot in a decade-long, Iraq-sponsored terrorist war against the United States.

The O'Neill suit claims that it will prove that Baghdad and al Qaeda—Saddam Hussein and Osama bin Laden—joined forces in 1998 and launched a new offensive against the United States. That wave of attacks included the bombings of the embassies in Africa, the

USS *Cole,* the Khobar Towers in Saudi Arabia, and ultimately the September 11 attacks.

Even if the lawsuit fails, the connections will stand in the minds of many Americans because they are supported by facts, and the facts make sense. The first Gulf War was deeply humiliating to Saddam Hussein; it would be foolish to believe he didn't want revenge. Saddam was, in fact, the only national leader in the world who praised Mohammad Atta's murder of nearly three thousand Americans—and the failed attempt to kill George Bush, Donald Rumsfeld, a few hundred members of Congress, and my friend Roy.

Strangely, Americans find themselves almost entirely alone in this conviction.

Most prominently, some Democratic candidates for president have rejected the idea. The Bush administration, pilloried at home and abroad for faulty prewar intelligence, the frustrating failure to locate Saddam Hussein's weapons of mass destruction, and for the deadly postwar chaos, now refuses to further stick its neck out by making allegations for which there is intriguing, even convincing, evidence—but which might expose it to further political attack and derision. The rest of the world is astonished that nearly 70 percent of the American public could believe such an idea and is convinced that the American public has been deluded into such thinking by an administration so desperate to create a reason for war that it intentionally lied to us about Iraq and Saddam Hussein.

The rest of the world can go to hell. It wasn't attacked. We were. And we'll judge who it was who plotted against us and who is plotting still.

France, of course, is the country that took a book calling the September 11 attacks a U.S. government plot—and sent it shooting high on their bestseller list.

One French author, Olivier Roy, set the tone of French thinking when he called Iraq a "mistaken target."

In an interview I conducted, the French philosopher and moderately pro-American writer Bernard Henri Levy quietly repeated Roy's claim, insisting that Iraq was "a mistaken target," and that the 69 percent of Americans who believe Saddam Hussein was behind September 11 were "prisoners of their own misinformation and media."

Levy may be pro-American, but he is still French. The September 11 attacks did not happen to him. Nevertheless, many others think precisely as he does.

Why? Some insist on incontrovertible proof—proof that could take years to gather and interpret before universal agreement could be reached on its meaning. But there are other reasons so much of the world withheld support for the war in Iraq. Distance was certainly among them. No other nation was reminded every day of our vulnerability in the way we were, by the sight of the hole in the ground, by the memory of loved ones lost.

They didn't know my friend Roy, and they didn't hear his story.

Fair enough. It was an American debate, and as we tend to do in this society, when the time came and an invasion was launched, Americans set aside their philosophical differences and supported the war.

We were alone in the world.

The first clues came on September 12, 2001. Reports from Europe expressed shock and sympathy, but the deep-horizon thinkers were already mulling the future, preparing to be shocked by the actions of a wounded giant. One European newspaper report quoted an academic from a major French institution who said he expected Europeans to be alarmed that Americans would not regard the attacks as "a parentheses," a completely isolated incident. "I think Europe will be shocked to find how seriously the Americans take this attack."

There was something terribly troubling in the remark—namely the attitude that outside America people would regard the attack as yet another isolated terrorist attack of the kind that happens fairly frequently around the globe, and the implication that the most notable result of the event was its inevitable effect on American behavior on the international stage.

I think many Americans thought the way I did: This *wasn't* like any other attack. It was crueler, more dramatic, more calculated to outrage our freedom-loving nation. It was a declaration of war. And as Americans we knew we could—*must*—do something about it. We could get the people who did it, and we could get the people who were planning to do it again. We did not have to take it.

Moreover, if a war was going to be fought, Americans could make certain it was fought in the aggressor's country, not our own.

Over the next year, the drumbeat began to build. President Bush issued his preemptive war policy, and the international commentators were outraged. A war against someone you think *might* attack you? Unthinkable!

I began to watch the overseas press with a morbid fascination, punctuated by bursts of outrage. The things that were being said about America and Americans were marked by an off-the-charts level of venom, a scandalous parade of mistaken assumptions of Americans, an endless font of suspicion, mistrust, and the promulgation of outright willful lies.

The viciousness of commentary on America was breathtaking. The purposeful refusal to understand Americans was incongruously coupled with a nearly constant repetition of the utter falsehood that the world knows America better than it knows itself. A resident of London who occasionally visits New York thinks himself as much an expert on America as a resident of Karachi who occasionally visits Los Angeles, and they both think they know America better than the 281 million people who have lived all their lives here.

Americans could not understand what was being said about them—the views that the populations of nearly every country on the planet hold to this day.

Americans could not understand that it was not merely a case of world opinion conflicting with American policy. Things had grown much worse.

It was a garish parade of hatred for America, open-throttle and full steam ahead. The world decided that the terrorists may have been bad, but America was worse. The international press decided, in virtual lockstep, that the question was not merely whether to hate America and Americans, but how strongly, how violently—how much.

This book is a result of those months and months I have spent watching this ugly groundswell, as it devoured the European, Arab, and Asian media. I turn special focus on those populations who practice a particularly vicious and unreasoning hatred of America. In many nations, they are not the majority, but they are present in virtually all of the rest of the globe's 190 countries, and they naturally color the thinking of even their opponents, the few erstwhile pro-Americans.

The anti-Americans have been speaking and writing about our nation and people in twists and turns of serpentine thinking that will probably astonish you, and should alarm you.

The great pageant of Hating America follows.

ONE

FRANCE'S WAR ON AMERICA

France does not know it, but we are at war with America. Yes, a permanent war, a vital war, a war without casualties, at least on the surface.

—Former French President Francois Mitterand
to his longtime confidant, Georges-Marc Benamou

AMERICANS THOUGHT WE COULD always count on France—and it turned out to be true. We could count on the French to be troublesome, to be haughty and demand respect, to threaten to refuse cooperation before eventually capitulating. That unflattering sketch was a picture of the France of old—before things got even worse.

In the weeks after September 11, France gave America good cause to wonder. John Rossant, who writes for *BusinessWeek* from Paris, noticed it two weeks after the 2001 terror attacks in New York and Washington. "Members of France's center-left coalition government also are starting to chime up," he wrote, and quoted

Green Party member Noel Mamère: "The reality is that American policy could only result in the kind of terrorism we've just seen."

Once again, for the French, even a vicious attack against America could be the fault of no one but the Americans themselves.

Ever since the United States evicted France's embedded Nazis at the end of World War II, the French have followed this predictable, if maddening, pattern—causing difficulty before eventually falling in line. But in the run-up to the war in Iraq, it was clear something had changed dramatically. The behavior of the French was beginning to sound more than merely cranky and irksome, until Americans had reason to wonder: Which side is France on?

The answer could be found in the Arab media, which reported intently on developing events and shaped the news into an almost mythical tale that every Arab would have recognized.

Their story went like this: The clouds of war were darkening a near horizon. As the Arab world stood in abject horror, an Armageddon of invader hordes promised catastrophe, with no army to stand in their way. The outcome was a foregone conclusion; to the proud and sensitive Arabs, the clash appeared to be over—in a cascade of humiliation—before it even began.

But as the long period of argument and debate dragged on, momentarily holding off the spectre of humiliation, one man stood to lead the Arab Nation, to speak eloquently and cleverly for the cause that would stave off the worst catastrophe in a millennium. Ultimately his mission failed, and the spectacle of outmatched defenders falling valiantly in the face of Western onslaught was salved only by the memory of that one man, who had the courage to throw himself before the inevitable conflagration. To the Arabs, his cause was in vain, but his defiance was noble and proud.

This man was proclaimed leader of the Arab Nation, from the Atlantic Ocean to the Persian Gulf—the man who shamed the ineffectual poseurs who pretended to lead the desperate Arabs, but who only grew irrelevant and fat in their weakness.

Who was this savior of the Arab people?

Jacques Chirac, the president of France.

So strenuous were Chirac's efforts to defend Saddam Hussein's regime that Iraq's state newspaper, *Babel,* awarded him the ceremonial title *Al-Munadhil al-Akbar:* Great Combatant.

One Algerian fundamentalist leader, Abdallah Jaballah, praised Mr. Chirac as "the only truly Arab leader today."

Imad al-Din Husayn, a columnist for *Al Bayan,* the government-owned newspaper in Dubai, United Arab Emirates, played with the idea. "I came to the conclusion that installing Chirac as president of the Arab League could bring about a solution to our problems," Husayn said, musing on the Gordian Knot Chirac could hack open for the Arabs. Unlike his Arab counterparts, Husayn reasoned, at least Chirac would make an attempt to defend against the American war machine. With the prospect of sure failure besetting the Arab peoples—invasion, death, carnage, humiliation, all at Western hands—miracles of salvation "would be wrought by the hands of our new *Saladin al-Chirac.*"

Saladin, the twelfth-century son of a Kurdish chief, born in Tikrit, Iraq, at a young age united the Arab world by force of arms, installed himself as the Sultan of Egypt and Champion of Islam. He eventually drove the Crusaders out of Jerusalem, which Muslims then held for centuries. In the Arab world, it is hard to pay a higher compliment than to enshrine a man's name as *Saladin.*

"Saladin al-Chirac."

As the Arabs contemplated the bleak future they had wrought— the coming Iraq war, of course, but also the continuing Palestinian conflict—they saw but one figure and one country on the world stage even attempting to stand in the way of the United States: President Chirac and his anti-American nation of France.

Chirac's behavior provoked a basic question: Why were the Arabs and the French working so hard to protect Saddam Hussein? The French certainly knew they were doing the Iraqi people no favor trying to stop a force that would drive Saddam Hussein out. As the war approached in 2003, the French, other Western Europeans—and, yes, the Arabs themselves—had seen a dozen years of reports from international human rights' agencies, including the United Nations, making it abundantly clear how agonizing the Saddam regime was for the Iraqi people. The United Nations Human Rights Committee had concluded in 1997 that Saddam's Iraq suffered a "high incidence of summary executions, arbitrary arrests and detention, torture and ill treatment by members of security and military forces." The Committee noted that Saddam's regime imposed retroactive laws, empowering security services to execute and torture people for newly declared crimes. It noted with particular disgust Iraq's Decree No. 109 of August 1994, which ordered criminals whose hand had been amputated as a punishment for their crimes be branded with an X on their forehead, so that amputees from Iraq's wars could be easily distinguished from criminals who had been maimed by the state.

In August 2001, Amnesty International weighed in with yet another of its many voluminous reports on Saddam's human rights' abuses. The report recounted a series of horrific tales from various individuals who had been taken into custody and tortured, some for a period of years. "Some of the victims have died and many have been left with permanent physical and psychological damage," the document reported. "Others have been left with mutilated bodies."

After the end of major conflict, enormous mass graves were found in Iraq, containing the bodies of more than 300,000 executed men, women, and even children. But the real tragedy was that these graves came as a surprise to no one: Arabs and Westerners alike had known of Saddam's murderous practices for a generation. Guest workers in Iraq came home in boxes, their bodies showing signs of prolonged torture before death. Indeed, France itself had spent years trying to convince Saddam to change his ways in order to help him rejoin the world economic community. France was especially eager to rehabilitate Saddam so that the U.N. sanctions against him would be lifted—allowing the dictator once again to sell Iraq's oil legally on the world market.

Europeans and Arabs alike may have been earnestly skeptical about Saddam's possession of weapons of mass destruction—but from the start they knew intimately what he was doing to his own citizens. And yet the prospect of the Americans launching a war to depose Saddam was deeply upsetting to the French.

Why? In part, because the French people had convinced themselves that America was the greater of two evils. As the war approached, French public opinion polls revealed dramatic anti-Americanism: 75 percent of the French public opposed George W. Bush's military action to end the regime of Saddam Hussein—even though a comparable number (73 percent) thought Iraq would be better off with Saddam gone.

According to the French, therefore, Saddam should be removed—unless it was the Americans who were stepping forward to make it happen. In that case, Iraqis would just have to suffer until someone else could get around to removing him.

"The French oppose the United States, quite simply, for what it is—the most powerful country on earth," observed Christopher Suellentrop in *BusinessWeek.* "The French are so concerned by the dominance of American power—militarily, economically, culturally, and technologically—that a former French foreign minister felt the need to coin a new word to describe it: hyperpuissance, or 'hyperpower.'"

That former foreign minister was a longtime self-proclaimed opponent of the United States named Hubert Vedrine. "I hate Americans," fumed Vedrine in an interview in 1995. He had just published a book, *France's Trump Cards,* in which he argued that the French could resume a leadership position in the world without a superpower military by virtue of the unique French culture, language, and elegant lifestyle. He summed up why the French so feared and resented the

United States: "The situation is without precedent. What previous empire has subjugated the entire world, including its enemies?"

What France feared, in other words, was American power. The French have spent a lot of time complaining about George W. Bush in recent years, but their reflex to oppose America began well before the Bush administration. As John Vinocur has noted in the *International Herald Tribune,* "it was during Clinton's presidency that France through its then foreign minister, Hubert Vedrine, defined American unilateralism as a principal problem for the world, and set a French course for mustering multilateral opinion to thwart it."

Indeed, Vinocur also reported, while Clinton was still in the White House, French political figure Bernard Kouchner "described anti-Americanism as the motor of French foreign policy."

During the Clinton administration, what bothered the French was the notion that America was trying unilaterally to spread its values through its popular culture and its economic power, which dominates the world economy. In other words, the problem was *globalism.* When the Bush administration arrived in 2001, their grousing about our "unilateralism" extended to complaints that we were abrogating treaties and showing a willingness to go to war without the approval of the United Nations.

Writing in the June 2001 *New Statesman* (two months and three weeks before 9/11), David Lawday argued that French anti-globalism was understandable. Globalism, Anglo-American style—including corporate expansion, higher productivity, lower taxes, and lower state spending—were not good for France, Lawday argued. The French were doing just fine with high public employment, high taxes, a thirty-five-hour work week, and a government-mandated system of vacations that gave French workers seven weeks a year off. "It is also accepted that America has gone wrong somewhere, and that big government, with judicious control of markets, strong social welfare, cultural independence and a brake on privatization, is the way to go," he wrote, adopting the same air of superiority exhibited by the French officials he interviewed.

The culture that George W. Bush brought to Washington prompted even more pronounced scorn from the French. The Bush White House endorsed public faith in God, tax cuts, the death penalty, and gun ownership—along with what the French saw as corporate wantonness; to the French, this was all met with contempt. Jacques Toubon, a former culture minister, scorned the new administration's profile to Lawday: "It is a parody of American social values. It can only lead to changing them."

And the French were itching to lead that movement for change. As Bernard Guetta, a columnist for *L'Express,* observed: "France has the ambition of creating a European Union that is a counterweight to the United States."

It wasn't the first time that call had been sounded. As early as 1997, Roger Cohen of the *New York Times* had reported that "France has set itself up as perhaps the nearest thing the United States has to a serious ideological rival in the last decade of the twentieth century."

The dashing and cinematic French foreign minister, Dominique de Villepin, played both sides of the fence. Even as he strove to maintain a consistent air of friendship with the United States, buried in his carefully crafted public statements were hints and glimmers of the French ambition to confront American power. In November 2002, just as the French were organizing the nations of western Europe to oppose the United States in the U.N. Security Council, de Villepin told an interviewer in Morocco: "We are convinced that the world can enjoy stability only if Europe exerts its full influence." Full influence, of course, meaning *concerted efforts to stand in the way of American interests.*

Throughout the year that followed, the French would make clear the lengths they were willing to go to stand in opposition to America.

As Victor Davis Hanson observed in March 2003 in National Review Online, "Maintaining the myth that France is really an ally and a NATO member is silly when its nuclear forces are not needed to provide wild-card deterrence against the Soviet Union and Frenchmen are nakedly trying to create a European axis against the United States, willing in the process to break with America over the safety of a psychopath"—Saddam Hussein.

Anti-Americanism is nothing new for the French. After the first outpouring of sympathy for the September 11 attacks (*Le Monde's* headline: "We Are All Americans"), the old complaints about American unilateralism soon bubbled back to the surface. Having held the United States in contempt for years over the death penalty, the antiabortion debate, President Bush's decision to withdraw from outdated or misguided treaties—the Kyoto Environmental Accord, the Anti-Ballistic Missile (ABM) treaty, the treaty establishing the U.N.'s International Criminal Court—the French weren't likely to change their tune for long. And America's support for Israel and its prime minister, Ariel Sharon—regarded by many in Arab-friendly Europe as a murderer and a war criminal—only made things worse.

Le Monde Diplomatique, a French journal of world politics and diplomacy, described the attitude of the French after 9/11 succinctly: "It's too bad for the Americans, but they had it coming."

In a post-9/11 report, *BusinessWeek* noted a surge of incensed calls to the popular Radio France Internationale. "What is so special about the American dead?" one caller asked about the September 11 victims. "Millions have died in Africa, but they never left messages on answering machines since they were too poor to have cell phones."

The French did their best to conceal official antipathy toward the United States, but the facts leaked out. As the *International Herald Tribune's* John Vinocur reported in April 2003, the French essayist and Chirac confidant Guy Sorman was present for some of Chirac's most important post–September 11 meetings. In November 2001,

Sorman participated in a discussion with Chirac and a small group of intellectuals at Elysee Palace, the headquarters of the president of the French Republic. In Sorman's view, Chirac was "the most anti-American of all of us."

According to Vinocur, Sorman described a President Chirac "who regarded American leadership as devoid of historical sense, lacking in patience, nuance, and profundity—attributes Chirac presumably considers as his own."

"Chirac is persuaded he is right on America," Sorman told Vinocur. "Pay no attention to what he might say about his affection for the United States from his student days," Sorman said, referring to Chirac's near-constant references to the pleasant summers he spent as a college student in America working at a Budweiser brewery and a Howard Johnson's roadside restaurant. "This is not the question. His view is deep, deep within him. For Chirac, Americans understand nothing."

This was certainly not the man Chirac himself wanted the Americans to see. But three events brought the French view of America into sharp focus at the start of 2002. The first was President Bush's State of the Union address on January 29, 2002, in which he identified an "Axis of Evil" that included Iraq.

Later that year, in September 2002, President Bush addressed the opening of the United Nations General Assembly, urging the body to confront the "grave and gathering danger" of Iraq—or become irrelevant. At that point, the United Nations sat up and took notice: The United States was prepared take action that would, in fact, render the United Nations irrelevant.

Just five days after that speech came the final straw for many Europeans—the French in particular. President Bush released his administration's "National Security Strategy," an official document that outlined a new U.S. military policy. The document laid out the case for "preemptive war," a military policy that allowed for first strikes to address emerging threats to the United States. This new policy also promised the world that the United States would allow no country, friend or foe, to develop the military capability to challenge the United States.

Le Monde, France's leading newspaper, reacted by charging the Americans with engaging in a "Soviet conception of international relations"; as they saw it, "[America's] safety is the insecurity of everyone else."

The voices of French opposition swung into action.

"If you ask me what will happen next I can tell you there will be no war," a senior French official was quoted as proclaiming in the November 2002 *National Review,* "President Chirac has taken personal charge of the Iraq dossier with the clear aim of preventing an unnecessary war that could destabilize the whole of the Middle East."

It was what journalist Amir Taheri called "the Chirac Doctrine": War on Iraq would require assent by the U.N. Security Council—which would look to its own U.N. weapons inspectors for guidance.

France was bent on mounting a moral argument against war in general, and extending it to this war in particular. An alumnus of the prestigious Ecole Nationale d'Administration (ENA)—whose graduates, known as *enarques,* are semi-revered as paragons of sensible public administration (and seldom challenged)—de Villepin devised plan after plan to allow the weapons inspectors greater rights and resources, in an effort to accomplish Iraqi disarmament without war. "War is always an acknowledgment of failure," he told the Security Council in March 2003. "Why should we now engage in war with Iraq? And I would also like to ask, why smash the instruments that have just proven their effectiveness? Why choose division when our unity and our resolve are leading Iraq to get rid of its weapons of mass destruction? Why should we wish to proceed by force at any price when we can succeed peacefully?" To be sure, France has legitimate historical cause to remain wary of war. The memory of more than a million and a half young men slaughtered during the futile stalemate of World War I still charges debates about war and peace in France. But contemporary French efforts to oppose American interests are motivated not by simple moral objection to war—and not even by political pandering to the fervently antiwar, pro-Arab French electorate.

For the French, a far more important motive was money. French officials hoped to hold off a war until Iraq's summer heat descended on the American plans—which might in turn force the Americans to table the war until after the 2004 election. That might prove long enough to prop up Saddam, clean up his reputation, get the U.N. sanctions lifted—and pave the way for France to help Iraq sell its oil on the world market.

Since his election in 2001, Jacques Chirac had been working eagerly to rehabilitate Saddam Hussein. In January 2002, around the time President Bush named Iraq as a member of the Axis of Evil, Chirac sent an envoy to Iraq to negotiate with Saddam. Pierre Deval, a bureaucrat with expertise in printing and counterfeiting, was sent to Baghdad under deep cover. For almost a year, Deval spent at least ten days a month in Baghdad, meeting with Tariq Aziz, and occasionally Qusay Hussein, about what Saddam could do to preserve his power.

When the story of Deval's meetings broke in November 2002, the Foreign Ministry of France tried predictably to deny it. "No French envoy tasked with such a mission to Saddam Hussein has gone to Iraq," a ministry spokesman said.

According to the London-based newspaper *Asharq al-Awsat,* however, Deval "has been regularly visiting Iraq for some time" to lobby for a change of "internal and foreign" policies, thus averting U.S. military action against Saddam's regime. The paper cited "authorized French sources" in its report.

"Saddam Hussein granted the amnesty to prisoners at the envoy's request," the newspaper said, providing an explanation for Saddam's sudden and mysterious release of prisoners held by the regime on October 20, 2002. Deval had evidently been pressing Saddam to release *political* prisoners, yet thousands of common criminals, rapists, and murders were also released at the same time.

Deval "openly spoke of the possibility of change without a war," and got "a more than encouraging response" from Iraqi authorities, the paper reported. Saddam even invited Deval to attend four cabinet meetings: "One of the ideas Deval raised was the formation of a 'new generation' government of technocrats headed by Qussay. [sic]"

Chirac's government proposed that a newly created, independent office of the Iraq government be charged with safeguarding human rights in Iraq, and that Saddam's son Qusay be presented to the world as "chief operations officer" of Iraq, while Saddam slipped into a murky emeritus status. "Chirac is convinced that he can persuade Saddam to talk the right talk and walk the right walk," columnist Amir Taheri reported.

Chirac had high hopes that his rehabilitation plan would carry the day, and his emissary Deval worked hard to achieve it. But Saddam himself wasn't eager to cooperate: As American forces later discovered, Saddam's regime was still carrying out executions the day before Baghdad fell.

Even as it was pursuing the idea of a second-generation Hussein regime, the French leadership was well aware of the moral depravity of Saddam and his family. In an interview with *France Inter* in November 2002—just as France was helping orchestrate the passage of the U.S.-sponsored Resolution 1441 (which demanded Iraq disarm or face "serious consequences")—de Villepin admitted that "given Saddam Hussein's attitude over the past few years, [we] feel, in the light of experience, that he might use the chemical, biological weapons" he possessed. De Villepin added, for emphasis: "And I want to repeat here that we also suspect there's an embryonic nuclear element he may possess. We can't run that risk."

De Villepin's comments leave little question: France knew the dangers of Iraq's military holdings and recognized the risks in allowing Saddam Hussein to proceed as he had for the eleven years since the Gulf War.

Ultimately, though, the French declared themselves satisfied with the weapons inspectors, claiming the inspections were working. Yet, as a *BusinessWeek* editorial noted, the twentieth-century idea of "containing" foreign threats through monitoring and sanctions has been rendered obsolete by technology and terror: "The Cold War policy of containment was based on rational states acting to preserve their own security. September 11 undermines this rationale."

The editorialists at *BusinessWeek* added: "So illogical is France's position on the U.N. that it raises the question of what the country's true aim is. Sadly, the answer increasingly appears to be nothing less than pure anti-Americanism."

The French determination to preserve the status quo in Iraq, then, was made in full knowledge of the horrific conditions Iraqis suffered under Saddam. For the French, obstructing the United States was more important.

In the October 2002 summit of French-speaking countries (*les Francophones*) held in Beirut, Lebanon, Chirac said *non* to the American push for war. "It should only be allowed in the case of legitimate defense, or by decision of the competent international authorities," Chirac said. By "competent," apparently, he meant to exclude the United States: "Competent international authorities" was code for the United Nations, where France held the power to block any action the United States wanted to take. (One thing it didn't reference was NATO, where France held much less sway, and the United States much more.)

The effort to overlook Saddam's offenses occasionally took a farcical turn. When Saddam Hussein was "reelected" president of Iraq with 100 percent of the vote, a reporter at the French foreign ministry impishly asked the spokesman, "Does France have any reaction to Saddam Hussein's 'good score' in Tuesday's referendum?"

The spokesman replied curtly, "No, I told you yesterday that I wouldn't comment on this point."

The French were working overtime to overlook not only rigged elections but torture, laws enacted retroactively to entrap the innocent, and murder under the guise of capital punishment.

Again, its reasons were partly economic. France had interests in Iraq: Saddam owed French banks, oil, and construction companies as much as $20 billion. (It also owed Russia, Germany, Saudi Arabia, and others, an estimated $200 billion, mostly in armaments Saddam used to fight the disastrous Iran-Iraq war in the early 1980s.) The French had already organized a 130-nation trade fair in Baghdad, and the French oil firm TotalFinaElf was lobbying to dominate the Iraqi oil business once sanctions were eventually lifted. Indeed, Chirac's minister of ecology was also the founder of the Franco-Iraq Association. Despite its public profession of friendship with America, and hollow condemnations of Saddam, France had long ago cast its lot with Saddam.

And theirs was no fleeting alliance: France saw a long-term opportunity in Iraq as well. Iraq, after all, had the world's second largest oil reserves, just behind Saudi Arabia. If France were to assume the position on the world stage that it wanted, a place from which to challenge the United States, it stood to have its own Saudi Arabia in Iraq.

On occasion, France made its long-term wishes known. On October 17, 2002, in a statement urging the Security Council to "demonstrate fairness by showing Iraq that war is not inevitable if it fully and scrupulously fulfills its obligations," the French ambassador pointed out that if Iraq should live up to its disarmament promises, it "would open the way to the suspension and then the lifting of sanctions, in accordance with Security Council resolutions." The line was dropped from France's later pronouncements on Iraq policy, because it indicated France's real goal—to put Saddam back in the world oil business.

But the deeper reason for France's obstructionism was its resentment over American power—military, economic, cultural—and France's desire to establish a world of "multipolar" power to replace the current "unipolar" power of the United States. In other words, its policy was motivated by dreams of the greater glory of France—by a desire to secure a prominent spot on the world stage for a country that thinks it richly deserves prominence.

It was a dream the French had nurtured for decades, though not always so obviously. During the Cold War, even as all of Western Europe was depending on American protection from the Soviets, France used what Leslie Gelb of the Council on Foreign Relations has called "a long lance" to express its contempt for America. Its jabs at American domination came from a distance; though annoying, they posed no serious threat to France's position in the Atlantic alliance.

This time, however, the long lance was abandoned in favor of daggers at close range.

The strategy was somewhat roundabout. The first step was to actually help the United States achieve a U.N. disarmament resolution for Iraq. Then, after appearing to be on the right side—even bringing along an Arab state, the Syrians—the French maneuvered to undercut the resolution itself by preventing its enforcement by military means, staving off war, and holding the line for their Arab friends. No American-sponsored regime change would be considered; only disarmament by U.N. inspectors would do.

The French plan was to tie up the United States in the United Nations, a rope-a-dope strategy involving great volumes of talk about intricate plans for inspections, and lots of superb lunches (with plenty of wine) designed to seduce other U.N. Security Council members and win them over to the French side.

French officials assisted U.S. Secretary of State Colin Powell's efforts to persuade President Bush and other members of the administration that disarmament was a matter best handled by the United

Nations. On November 8, 2002, the U.N. Security Council unanimously approved Resolution 1441, which required Iraq to admit weapons inspectors and submit to full inspections. But France planned to stop the march on Iraq at Resolution 1441: the French were confident that the United States would go no further.

"There will be no automatic triggering of the recourse to force," Jacques Chirac said the day before the Security Council vote. "The Security Council will, I repeat, have to reconvene to consider any possible violations by Iraq of her obligations."

The Bush administration saw things differently. The resolution promised "serious consequences" if Iraq should fail to comply fully, and to President Bush (and the American people) the resolution was meaningless if its threat of force was empty.

All along, of course, the French had been maneuvering to save Saddam Hussein. The French proposal for two U.N. resolutions on Iraq had one purpose: to thwart the United States in its drive for "regime change." The French were content to settle for Iraqi disarmament and nothing more. Under the French plan, Saddam would be obliged to give up any weapons of mass destruction, but Iraq would remain in his grip. "The objective," President Chirac said as he embarked on a Middle East trip while the U.N. debate boiled, "is to disarm Iraq, not to change the regime."

Chirac began issuing public admonitions to Saddam as soon as Iraq announced it would agree to allow weapons inspectors to return, and the U.N. Security Council passed Resolution 1441. Iraq must not make any mistakes, Chirac warned; it must cooperate fully with the inspections, scheduled to begin in mid-November 2002. "Iraq must not commit any error this time," said Chirac. "Its full and total cooperation with the international community is indispensable."

But Iraq's systematic flouting of the requirements of disarmament continued through the end of 2002. Weapons inspectors resumed their work at the end of November, and on December 7, Iraq submitted a 12,000-page declaration on its chemical, biological, and nuclear activities, claiming it had no banned weapons, but refusing to explain how they were destroyed.

The French recognized immediately that Iraq's declaration was so inadequate, so obviously a ruse, that it could constitute a tripwire for the Americans to go to war. "I solemnly reaffirm here that war is not inevitable," de Villepin told the National Assembly on December 11, 2002, "that our action is based on the primacy of law and moral values over force; it remains guided by the conviction that a peaceful political solution is possible."

The Bush administration wasn't buying it. Four days before Christmas, President Bush approved the deployment of an estimated 200,000 troops to the Gulf region, to be stationed there by March.

In the first days of 2003, as American war preparations continued, France quietly hardened its position. Even though Colin Powell thought he had a promise from France not to use its veto in the U.N. Security Council to block a U.S.-sponsored war resolution, that's exactly what the French had in mind.

De Villepin was scheduled to host an antiterrorism meeting for foreign ministers of U.N. countries in New York on January 20, 2003. It was a meeting Colin Powell had planned to skip, but de Villepin personally interceded and persuaded Powell to attend. After all, de Villepin had been helpful in securing a unanimous vote on Resolution 1441 just months before; Powell was still eager to maintain French support, as troublesome as it might be. As a courtesy to de Villepin—who had extended his assurance that the French would not veto America's plans for Iraq—Powell changed his schedule.

On January 20, at the U.N. headquarters in New York, the terror conference quickly turned into a debate on the Iraq war—and an ambush. Germany hardened its antiwar position, and de Villepin humiliated Powell publicly—insisting, loudly and grandly, that there was no reason to go to war while the weapons inspectors were still working.

Caught off guard, only lightly prepared, Powell was stunned to hear de Villepin threaten the precise move Powell had thought was off the table: the French veto.

Only a week before, de Villepin had promised that France would face its "responsibilities" if Iraq did not cooperate with disarmament. Now, at the end of the conference, he declared: "Nothing [that happened] today justifies envisaging military action," and accused the Bush administration, and Powell in particular, of "impatience" to wage war.

As Tony Allen-Mills and David Cracknell reported in the Sunday *Times* of London, "American sources said that . . . Powell was 'incandescent with rage' at what he regarded as French treachery in luring him to a meeting and then publicly stabbing him in the back."

Did the French regret treating its longtime ally and protector in such a shabby fashion? No. Not long after the U.N. ambush, the French claimed *they* were the real victims. "What worries us is that Francophobia is becoming commonplace and could lead to physical attacks on individuals," foreign ministry spokesman Francois Rivasseau told a news briefing in Paris.

By now, the antiwar movement was moving from the French foreign ministry to the streets of America and Europe. On December 10, 2002, International Human Rights' Day, protestors marched against the war all over America. On February 15, 2003, millions of people took to the streets of Europe to protest the coming war and condemn George W. Bush.

On PBS's *News Hour with Jim Lehrer,* commentator David Brooks questioned the judgment of the protestors. "Here's a regime that has professional rape teams in their military where they rape women and send the videotapes to the fathers. Here's a regime that imprisons mothers and babies in the next cell and forces them to watch their babies starve to death. What is your defense for preserving that regime?"

In the *Wall Street Journal,* Mike Gonzalez pointed out that de Villepin had been fanning centuries-old anti-English sentiment in his quest to block the road to war: "He told legislators that the fight over Iraq was actually one against 'Anglo-Saxon liberalism,' one [National] Assembly member told me." And Gonzalez noted that the phrase "Anglo-American forces," used consistently in French media reports on the Iraq war, came directly from pro-Nazi Vichy propaganda during World War II.

De Villepin repeatedly noted in an interview with *L'Express:* "Let's make no mistake about it: The choice, for sure, is between two visions of the world." France's vision, and the American vision.

Wherever it could, France insisted on challenging America. Could it be, as the *New York Times'* Thomas Friedman finally concluded, that France had become America's enemy?

France's inclination to embrace whatever America condemned reached tragicomic proportions in February 2003, when Jacques Chirac welcomed the rapacious, genocidal murderer Robert Mugabe of Zimbabwe to a conference on Africa hosted by France. It was deja vu all over again: Chirac had once hosted Saddam Hussein himself during his visit to the City of Light shortly after he had seized power. (Saddam came on business: Chirac was helping arrange for him to purchase the Osirak nuclear power plant, which was nearing completion before the Israelis preemptively bombed it.)

The dictator Mugabe said he felt "at home" in Paris, even as French police were beating anti-Mugabe protestors in the streets of Paris. "President Chirac insisted that we attend," said Mugabe. "He held firm to his principles. We need leaders of his stature."

Chirac later sought credit for his restraint in not kissing Mugabe on both cheeks at the opening of the conference, which Mugabe and his wife and entourage used as cover for an extensive Parisian shopping spree. The United States was not the only country outraged at Mugabe's visit to Paris, but France seemed to especially relish parading its independence to the Americans.

That same month, on February 5, Colin Powell appeared before the United Nations Security Council to present America's case that Saddam had failed to comply with Resolution 1441. The French received his argument coldly, insisting that the inspections were working and should continue.

From February 14, when the United States submitted a second U.N. Security Council Resolution authorizing military force against Iraq, until March 14, when the United States realized it would not pass, Chirac and de Villepin made speeches to the Security Council against war and American unilateralism, and spoke out in interviews on the success of the weapons inspectors. Their performances may have swelled the pride of the French back home; certainly they must also have cheered Saddam himself.

On March 9, de Villepin made an impassioned speech to the Security Council, outlining his proposal to increase the authority and effectiveness of weapons inspectors. "And I say this in the name of our friendship for the American people," he said, "in the name of our common values: freedom, justice, tolerance."

The American people were being told by France to extend to Saddam Hussein the common values of freedom, justice, and tolerance— virtues he had banished from his own country decades before. It was a ludicrous challenge, and one that hardly resonated with the American people: Polls showed that Americans overwhelmingly supported the Bush administration's determination to remove Saddam.

But de Villepin's grandstanding played well in Paris, not to mention Berlin and Rome and Cairo and Damascus and Gaza. The French were especially proud of their antiwar warriors. The *Journal du Dimanche* proclaimed that "France has spoken, resisted, laid down the law, and its voice has been heard."

"The arrogance of many Bush administration officials—particularly Secretary of Defense Donald Rumsfeld—has undoubtedly stirred an attitude of defiance among French academics, who drive the political debate in France," reported Pierre Taminiaux, an associate professor of French at Georgetown University. "Both France's left and the right are united in their dislike of the Bush administration's habit of striding the world stage with minimal humility." Americans who heard such comments could only blink in disbelief.

At the core of France's position was the notion that the world could trust Saddam Hussein to disarm. Prime Minister Raffarin declared: "As Dominique de Villepin said, 'take Iraq at its word.'" The French dismissed America's fears of a malevolent Iraqi regime plotting against the United States. "We could have disarmed Iraq differently," Raffarin insisted, though he appeared flummoxed when pressed to say just how that might have been achieved, considering the failure of twelve years of peaceful coercion. The French view, apparently, was simply as long as Saddam's regime was preserved, the mission of the inspectors was working.

In his "Letter From Paris" dispatch, Douglas Davis of the *Jerusalem Post* observed: "Buoyed by the huge domestic popularity of his message, Chirac must have drawn satisfaction from the eve-of-war polls which showed that not only did an overwhelming majority oppose the war but that fully one-third of French opinion actually hoped for a Saddam victory."

By March 20, the day after the first bombing on Baghdad, opinion polls showed that 92 percent of French citizens polled supported Chirac and de Villepin. Significantly, 62 percent said they also believed that France's position on the international stage had been boosted as a result of its stance on the crisis.

Among the French, almost half of those polled said they believed the main goal of the U.S.-led war was to take control of Iraq's oil fields. Another 17 percent said Washington was seeking to impose U.S. domination on the Middle East.

Only 3 percent said they thought the goal was to disarm Iraq of weapons of mass destruction—one of several U.S. justifications for the war.

Interviewed by the French newspaper *Le Figaro* on February 24, de Villepin had been asked, "Aren't you worried about appearing to defend Saddam Hussein?" Not at all, de Villepin answered. "We are adhering in a determined and responsible way to the goals set by the United Nations. We have to know how to stick to our goals. With the best of intentions, we could become embroiled in objectives contrary to those sought. Premature action, especially a military operation, would entail dangers of destabilization and a revival of terrorism." The interviewer failed to ask whether de Villepin really believed a "revival" of terrorism was not already well under way.

Such military conflict, de Villepin claimed, "would risk aggravating certain conflicts and so, in the end, bring disunity to the international community and compound the uncertainty in the world. We would find ourselves in a situation where the concept of developing a model for future action through what we're doing with the inspections would be destroyed." Apparently de Villepin had been hoping that the weapons-inspections "model"—an ineffectual disaster when applied to Saddam's Iraq—could be extended to other rogue nations as well.

But the French didn't really seem to care about bringing such rogue nations to justice. Their leaders seemed far more concerned about standing in the way of the American plan for war. "Is the purpose of the second resolution being talked of to sanction the failure of inspections, when we see they are making progress, or is it aimed at getting support from the international community for a scenario which seems to have been written in advance?" de Villepin asked rhetorically.

"They are going to get screwed. We are at the start of a hundred-year war," seethed Jacques Myard, a member of the Chirac government, in a rage directed at the United States.

If the Americans were unclear about whether the French would exercise their veto power in the United Nations to defeat the second American resolution—the authorization for war—they only had to hear President Chirac's interview with French television on March 10. "I repeat: France will oppose that resolution. For a resolution to be adopted, it must have a majority of nine members. This resolution won't get a majority of nine members."

Colin Powell and the U.S. ambassador to the United Nations, John Negroponte, were working hard for those votes. So why would Chirac be so confident they could not succeed? Because de Villepin was flying all over the world to organize international opposition to the United States. He had a potent argument: If France was threatening to use its veto, why should any of the other nations on the U.N. Security Council stick their necks out and side with a very unpopular America? Answer: They shouldn't.

"In other words, France wouldn't need to use her veto?" the interviewer asked Chirac.

"In this scenario, that's exactly right," said Chirac.

The interviewer pressed Chirac. "Some people, including some members of the governing party, have said [that exercising the veto] would be firing a bullet in our allies' back . . ."

"Don't let yourself be influenced by polemics," Chirac replied, shying away from so potent an image of betrayal. "I repeat: War is always the worst solution."

It's intriguing to realize that Chirac's new vision of his nation's role in world politics flew in the face of the beliefs of his legendary forebear, General Charles de Gaulle. It was de Gaulle who said of the United Nations, "It goes without saying, that under no circumstances will France accept that a collection of more or less totalitarian states and past masters of dictatorship and newly invented states . . . should dictate the law to it."

It was just such a collection of countries that de Villepin was organizing to support France and oppose America.

Dumping de Gaulle's strict rule about the United Nations, the France of Chirac and de Villepin instead issued a steady stream of statements, speeches, pronouncements, and position papers insisting that the United Nations was the world's primary lawgiver, that action taken without U.N. sanction was in all cases illegal, and that France, naturally, would obey any law set down by the United Nations.

It was a fascinating historical moment: George W. Bush stood firmly within the de Gaulle camp, and France's current leadership outside it. It was Bush who followed de Gaulle's principle that "no collection of totalitarian states and past masters of dictatorship and newly invented states" would dictate law to the United States. And it was Chirac who bent his nation's knee to that motley collection of countries and urged the United States to do the same.

The Americans saw the writing on the wall. On March 14, the United States withdrew its proposed second resolution; three days later, President Bush issued an ultimatum, giving Saddam Hussein and his sons Uday and Qusay forty-eight hours to leave Iraq.

On March 19, almost to the moment of that deadline, the United States attempted a decapitation attack on Baghdad, bombing an installation where the CIA believed Saddam would be sleeping the night. The building was destroyed, but it appeared Saddam escaped alive.

On March 20, seven and a half hours after the first bombs were dropped, France denounced the "illegitimate and dangerous war." That evening Britain's prime minister, Tony Blair, flew to Brussels for dinner with Chirac. The two European leaders, one pro-American and one anti-American, compared notes. It could not have looked very good for either. Chirac had broken faith with an alliance that had saved France from the Germans twice and kept the Soviets at bay four decades. And Blair, whose solidarity with Bush put him at tremendous political risk, doubtless foresaw the seething anger among at least half his people over his decision.

Chirac said in a written statement that "Right to the end, France, with many other countries, strove to convince that the necessary disarmament of Iraq could be obtained by peaceful means." He promised that France would continue to work "in the framework of the United Nations, the only legitimate framework for building peace, in Iraq as elsewhere."

In the very first days of the war—while warplanes were bombing Baghdad, and American armored vehicles were driving north toward the Iraqi capital—de Villepin went to Britain for a speaking engagement at an international relations institute. For all the prewar debate in Britain, once British men were in the fight, the public stood stoutly in support of their efforts. So when de Villepin was asked who he was hoping to win the Iraq war—the British and American forces or the Iraqis—he stepped into a trap. He irritably tried to avoid answering, but was pressed by a British reporter. "I'm not going to answer," he said, "because you have not listened carefully to what I have said before."

Pressed repeatedly to say which side he was actually rooting for, de Villepin continued to avoid any actual endorsement of the "Anglo-American" coalition forces. "I naturally wish that this conflict finds a swift conclusion with the minimum possible number of casualties."

When the anger from Britain and America forced the issue into a second day of questions, did the minister's spokesman assure the Americans it was all a misunderstanding? Not quite: "We are outraged by the presentation that was made of the minister's comments. His remarks are totally devoid of ambiguity," de Villepin's spokesman Francois Rivasseau said. "It is not acceptable in these circumstances that France's position should be deformed or misrepresented."

What could de Villepin have been thinking of, with his cowardly evasions? His audience at home, for one thing. At that early point in the Iraq conflict, a full third of the French public told pollsters they wanted Iraq to win and America to lose. The remaining two thirds was less committed to rooting against the Americans, but still opposed the war vehemently.

On April 9, eighteen days into the ground campaign, American tanks rolled into Baghdad.

"France, like all democracies, expresses satisfaction at the fall of the dictatorship of Saddam Hussein and hopes for a quick and effective end to the fighting," the office of President Chirac said in a written statement. "It is necessary now to create conditions that would return to the Iraqi people their dignity in rediscovered freedom."

De Villepin seconded the motion. "Together, we now have to build peace in Iraq and for France that means the United Nations must play a central role," the foreign minister said on April 10.

The BBC correspondent Emma Jane Kirby, in Paris the day Baghdad fell, reported that "many French people, who believed this was an illegal and hot-headed war, have been stunned by the welcome American forces received in Baghdad on Wednesday." And she confirmed that Chirac's government had reaped the political rewards of his anti-war stance: "The left-wing *Liberation* newspaper said Chirac had become the 'king of peace without a crown.' "

Even the Arabs were mystified by the drive-over-the-cliff moves of *Saladin al-Chirac*—by just how thoroughly his government had been willing to alienate its longtime allies in the name of "peace." Columnist Amir Taheri quoted a senior Egyptian official just before the fall of Baghdad: "We cannot understand Chirac. It is a mystery why he wanted to save Saddam when that meant wrecking relations with Washington and London." According to Taheri, many Arabs viewed Chirac's behavior as a "forlorn attempt" to prop up Saddam.

"Iraq also has unearthed a world of European frustration at its own continued political and military impotence while American power appears to swell," wrote Frederick Kempe in the *Wall Street Journal* after the first weekend in which American troops suffered significant losses. "I sense among many Europeans a desire to see America fail and even smug self-satisfaction at some of the weekend's bloody setbacks."

But the leaders of France and several of its Western European neighbors—Belgium, Germany, and Luxembourg among them—had military concerns of their own. The entire debate over the Iraq war was colored by one glaring truth: none of the nations arrayed in opposition to the United States possessed more than minimal military capability. Not only did they lack the military power to pose any serious deterrent to the coalition—whatever support they might have offered wasn't even worth bargaining for. They were entirely out of the game.

In late April, the aforementioned nations convened a mini-summit in Belgium to make a show of discussing their defense capability and future plans. The "Praline Summit," as it was derisively called, was a transparent attempt to give the Belgian prime minister (who hosted the summit) a few seconds on the world stage. But building any kind of significant military "capability," even a small reactionary force of some sixty thousand, would require pinching the Europeans' social welfare systems—a threat that would doubtless have provoked hundreds of thousands of protestors to gather at rallies and ballot boxes to toss out the leaders who suggested it.

Despite French ambitions to dominate a United States of Europe, no one believes that any single European country—or even a USofE—could muster the budget to challenge the U.S. military. America spends more on defense than the rest of NATO combined—$322 billion in 2001, rising to $600 billion in the foreseeable future—while most recently France and Germany together only kicked in $59 billion, five to ten times less than their counterparts across the Atlantic.

In the end, Germany, France, Belgium, and Luxembourg avoided the question of military buildup altogether, deciding instead to construct a new European defense headquarters down the road from NATO Headquarters in Brussels. Yet another grand salon of polished wood and glittering chandeliers, ready to host the parade of European dignitaries to meet and resolve to hold more meetings.

In his book *Of Paradise and Power,* Robert Kagan (who famously coined the phrase "America is from Mars, Europe from Venus") observes that the Europeans are frightened and jealous of American military power because they are helpless to match it—and are left searching desperately for other methods to constrain it. According to Kagan, the French (and Germans and Belgians, and even to some extent the Brits) have created a soft-life Euro-paradise for their populations, and a dependence on what he calls "soft power" in its dealings with the world. The French military may be competent at peacekeeping and regional interventions, but the French government avoids the budget outlays required to build a world power military, preferring to put its money into endless social programs and shorter work weeks. They choose to counter America's "hard power" (the U.S. military capability and the economy that drives the world) with the soft power of diplomacy, international law, economic deals, and the United Nations, where France parades its veto power.

It was a system that worked well until America awoke to the threat of global terror, and George W. Bush resolved to counter that threat by every means necessary—whether the United Nations chose to join the battle or not.

As American newspapers howled at the French, dubbing them an "axis of weasels," French officials recoiled. The French ambassador to the United States, Jean-David Levitte, bristled at American reactions in a column he wrote for the *New York Times:* "Reading the papers from both sides of the Atlantic, I sometimes wonder whether the impending war is not between France and the United States."

Jacques Chirac also noted the rhetoric, but with less alarm. "I was struck by this hostility coming out of Washington and it saddened me. But I regard this as the chattering of a few people, which has been picked up by the media . . . frankly I don't lose much sleep over this."

Somehow, the French had managed to convince themselves that the political battle over the Iraq war had ended in victory—at least on moral terms—for their side. "In the run-up to the Iraqi conflict, France thwarted the U.S.-led attempt to convince the U.N. Security Council to authorize the opening of hostilities," Francois Heisbourg of the Foundation for Strategic Research said in the London *Financial Times.* "Although Jacques Chirac's government recognizes that the damage to the transatlantic relationship must be repaired, it is a sense of diplomatic victory that informs France's postwar choices, not a feeling of failure."

De Villepin, in particular, was lavished with praise for his diplomatic style and cosmopolitan flair. A self-styled poet who has privately published several volumes of verse, de Villepin seemed to capture the imagination of Britain's antiwar, anti-American *Guardian* newspaper; in June 2003, the paper observed that "Now vulpine de Villepin is being tipped as Chirac's successor. He would bring poetry to the post because, as he has said, diplomacy and poetry 'both rely on the alchemy of paradox.'" One French magazine, *Le Point,* described de Villepin as the "silver wolf with burning eyes," as if he were a Gallic movie idol.

In the wake of this "war before the war," America vented its own frustration in a sudden groundswell of French insults. Groundskeeper Willie of *The Simpsons* had given the world the immortal phrase "cheese-eating surrender monkeys," and in the late winter of 2003 it became instant common usage. "I am called a monkey; I am called a weasel, and I am called a rat. What the hell is going on here?" Francois Heisbourg complained. "Now I know what it's like to be called a dirty Yid."

It was no accident that such a slur should come to Heisbourg's mind. Hate speech—aimed especially at Jews—has become common currency in his native land.

Influenced in part by their six million Muslim citizens, the French have allowed anti-Semitism to run amok within their borders. As the Associated Press reported on March 28, 2003, violent hate crimes in

France jumped by more than 400 percent in the previous year, to their highest level in a decade—and more than half the assaults were aimed at Jews. Two days after that statistic hit the news, French Interior Minister Nicolas Sarkozy was forced to issue a strong condemnation of a street attack on two Jews by antiwar demonstrators.

A number of fundamentalist Muslims had recently been elected to the Paris city council, and Sarkozy took the occasion to issue a warning that the French would have condemned had it come from John Ashcroft: "We want to say very simply: imams who propagate views that run counter to French values will be expelled," Sarkozy told the Europe-1 radio network. But the French government's claims to have cracked down effectively on Muslim anti-Semitism rang hollow. As the *New York Times*'s Alan Howell reported, one former American journalist who has lived in France for twenty-five years observed that "Anti-Semitism, anti-Americanism, and anti-globalization, they mix it all up here."

One consistent complaint emanating from the French camp was that America's foreign policy had been hijacked by the "neo-conservatives"—a term many took as code for "the Jews." According to Mike Gonzalez of the *Wall Street Journal,* de Villepin told members of the National Assembly that "hawks" in the Bush administration are "in the hands of [Israeli Prime Minister Ariel] Sharon," and went on to attack a "pro-Zionist" lobby comprising U.S. Deputy Defense Secretary Paul Wolfowitz, White House staffer Elliot Abrams, and former Pentagon advisor Richard Perle, all of whom are Jewish. The French pointed to the "Northeast Corridor" of the United States—the opinion belt stretching from Washington, D.C., to Boston—as the implicit locus of Jewish influence. Distrustful for years of Israeli influence over U.S. foreign policy, the French have now let institutional Jew-bashing run unchecked.

France's former environment minister, Corinne Lepage, recognized the hate-filled tenor of the antiwar movement in France. Writing in *Le Figaro,* she expressed her dismay at the so-called "pacifist" demonstrations in the streets of Paris, which she said "have nothing peaceful about them."

"Having attended them," Lepage wrote, "I can bear witness to the fact that these demonstrations are far from gatherings of real defenders of the rights of man or of peace. These are hordes orchestrated by the security services of Islamicist groups which, perfectly organized and armed with loudspeakers, shout extremely violent slogans in which racial and anti-Semitic hatred is expressed without the least taboo."

As Mike Gonzalez reported, demonstrators at these rallies made their feelings clear: "Long live Chirac," they chanted, "stop the Jews!"

"The French are terrified that the Iraq conflict will turn their own Arab population against them," John Cruickshank of the *Chicago Sun-Times* observed just before the fall of Baghdad. "They are hostage to their own minority citizens and they will do practically anything to placate them." Cruickshank's point is critical: Six million Arabs in France constitute not only a voting bloc, but also a disaffected minority—French in name only—whose status as second-class citizens has already bred resentment and anger, boiled over into street confrontations, and could erupt into terror attacks.

As Salman Rushdie himself has observed, anti-Americanism is a phenomenon that is sweeping the world. As the buildup to the war in Iraq proved beyond doubt, it is already well-entrenched in France.

"Most French people will cheerfully admit to being anti-American," wrote Sophie Masson in the *Sydney Morning Herald*. "France has a sense of destiny, a 'civilising mission,' just like the United States." Masson, a French-born Australian, described anti-Americanism as a central tenet of French life, one of the many ways the French define themselves. "It is as a rival, not as a client, that French anti-Americanism expresses itself."

A month before the first shots were fired in Iraq, Robert Kagan used a column in the *Washington Post* to issue this warning to his fellow Americans: "Here's what Americans need to understand: In

Europe, this paranoid, conspiratorial anti-Americanism is not a far-left or far-right phenomenon. It's the mainstream view."

When Gerhard Schroeder campaigned on an anti-American platform in Germany, Kagan pointed out, he was not simply following the familiar dance steps of all politicians, mobilizing his base or reaching out to Greens and socialists. Schroeder was talking to the man or woman on the street—whatever his or her political stripe.

"When Jacques Chirac and Dominique de Villepin publicly humiliate Colin Powell, they're playing to the gallery. The 'European street' is more anti-American than ever before," Kagan wrote.

In Paris, a hit stage revue called *George W. Bush, or God's Sad Cowboy* was packing crowds. (Not to be outdone, Britain's West End offered *The Madness of George W.,* likening Bush to England's mad George III; as *Newsweek* pointed out, the play portrayed POTUS as a "childish dimwit" given to malapropisms like "Sadamma bin Laden.")

A week into the war, *Newsweek*'s Robert Samuelson reported that European disapproval rates "approach unanimity: 87 percent in France, 85 percent in Germany, 83 percent in Russia, 79 percent in Spain, and 76 percent in Italy. Polls in Asia and Latin America find similar hostility."

Public opinion surveys conveyed the dramatic truth. According to a poll by the Pew Global Attitudes Project, regard for the United States has dropped in almost all European countries since 2000, the year of George W. Bush's election and the end of the Clinton era. It is down seventeen points in Germany, eight in Britain, six in Italy.

When it comes to the Iraq war, the numbers are even worse. According to the Pew poll, 76 percent of Russians, 75 percent of French, 54 percent of Germans, and 44 percent of Britons believed that Bush's true motive was his desire to control Iraq's oil assets. In America, only 22 percent held this view.

In the *New Yorker,* noted historian Simon Schama tried to explain why Europeans in general—and the French in particular—have maintained this studied dislike for America for so long. In addition to aligning itself with the British over the French at the end of the eighteenth century, Schama observed, America had engendered lasting enmity among the French by waiting too long to enter World War I. "Why, it was asked, had the engagement of American troops on the western front been delayed until 1918? The answer was that the United States had waited until it could mobilize a force large enough not just to win the war but to dominate the peace." Thus, the Americans became a welcome scapegoat for the carnage of the war.

After the Americans returned to evict the Germans from France in World War II, Schama wrote, "the greatest 'American peril' (a phrase that became commonplace in the literature) was the standardization of social life (the ancestor of today's complaints against globalization), the thinning of the richness of human habits to the point where they could be marketable not only inside America but, because of the global reach of American capitalism, to the entire world." The Americanization of the globe was particularly loathsome to the French because they considered themselves to have a kind of monopoly on cultural sophistication.

Philosopher and author Bernard Henri Levy traces the birth of modern French anti-Americanism in the extreme political right of the 1920s. "Because for the extreme right of the 1920's and '30's, they have a certain idea of what nationhood must be: roots, purity, homogeneity, get rid of Jews, get rid of black people, and so on. And America[,] to them, was contrary of that. A country where there were Jews, where there were blacks, where there was a melting pot, where there was a recent or new nation."

Whatever it was that rankled the French most profoundly after World War II (*Le Coca Cola? Le hamburger?*), the French also began to recognize that the long arms of global capitalism would spread other American values the French detested—from junk culture and raging corporate business tactics to the ability to act without

French permission. In the late twentieth century and the first years of the twenty-first century, France has shown ample evidence that it was more than a little embarrassed—and not the slightest bit grateful—to think that the Americans had saved it from German aggression twice in one century. It didn't matter if the Americans were right (deploying Pershing missiles in Europe, for instance). To the French, all that mattered was that the Americans had presumed to trump French opposition by going it alone.

Most Americans fail to appreciate just how checkered Franco-American relations have been. But we have been at loggerheads with the French more often than we have been allied with them: the history of tensions between the two nations extends back to the turn of the nineteenth century.

We do owe it to the French for sending Lafayette to help George Washington prevail in the American Revolution. But the French began their double-dealing immediately after the British loss at the Battle of Yorktown. After the Americans had won their war, the French convinced Britain to deny the American colonies' claims west of the Alleghenies. In the early days of the American republic, post-revolutionary France sent Citizen Genet to the United States to undermine President Washington's neutrality in a fresh French-British war. The French Foreign Minister Talleyrand, Napoleon's minion, created a storm called the XYZ Affair by demanding a bribe before he would meet with American diplomats. This led to America's first war against a foreign power—a series of naval clashes with France.

The story continues:

- Andrew Jackson almost declared war on France in the 1830s.
- During the Civil War, Napoleon III assisted the Confederacy.
- French and American negotiators bickered at Versailles at the end of World War I over German reparations (France insisted on

raiding German coffers and was rewarded two decades later with Hitler).

- The Vichy government shelled American troops storming ashore at Normandy on D-Day.
- In 1961 de Gaulle pulled out of NATO in a spat with the United States.

Recalling this sorry history in the *Wall Street Journal* in mid-2003, John Miller brought the story up to date: "In 1986, as a kind of dress rehearsal for its latest recalcitrance, France refused to let American jets fly over its territory on the way to attack Libya."

Confronted with such a list, who can be surprised at the events of 2003?

Colin Powell may or may not have been surprised, but he was surely aggrieved by the behavior of the French throughout early 2003. Asked by PBS's Charlie Rose after the fall of Baghdad whether France would suffer the consequences of its actions, Powell—the Bush administration dove—bluntly replied, "Yes."

The French, at that early date in the American backlash, were still in denial. Elisabeth Bumiller of the *New York Times* reported the wishful words of one French diplomat: "It's a concern to see that some people in the administration are still fighting a war against France that is completely irrelevant." But when confronted with Powell's answer to Charlie Rose, the diplomat's expression sank, and he could only mutter, "Wow."

Wow indeed.

Later, looking back on this seminal moment, Britain's foreign minister, Jack Straw, could only shake his head ruefully. "Decisions have consequences," he said, diplomatically drawing a thin gauze over his dismay at France's attempt to challenge the United States. After all, the French had created a breach with America that could take years, at least, to repair. "Some of the approaches which were taken by some of our continental colleagues were simply inexcusable to most people in the United States," Straw observed—though he specifically exempted the Germans from this assessment. It was the French who had burned the trans-Atlantic bridge.

The French suffered some economic repercussions as well. French wine sales and travel bookings fell off 15 to 30 percent, as average Americans chose to invest their disposable income elsewhere. American tourists stayed away, costing the French economy $1 billion in the first half of 2003. And the Bush administration formulated plans to lower the temperature on the relationship with France, disinviting the French in certain key arenas.

There were signs that France will be punished in any number of ways for dissociating itself from the United States—not all of them diplomatic. In one recent court case, involving a fraud charge against Credit Lyonnais and the French government entity Consortium de Realisation, the U.S. Justice Department insisted that the French government plead guilty to a criminal charge and pay a $585 million fine. In other circumstances, the French government might have been allowed to slide, left out of the prosecution altogether. But in these changing times, the French government was given no special consideration in the U.S. District Court.

In the aftermath of the war, France insisted that the United States hand over control of Iraq to the United Nations. Considering how fully the U.N. Security Council was a *provence* of France, that was tantamount to letting Chirac and de Villepin take the spoils of a war in which another nation's soldiers had fought and died.

America said no. France continued to criticize American "unilateralism" from the sidelines—even as it returned to its own unilateral habits, ignoring its beloved United Nations when it saw fit.

In the broiling summer of 2003, as temperatures in Baghdad reached 140 degrees and American soldiers confronted renewed and deadly attack, events in faraway Paris belied French claims to a superior system.

An unexpected heat wave began affecting the elderly of Paris; soon it was killing them at a rate of three thousand a week. The French government would eventually put the death toll of French senior citizens during this heat wave at 15,000. As the bodies piled up, however, French officials had to be summoned back from their August holiday to deal with the deadly crisis. As thousands of vacationing Frenchmen refused to return from their resort vacations, hapless authorities back home were obliged to store the bodies of their loved ones in morgue refrigerators.

France's proud system of nuclear power plants, built to ensure independence from Middle Eastern oil, had to be shut down after water being expelled from the plants was found to be heating entire rivers to dangerous levels.

In the midst of this abiding national crisis, Dominique de Villepin was caught red-handed—and red-faced—directing a secret military mission in South America that went so disastrously wrong the newspapers dubbed it "the Bungle in the Jungle." Those who asked what America was doing in Iraq were now confronted by a far thornier question: What was France doing in Brazil? Why would a French military transport plane, loaded with French commandos and secret agents, turn up on a jungle airstrip in Brazil, bound for a strange and ill-advised rescue mission into neighboring Colombia? Whose rescue was so important to France that an envoy with armed support would be dispatched to the jungles of Colombia, using a Brazilian airstrip as a jumping-off point to disaster and embarrassment?

The answer had little to do with French national interests and everything to do with personal friendship. Without informing either Brazil or Colombia, de Villepin had sent the French secret agents to try to rescue Ingrid Betancourt, a Colombian political figure and dual Colombian-French citizen—and a former university student of de Villepin's twenty-five years earlier. Betancourt had been held captive by Colombian rebels for seventeen months; de Villepin made a personal promise to Betancourt's family to intervene, and authorized the launch of "L'Operation 14 Juillet," no doubt in hopes of orchestrating Betancourt's triumphant and dramatic return in time for Bastille Day celebrations in Paris.

De Villepin, who had argued so eloquently and passionately for the sanctity of unified action by international authority, against the "illegal, and illegitimate" go-it-alone policies of George W. Bush, had embarked on a secret unilateral mission of his own. De Villepin dispatched a French commando force to a remote airstrip in Brazil, to jump off into Colombia just across the Amazon River. The French Hercules C-130 military transport dropped off four French secret service commandos and one high-ranking government official in the jungles of Brazil along the Amazon River, which forms the border with Colombia.

It could have been a triumph, a new occasion for the French to take pride in their valiant national spirit; instead, it was a disaster. The five-man team, backed by an unknown number of commandos, aroused the suspicion of their hired pilot when they claimed to be wilderness trekkers. When the Brazilians got wind of the French secret agents, they suspected them of running weapons to local narcotic-trafficker guerrillas as ransom for Betancourt, and tried to arrest the entire contingent. The French team produced diplomatic passports and claimed immunity, and the Brazilians ordered them out of the country. The five-man team came back across the river without Betancourt, and the rebels later issued a statement that it had no intention of releasing their hostage. The clandestine C-130 flew home with a cargo of disappointment and dismay.

To make things worse for the foreign minister, it seemed de Villepin hadn't bothered to tell either of his two superiors, the president or the prime minister. "This sort of operation would not have happened without me being informed, and I was not informed," said

President Chirac; after reportedly flying into a rage at his *protégé,* though Chirac circled the wagons, claiming that the aborted plan was an approved humanitarian mission.

In the case of the Bungle in the Jungle, France made clear that it claims *the French exception* in the very same situations in which it demands the United States subject itself to international oversight and international law. The French may not have agreed that American self-interest was sufficient reason for the United States to take unilateral action, but when it comes to the personal self-interest of the French foreign minister and his friends—well, that's a different story altogether.

The French, of course, bridled at the comparison. Bernard Henri Levy complained, "It is not the same scale. . . . a humanitarian operation, in order to rescue [a] half-French citizen—you cannot compare this to war." The failed rescue mission "didn't hurt anybody," Levy added.

The Bungle in the Jungle may have been overlooked by Americans, but not the general hypocrisy of the French. As average Americans noticed, the French had begun acting like our adversaries—cowardly adversaries, who wouldn't even own up to their mistakes when caught in the act.

"The next pleasant French person [I meet] will be my first," wrote Josh Thomas of Portland, Oregon, in a letter to the editor. Thomas, who lived in France as a youth, wrote that "The French continue to be small-minded with big chips on their shoulders; they manifest the classic 'small man' complex toward Americans at every opportunity."

"I'm not surprised," Thomas concluded, but "I'm ashamed of the many [American] tourists who tout France as an ideal tourist destination."

And from Germany, a pro-American reader of the *Wall Street Journal* wrote to call the French "the New Soviets—power-seeking mischief-makers with a vision of global leadership. Americans should be resolute, not magnanimous, and recall that rapprochement with the Soviet Union came after the collapse of communism." In the opinion of Ludwig von Reiche, "The French have long known that to wield clout they must build a base of political support in Europe, North Africa, and the Mideast. This means running the Americans out."

President Chirac has dreamed of leading a United States of Europe, which in his vision would allow France to dominate the economy, foreign policy, and general direction of 500 million Europeans. It is just this brand of naked ambition, manifesting itself in France's stated desire to serve as a counterweight to American hyperpower, that has percolated down to the French people: *l'homme dans la rue.*

Both Jacques Chirac and Dominique de Villepin have spent years living in the United States; both claim to be fond of Americans. And yet their actions speak louder than words: they have sounded the chord of hatred for America that has resonated within French culture. The cab drivers in Paris don't like Americans; the waiters don't like Americans; the religious leaders, what few there are, don't like Americans. French opinion polls show a strong and growing bias against all things American; it's a subject of constant conversation.

What is the French problem with the United States?

Power, pure and simple. America has it, the French do not—in their view, largely because America is always present to trump whatever power the French can manage to put together.

In his 2002 satirical novel *The Edict of Carcalla,* the veteran anti-American French writer and activist Regis de Bray put his finger on the problem.

The hero of de Bray's novel surprises his friends by revealing that he has become an American and proposes that France and the rest of Europe become America's fifty-first state—as quickly as possible. *Mais pourquois?* His friends are stunned. The answer is simple: Because that would give the people of Europe the right to vote for the U.S. president.

"By electing the president directly, the integrated Europeans will at last be able to exert some influence over what happens to them," the hero says. "They might even rediscover the feeling of having a collective manifest destiny."

De Bray's leftist Parisian friends ignored the book. Aiming to amuse, de Bray had apparently struck a little too close to home.

W HAT DOES THE FUTURE hold for Franco-American relations? One thing is certain: no lasting reconciliation should occur without a true reckoning of France's role in aiding and abetting the enemy in the buildup to the Iraq war. Two months after the end of major combat, the French ambassador to the United States publicly complained about a long list of lies he claimed the Bush administration had spread about France. In a tally of eight American media stories the French claimed were patently false, however, conspicuously absent was any denial of the most dismaying discoveries of postwar Iraq: That French intelligence agents had been keeping Saddam Hussein advised of the most sensitive discussions between Jacques Chirac and George W. Bush, and Chirac and Tony Blair, up to just a few days before the war. Nor did they deny that French security services had long helped to suppress opposition groups seeing to depose Saddam, or that figures in French media and politics had taken oil payments from Saddam that clearly amounted to bribes, or influence-peddling.

Anti-American rhetoric is one thing; even antiwar demonstrations fall within the bounds of civilized dissent. But if the French government ever expects to be trusted again on the world stage, it should halt its petty allegations about American press leaks—and start explaining its own, far more serious, efforts to compromise the security interests of its strongest ally.

Chirac and his government should also give new thought to sending troops and funding to help ensure the future security of

Iraq—although this now seems unlikelier than ever. "Forget it," Bernard-Henri Levy told me in our interview. "Villepin won't send French troops to Iraq now. He wants no part of it." Iraq had become too messy; too many Americans and Iraqis were already dying. The French would stay home. When the Donors Conference assembled in Spain in October 2003, America contributed $20 billion in grants to Iraq to rebuild. France offered nothing.

Even as it continued to withhold such aid, however, the French signaled that they wanted in on the business opportunities of postwar Iraq, insisting that the United Nations—where France exerts control in the Security Council—must play a "central" role in the nation's economic redevelopment.

When cornered by an anti-France backlash from angry Americans, France shrugged: *But we are friends! Friends owe it to each other to tell the truth, even if the truth hurts. Why are you so offended by our honesty, which is a sign of true friendship?*

Americans could only mutter: *How stupid do you think we are?*

THE ARABS' MINDLESS HATRED FOR AMERICA

Today the United States is governed by a junta of war criminals who took power through a kind of coup. That coup may have been preceded by (dubious) elections: but we should never forget that Hitler was also an elected politician. In this analogy, 9/11 fulfills the functions of the 'burning of the Reichstag.' It is vital that we have the courage to tell these truths, and stop masking them behind phrases such as 'our American friends' that have by now become quite meaningless.

American political culture is clearly different from that which has emerged from the history of the European continent: it has been shaped by the establishment of New England by extremist Protestant sects, the genocide of the continent's indigenous peoples, the enslavement of Africans, and the emergence of communities segregated by ethnicity as a result of successive waves of migration throughout the nineteenth century.

—Columnist Samir Amin in Egypt's
Al-Ahram Weekly, May 21, 2003

S THE IMAGES FLASHED around the world of American jetliners knifing into New York's World Trade Center towers, two taxi drivers in faraway Cairo watched on a tea shop television.

"Bullseye," said one, his eyes riveted to the pictures.

"Nice work," agreed the other, sitting alongside.

These quotes were reported in a news agency dispatch from Cairo, but if they were seen at all it was only after a long delay: They were censored by Egyptian authorities on September 11, only to be released months later, inexplicably, on an Egyptian newspaper website. No explanation was given for the long months in which the stories including those quotes were kept hidden, as if they were a state secret. Clearly, government authorities were embarrassed by such remarks. But within a few months, their embarrassment had been replaced by anger, and the Egyptian censors evidently changed their minds. Now they seemed to *want* America to see what Egyptians had been saying that terrible day. Or perhaps they wanted Egyptians to see what other Egyptians were saying, for there is no evidence they hold back any of the normal venom that spews forth from Egyptian media every day.

Fast forward a year and a half. Iraq had been invaded—liberated—with lightning speed, and Baghdad was in American hands. It was late April 2003, and David Lamb, correspondent for the *Los Angeles Times,* was trying to interview Mahmoud Shazli, a member of Egypt's parliament. The first-term parliamentarian was disinclined to do the interview, but after further consideration he changed his mind.

He told Lamb he wanted to send a message to the American people. "The message is, we really hate you," he said.

"To the people [of America] I say, if you support what America is doing in the humiliation of Arab citizens, if you don't stand up to your rulers, we will boycott you and not deal with you, and go to hell with your own fake civilization."

After the Iraq war, C. David Welch, the American ambassador to Egypt, complained publicly about the general tenor of discussion of

the United States in the Egyptian media, particularly the open cele-
bration of suicide attacks on American troops in Iraq. Part of what
the ambassador was trying to point out to Egyptians was simply the
obvious: that Iraqis are glad to have been relieved of a dictator who
subjected them to a governmental torture and murder machine. The
ambassador might as well have stayed in bed that day.

Responding in a weekly *Al-Arabi* article titled "The Ambassador from Hell in Cairo," columnist Jamal Fahmi wrote: "Welch
deserves to be punished for being the representative of the gang that
escaped from the Trash Museum of the Old Colonialism and en-
trenched itself in the White House. 'Brother' Welch has the arrogance that befits an ambassador representing that imbecile in
Washington, George W. Bush."

Let's go back to mid–September 2001.

"It is a quiet morning in Maadi, a residential section of Cairo,
and a favorite with Americans," reported Fatemah Farag in Egypt's
Al-Ahram Weekly a month after the 9/11 attacks. "A few days after
September 11, an obviously foreign couple are walking down the
street. A little boy in a mechanics shop watches them intently. After a
few moments of deliberation he makes his move. Spreading his arms
to mimic an aeroplane, he veers across the road in front of them.
'*Zoom!*' he cries, before running off. . . . He does not pelt them with
stones, he does not scream abuse at them or jeer, but he cannot resist
telling them that he has seen their vulnerability."

Farag's article went on to explore the casual cruelty—nascent
terror—exhibited by even a child, which extends an unbroken tradition that dates back well before September 11 (shall we say back
to 1948 after the founding of Israel?), through the dismantling of
the Taliban and al Qaeda in Afghanistan, right up to the period
of postwar Iraq. "As Egyptians across the nation watched the twin
towers of the World Trade Center crumble to dust . . . pent-up feelings of humiliation and anger for all the images of Arab suffering
they had powerlessly watched for years gave way to something akin

to gloating. 'They had it coming' and 'it is about time they had a taste of our pain,' were some of the catch-phrases," she wrote.

On the first anniversary of September 11, Egypt's *Al-Ahram* reported the results of a poll of Arab opinion on the attacks. Fifty-two percent of those polls said that "the Americans deserved it." Thirty-nine percent blamed Israel's Mossad spy agency for the attacks; only 19 percent thought al Qaeda was responsible. This startling notion had gained traction despite al Qaeda's own repeated public statements either openly or implicitly seeking credit for the terrorist attacks.

In Arab societies such as Egypt and Saudi Arabia, such sentiments were more than casual asides or cynical jokes. Among the America-hating Arabs, the argument was made by Islamists and their sympathizers that because America supported the killing of Arabs (in Palestine, Afghanistan, Iraq), the murder of American civilians in attacks like September 11 was morally justified. As this self-serving reasoning went, since the United States is a democracy, its citizens can be held responsible for the immoral or illegal actions of its leaders. Therefore, U.S. civilians were legitimate targets, as much as the American leaders whom the 9/11 hijackers had also targeted. Unlike the well-protected leaders, the U.S. civilians were considerably more accessible.

In fact, the attacks of September 11 were predated by considerable discussion in the Arab world in which America was portrayed unequivocally as the enemy. In Egypt's *Al-Akhbar* newspaper, columnist Mahmoud Abd Al-Mun'im Murad wrote on August 26, 2001: "The issue no longer concerns the Arab-Israeli conflict . . . the real issue is the *Arab-American* conflict" [emphasis added].

In another article two days later, Murad elaborated: "The Statue of Liberty, in New York harbor, must be destroyed because of following the idiotic America policy that goes from disgrace to disgrace in the swamp of bias and blind fanaticism." Boldly, the columnist declared: "the age of the American collapse has begun."

Among the most fanatical of the Wahhabi *jihadis*—Osama bin Laden among them—killing Americans was also justified on the grounds that Americans are seen as *polytheists,* infidels. More point-edly, Americans had sullied the Arab landscape by placing military outposts in Saudi Arabia, the land of Islam's two holiest cities, Mecca and Medina. "The ruling to kill the Americans and their allies," bin Laden said in his now-famous 1998 *fatwa,* or declaration of war on the United States, "is an individual duty for every Muslim who can do it in any country in which it is possible to do it."

Later, one of bin Laden's principal religious theorists, Sheikh Yousef Al-Ayyeri, instructed al Qaeda followers that the real enemy of Islam is "secular democracy." According to him, democracy was synonymous with polytheism, the worship of gods other than Allah, because a secular democracy makes people believe they are capable of making decisions about their lives that are properly left to Allah and the commandments of the Koran. "They worship themselves rather than Allah," Ayyeri wrote shortly before he was killed in a gun bat-tle with police and security forces in Saudi Arabia in mid-2003. And beyond self-worship, the American consumer's worship of material goods only doubled the offense.

Only a small percentage of Muslims are followers of the fanatical Wahhabi and Qtubi sects that spawned al Qaeda and the Egyptian Muslim Brotherhood, and which subscribe to the deadliest of anti-Western religious creeds. Still, even many moderate Arabs found themselves cheering the attacks on America. "Most Arabs, and per-haps also most of the Third World, did rejoice, not because of the killing of thousands of innocent Americans, but because of the pene-tration of the bastion of American colonialism and the offensive within its home turf," wrote University of Lebanon lecturer Mustafa Juzo in London's Arabic newspaper *Al-Hayat* on September 17, 2001. "No one thought for a moment about the people who were in-side the tallest of the world's towers as they burned," Juzo said. In-stead, he said, "Everyone thought of the American administration and rejoiced at its misfortune, while its leaders scrambled to find a place to hide."

In the immediate aftermath of September 11, Juzo continued, "Does anyone think that the CIA does not know how much it is hated by the Arab people, and how happy the oppressed people in the Third World are at the tragedy that has struck it? [Therefore, there is no point] in our trying to prove to them that the Arab people are not gloating over the American misfortune. Can anyone really believe that a people of whom the U.S. has killed hundreds and thousands times the number of people killed in New York and in Boston [sic] is sorry, and is not happy, when he witnesses this smack to the face of its most bitter enemy?"

Two months and two days after September 11, Taliban- and al Qaeda-ruled Kabul, Afghanistan, fell to American-led coalition forces. The last remnants of the regime were subdued by early December 2002. In his book *Jihad: The Trail of Political Islam,* Gilles Kepel wrote, "Among demonstrations of joy and liberation, residents of Kabul rushed to barber shops for a clean shave and waited in long lines to reclaim old TV sets, as Kabul television programming was soon to be back on the air. Images of Arab prisoners traded to U.S. troops by Afghans, and of Pakistani and foreign Islamists spat upon, molested, or killed by locals, went around the Community of the Faithful (the Muslim world)."

When American forces liberated Afghanistan, they removed one of the harshest and most brutal regimes on the planet. Until September 11, most of the people the Taliban killed and oppressed were Muslims.

And yet, as the memory of September 11 grew more distant, as the pictures of liberated Afghans receded in the public mind, Arab anger with America increased. The plight of the Palestinians, slaughtering themselves in the futile war with Israel they foolishly started; the fate of the mud-hut Taliban; the toppling of the cruel regime of Saddam Hussein: It all added up to a series of painful and humiliating Arab losses, even though the Arabs knew the Taliban and Saddam were not worth supporting.

In late summer 2003, Fatma Adballah Mahmoud published a column in Egypt's *Al-Akhbar* in which she described Americans as "cannibals." "Cannibals . . . were barbaric creatures similar to beasts of prey, [which] took vengeance upon their enemies. They would slaughter them, tear them limb from limb, and mutilate the corpses, exactly as the American forces did to the bodies of Saddam Hussein's two sons Uday and Qusay, whose distressing and shocking pictures were circulated by the world media. [In] every place [which] it destroys, annihilates, and plunders treasure and oil, America does no less than what primitive cannibal tribes did in the prehistoric era."

Ms. Mahmoud, whose newspaper is owned and operated by a government that has received $60 billion in aid from the United States since 1979, called for further war against the United States of America and its citizens. "The fight against America will be continued, Allah willing, by the peoples waging Jihad against the original pirates and criminals—or, to be more precise, against the cannibals and the human corpse-disembowelers."

To many in the Arab world, the first anniversary of September 11 was seen as an important pause in the American War on Terror. The Taliban had fallen quickly, as expected, and though the Arab world bemoaned the loss of innocent life, there was not much in the way of serious mourning for the Taliban. Among many Arabs, there was a rebellious but largely sentimental and thoughtless admiration for bin Laden. The al Qaeda leader, after all, sought not only the fall of America, but also the end of the semi-secular lifestyles of modern Egyptians and Saudis, and the fall of their rulers as well.

After the war in Afghanistan, Laila, a devout sixty-year-old Muslim housewife in Cairo, looked back on 9/11 in conversation with a columnist for *Al-Ahram*. "Whoever did this is not Muslim. These people with beards who want us to live in caves—they don't understand the religion. Islam tells you to modernize. Modernity is good. They are backwards. That's why al Qaeda could never have done this—it required tremendous planning. They might be able to rob, or slap me in the face, but they could never do something like this. This needs something as strong as the United States."

Laila's confusion about the goals and capabilities of al Qaeda—not to mention her ludicrous implication that America would attack itself—followed a certain absurd logic: "Everything after [9/11] was meant to put Muslims down. Like those Bin Laden tapes. They were meant to defeat the Muslim world by showing us that these people who supposedly represent us have no hearts."

For other Arab commentators, the anniversary was an occasion to diminish the enormity of the terror attacks and contrast them with what they characterized as a disproportionate American response.

"I believe that when in the future historians come to write about the effects of 11 September," wrote Gamil Mattar, director of the Arab Center for Development and Futuristic Research, in *Al-Ahram Weekly* in September 2002, "they will judge that what U.S. politicians did with that calamity was far more brutal, and of more extensive and lasting consequence, than the immediate loss of life and trauma caused by the calamity itself.

"I am disturbed by the opinion, which is increasingly widespread in this part of the world, which holds that 11 September has functioned as a call to *jihad* (holy war) for growing numbers of 'Islamists' and radical youths in the Islamic world. In my opinion, the true reason for this unexpected upsurge in zealotry is that America's response was grossly out of proportion to the event and exceeded all acceptable bounds."

At the time Mattar's piece was published, the United States had recently wrapped up a quick war in Afghanistan; British and American warplanes had stepped up attacks on Iraqi installations in the northern and southern no-fly zones; most important, President Bush was preparing to address the U.N. General Assembly and make the case for invading Iraq.

In the Arab world, the prospect of a war in Iraq was the greatest fear. Saddam Hussein was a villain, the Arabs would admit if pressed, but there was simply no way Arab leaders could publicly support an American invasion of an Arab land—especially one as historically important as Iraq. Plainly, it would be too much: too many "Crusader" invasions, too many Arabs killed by Christian bombs, too many Arab leaders trampled under Western infidel boots. It would be just the calamity about which Osama bin Laden had warned the Arabs and Muslims.

Egyptian foreign minister Ahmed Maher, interviewed in an Egyptian newspaper on the eve of Bush's U.N. address, addressed his comments directly to the president. "You confuse terrorism and freedom fighting," he said. "You confuse your relations with every country with the fact that some of the terrorists come from this country or that country," referring to Saudis and Egyptians who were hijackers aboard the doomed September 11 flights.

"This should be a period that passes and is overcome. It's finished, you cannot live and think only of 9/11," Maher said. His comments demonstrated the Arab world's tin ear for American sensibilities: The last funeral for a New York City firefighter killed in the 9/11 attacks was in the summer of 2003. Whatever the expectations of others, Americans would consider the attacks an open wound for years.

For the Egyptians, the frustration of not being able to influence American policy clearly weighed heavily. It was, in fact, yet another U.S. policy Egypt was powerless to influence.

Yet, the Egyptian foreign minister demonstrated a tendency to see an Israeli conspiracy in all events, even September 11. "What is disturbing is that very soon after 9/11—of course the American people were in shock, which was to be expected—the Israelis took the opportunity to mix the cards; to confuse the whole issue and present themselves as if they were in the same fight as America."

Two months after Maher gave his glum interview, the U.N. Security Council voted to accept U.N. weapons inspectors after a four-year absence and to require Iraq to give up its weapons of mass destruction. The vote was unanimous, including even the support of Syria. Though France and Germany promised Egypt and the other Arab nations that the resolution would not allow the Americans and the British to go to war against Iraq, their promise was clearly hollow. The Arabs were well aware that the U.N. Security Council could not stop America; it could only force President George W. Bush to proceed without their support.

"The Arabs, today, appear weaker and more helpless than ever before in their modern history," wrote Mohamed El-Sayed Said, *Al-Ahram*'s Washington bureau chief, just before the anniversary. "They make no impact whatsoever, because of their failure in economic and social development and the prevailing despotism and tyranny of their governing systems. Above all, they have no influence worth mentioning among the American people and their political system. As a result, in spite of the fact that the Arabs cooperated in the campaign against terrorism, they reaped no political returns, not even in terms of sympathy for their problems and causes. Worse, they seem incapable of explaining their most straightforward and obvious cause: the plight of the Palestinians."

The plight of the Palestinians is a sorry situation indeed, even if it is of their own making. George W. Bush has demonstrated virtually no interest in immersing himself in negotiations to settle relations between the Israelis and the Palestinians. To the Arabs it is no mystery: The Israelis, in their view, own the U.S. Congress and the American media and have shut out any discussion of what they consider the obvious injustice of the Palestinian situation.

But the American people see things differently, taking a view the Arabs refuse to recognize as legitimate. Americans have watched their presidents try to mediate the Arab-Israeli dispute for decades.

They watched Jimmy Carter bring Anwar Sadat and Menachem Begin together—and watched as both Sadat and Begin's successor, Yitzak Rabin, were killed in the ensuing years.

They watched Yasser Arafat parade through Bill Clinton's White House as if he had a permanent pass—extraordinary treatment for a terrorist who was overheard by CIA agents ordering the murder of an American diplomat in Khartoum in 1970. Buoyed by the apparent success of the Oslo Accords, Americans watched in cautious anticipation as Clinton brought Arafat and the Israeli "peace" prime minister, Ehud Barak, to the Wye River Plantation in Maryland for a series of intense negotiations in 2000, resulting in a deal for a Palestinian state that many thought was the best Israel was ever going to offer. But the Palestinians under Arafat have been beset by an "all-or-nothing" mind-set for decades and, at the moment of a historic decision, Arafat could not bring himself to choose peace and nationhood. He rejected the last deal Bill Clinton had time to negotiate before leaving office, and Arafat returned to his West Bank headquarters having chosen war, intifada, suicide bombers. Arafat had apparently concluded that Israel could be pressured into further concessions by a campaign of terror and death.

Naturally, there were doubts that the deal would hold: If Arafat accepted, would he be killed the moment he stepped off the plane in Gaza? Would Barak be able to sell the deal to a skeptical Israeli public and Knesset when he arrived home? Both sides knew it wouldn't be easy. Because of Arafat's recalcitrance, however, the deal never had a chance.

It was a fatal decision. In consequence, the Israelis appeared to give up on peace with the Palestinians, electing one of the most hawkish prime ministers in Israel's history. Ariel Sharon came to office with the clear vision that his country was at war; his intention was to fight back and make the Palestinians suffer for their decision. The Palestinians also lost the United States: The American public stopped paying attention, and a new president came to office obviously intent on staying out of the mess. If Arafat could reject what most judged to be the best deal Israel would ever offer, what was the point of returning to the table?

If Arafat and the Palestinians were going to choose war, Sharon and the Israeli military were happy to oblige. The Israelis vigorously and often brutally returned fire on the Palestinian organizations that were behind the relentless campaign of suicide bombing. Americans grew exasperated and lost interest, turning away from the reports of mayhem and death with a shrug: "Don't tell me anything until you can tell me it's over."

The attitude of the Arab world has been precisely the opposite. Arabs have watched in horror as the Palestinians have lost ground and lives in their war, sending scores of suicide bombers to their deaths; maiming many young Palestinian stone throwers; and destroying Palestinian homes, villages, and orchards.

In June 2001, King Fahd of Saudi Arabia published an open letter addressed to the Arab World. In it he said, "The whole world is witness to the practices of the Zionists against the Arabs of Palestine, their territories and their Holy Sites. The aggression has taken the form of a real war as the Zionists use all types of lethal weapons. We call upon the international community to put an end to these practices committed against the unarmed Palestinian people." In his plea for justice, the king failed to mention the Palestinians' liberal use of suicide bombers against Israeli civilian targets, such as buses, cafes, and public markets.

But King Fahd pointed to the Americans as a cause of the Israeli domination and the Palestinians' losses and suffering: "And we call in particular on the United States to take a decisive stance toward ending this situation, especially since the enemy [the Israelis] is ignoring all conventions, charters and principles upon which human rights have been founded." Instead of condemning the Palestinians on similar terms, of course, Fahd announced that he would donate yet more hard currency in support of Palestinian efforts against "the enemy." In the very same announcement, Fahd established an $800 million Al-Aqsa Fund with an immediate Saudi contribution of $200 million.

In 2001 alone, the Saudi kingdom contributed over $4 billion to the Palestinian *intifada*. As he was announcing another cash grant to the Palestinians, Crown Prince Abdullah (the regent running Saudi Arabia during his brother King Fahd's incapacitation) proclaimed: "It is high time that Israel realized that the Palestinian Jihad will continue until they regain their legitimate rights, including the right to return to their homeland and establish an independent state." Abdullah also failed to mention that the Palestinians' latest difficulties started when their leadership rejected a proposal for an independent state offered by Israelis and at the insistence of the United States.

As Ibrahim Nafie wrote in *Al-Ahram Weekly* at the end of August 2001, "Bush's hands-off approach to the Arab-Israeli conflict also stems from an attitude, espoused by the more reactionary elements in the current administration, that any attempts to mediate a settlement will automatically lead to the United States getting its hands burned. Simultaneously Bush, like his predecessor, has fallen prey to Israeli propaganda blaming Arafat for the failure of the Camp David talks. The opinion in Washington, therefore, is that the situation in the Middle East is not yet 'ripe' for peace talks because the Palestinians in particular are not yet ready to make the necessary concessions, for which read kneel to Sharon's dictates. Tragically, this U.S. policy of 'benign neglect,' as it has been called, has left the Palestinians increasingly vulnerable to the unrestrained brutality unleashed by Israel's war cabinet."

It should be said that the Arabs are not lacking in voices of reason among their own people. After being fired from the Saudi-supported London daily *Al-Hayat* for calling the Saudi regime "barbaric" during an Al Jazeera broadcast, Tunisian intellectual Al-'Afif Al-Akhdar published a self-critique in which he concluded that his fellow Arabs were the "masters of the missed opportunity." He questioned why Arabs were "obsessed with vengeance."

"Delusional with the solitary, fixed idea of military vengeance for two centuries of defeat at the hands of the West and Israel, [Arab] political and intellectual elites became crippled," he wrote. Addressing his fellow Arabs, he said, "You are resolved to achieve through terror what others have achieved through diplomacy."

"This insane obsession with vengeance," Al-Akhdar concluded, "has robbed [Arabs'] minds of the ability to think reasonably."

Why? Part of the answer is illustrated in an observation of Tariq Ali, a British political activist and writer. In his book *The Clash of Fundamentalisms,* Ali points out that "The brutal punishment being inflicted on the Palestinians for refusing to accept Israeli suzerainty *can be seen every day by the entire Arab world on Al-Jazeera television*" [emphasis added].

Ali is correct in identifying the Arab media, particularly satellite television networks such as Al Jazeera, as a major contributor to the pan-Arab sense of outrage. These media outlets feed and nurture the Arabs' conviction that they are completely innocent of their own suffering, and that others—Americans and Israelis—are completely to blame. "The large-scale sufferings of the Palestinians are not perceived as being simply the work of Israel," Ali wrote. "Many Arab intellectuals see Israel as the biblical ass whose jaw has been borrowed by an American Samson to destroy the real and imagined enemies of the empire."

Tariq Ali gained fame as a young writer in the early 1970s decrying American policy in Vietnam. By 2003, he had lost none of his youthful anti-Americanism. "Some of the Bush ideologues in the media compare Washington to ancient Rome. It is a permissible fantasy, but they should remember that (a) the Romans never expected to be loved and (b) that Rome, too, fell."

Americans were on notice: You will not be "loved."

America has "no regard to our dignity and our issues while at the same time it talks about freedom, peace and human rights," Ali Saad Al-Moussa, a columnist for the daily *Al Watan,* wrote in the early days of the Iraq war.

Dignity, humiliation, honor—these were the basic considerations in any Arab discussion of America and the Arab world. The new Arab media made them the central themes of their coverage of the Palestinian uprisings, the Israeli military response, and the American war on terror. A new generation of Arabs devoured the hurt without the slightest hesitation.

But that younger generation of emotionally charged viewers was too young to remember a previous period, before they were born, when Arab media was completely untrustworthy. In 1967, an Egyptian broadcaster named Ahmed Said held the Arab world on the edge of its seat with dramatic eyewitness accounts of Egyptian tank formations rolling over the hated Israelis, of Israeli air force jets "swatted out of the skies like flies." For a few days the Arab public was led to believe the Arabs were winning the war—until reality suddenly crashed through the front door of every Arab household. The Egyptian air force had been destroyed on the ground. The Israelis not only controlled the skies, but the battlefield below. The 1967 Six Day War was over in precisely that—six days—and the Arabs had been completely defeated.

The Arab public was crestfallen and doubly betrayed: Not only had the Egyptians failed to organize an effective military campaign, but the 300-million member Arab world had been led to believe by government broadcasting that they were winning when in fact they were suffering total, humiliating defeat. When that reality dawned, the sense of betrayal was crushing. The Egyptian people had been lied to, cruelly, by their own government—by Arab brothers they had put their faith in.

For several decades thereafter, the Arab public viewed its own Arab broadcast media with extreme skepticism. This suspicion and doubt lasted for roughly a quarter century—until the arrival of Al Jazeera. With its dashing look, regular influx of inflammatory video, and skillful exploitation of Arab dignity and pride, Al Jazeera became the must-see TV of the Arab world—and ultimately spawned several fiercely competitive imitators.

For Arab television, the Palestinian *intifadas* and the American war on terror in Afghanistan were rehearsals for what turned out to be the real show: the war in Iraq.

Al Jazeera and its pan-Arab television brethren came into their own during the debate over the war in Iraq. As the first anniversary of September 11 turned the world's attention from the expulsion of the Taliban and toward the lurking dangers of Saddam Hussein, pan-Arab television framed the discussion in terms of the thirteenth-century conquest of Baghdad by the Mongol warrior Hulegu, the grandson of Ghengis Khan. In 1258, Baghdad was a dusty backwater of the Abassid caliph (successor to the Prophet), with little to defend it, since the once-powerful caliphate had become moribund and weak. The Mongul armies sacked the city, killing 700,000 inhabitants. The prodigious work of slaughter actually forced the Mongol warriors to take a two-week hiatus from the gore and stench before returning to finish off the stragglers.

In 2003, almost 750 years later, the Americans were cast as the new horde of Hulegu—the very definition of pitiless and bloody killers.

The war in Iraq, initiated March 20, 2003, became Al Jazeera's bloody canvas.

Faisal Bodi, a British journalist who identified himself as an "Islamist" and who joined the war from Al Jazeera's Internet newsroom, wrote in Britain's *Guardian* newspaper: "Of all the major global networks, al-Jazeera has been alone in proceeding from the premise that this war should be viewed as an illegal enterprise. It has broadcast the horror of the bombing campaign, the blown-out brains, the blood-spattered pavements, the screaming infants and the corpses."

Al Jazeera's view that the war was an illegal enterprise permeated every part of its coverage and was mirrored in virtually all of the Arab media coverage. Bodi said: "There is . . . a marked difference when reporting the anger the invasion has unleashed on the Muslim street. The view from here is that any vestige of goodwill toward the United States has evaporated with this latest aggression, and that Britain has now joined the United States and Israel as a target of this rage."

Al Jazeera aired the most raw and incendiary images of Iraqi, American, and British blood and death, virtually splashing buckets of blood on the television screen to incite its worldwide audience in what one of its own producers confided was nothing more than "political nudity"—that is, pornography. It was a formula that worked well in Al Jazeera's coverage of the Palestinian uprisings against the Israelis, and again when U.S. forces routed the Taliban in Afghanistan. So Al Jazeera followed the same strategy for the Iraq war, with Americans and British standing in for the Israelis. The images of scorched and dismembered bodies, the bloody clothes, the red-stained sheets, the bloodied pavement, dust, and mud all electrified the Arab world.

The screen told a tale all too familiar to Arabs: Crusader armies, invasion, defeat, humiliation, death, and rivers of blood. It *was* as transfixing as pornography, both repulsing and enticing, designed to dissolve passivity and torch the passions of hate. Running roughshod over the truth (implying that civilian casualties were intentional; blaming American forces for actions perpetrated by Saddam's regime) was not only good television but it was world-class propaganda.

The aforementioned Al Jazeera producer, who confessed that his station's bloody, hate-inspiring coverage was merely political pornography, was interviewed by columnist Mamoun Fandy of the London newspaper *Asharq Al-Awsat*. Fandy, who also taught media and politics at Washington's Georgetown University, revealed in the *Washington Post* in late March 2003 that Al Jazeera's political pornographers were its reporters and producers, who work tirelessly to enrage their audience.

Fandy wrote: "They also want to see what Hussein's information minister, Muhammed Said al-Sahaf, calls 'teaching the Americans a lesson.'

" 'We are no less than the Vietnamese. Just make it costly in body bags and the Americans will run,' said a retired Arab general who comments regularly on al-Jazeera."

Fandy also described the internal reviewing process—a kind of Arab political-correctness censorship—at Al Jazeera, which ensures that this outlook of fear pervades every frame of video, every word spoken on the air.

Some Arab journalists claim they had little choice but to go along. "The cost of speaking out now—even to simply say that Saddam is partially responsible for what is taking place—is very high. It could cost you your job and could even cause you physical harm," said one.

What Fandy was revealing about Al Jazeera—and the other networks that aim for the pan-Arab audience—was hardly a state secret. One need not be fluent in Arabic to see it. Al Jazeera, along with Abu Dhabi TV, MBC, and several other rival Arab networks— would be just as comprehensible to non-Arabic speakers as they are to their core constituency. The visual images speak abundantly well for themselves.

In the September 2003 issue of *Foreign Policy,* Fouad Ajami tried to point out the absurdly mixed messages of Arab satellite television. "The world rails against the United States, yet embraces its protection, its gossip, and its hipness. Tune into a talk show on the stridently anti-American satellite channel Al Jazeera, and you'll behold a parody of American ways and techniques unfolding on the television screen," Ajami wrote, pointing out the highly coiffed, impeccably suited, flawlessly made-up men and women anchors, modeled directly on American television news anchors. "That reporter in the flak jacket, irreverent and cool against the Kabul or Baghdad background, borrows a form perfected in the country whose sins and follies that reporter has come to chronicle."

Whether in broadcast or print form, the purpose of most, if not all, Arab media before and after the Iraq war has been to inflame passions against the United States. There was quite a significant debate about precisely that in the Arab press in late October 2003. Abd Al-Bar Atwan, editor of the London Arabic daily *Al-Quds Al-Arabi*, wrote an op-ed column putting forward the rather typical claim that the United States has earned the Arab world's hatred. That provoked a response from columnist Munir Al-Mawari of London's *Al Sharq Al-Awsat*, who argued that hypocritical Arabs like Atwan were to blame.

"The Atwan [who appears] on CNN is completely different from the Atwan on the Al-Jazeera network or in his *Al-Quds Al-Arabi* daily," Al-Mawari wrote. "On CNN, Atwan speaks solemnly and with total composure, presenting rational and balanced views. This is in complete contrast with his fuming appearances on Al-Jazeera and in *Al-Quds Al-Arabi,* in which he whips up the emotions of multitudes of viewers and readers."

"Atwan is part of the problem . . . and our problem is that it is not only America that we hate. Our Arab societies are societies of hate; we were raised to hate each other even before we hated others."

To be fair to Mr. Atwan, he was certainly not alone among the Arab media. On March 28, just over a week into the war, the Arab press and television reported the news that fifty-eight people had died in a vegetable market in Baghdad, reportedly victims of a U.S. air assault.

"Monstrous Martyrdom in Baghdad" screamed a headline in *Al-Dustur,* a newspaper in Amman, Jordan.

"Dreadful massacre in Baghdad" read a banner headline in the Egyptian paper *Akhbar Al-Yawm*. A lurid photograph of two child victims of the blast took up half the front page.

"Yet another massacre by the coalition of invaders," read the headline in Saudi Arabia's *Al-Riyadh*.

Emily Wax of the *Washington Post* foreign service news desk, who reported on these headlines the day after the bombing, also reported the predictable reaction among Arabs. "Mr. Bush has lost us. We are gone," said Diaa Rashwan in Cairo. "If America starts winning tomorrow, there will be suicide bombing that will start in America the next day."

George Elnaber, an Arab Christian and operator of a supermarket in Amman, said, "We hate Americans more than we hate Saddam now."

The Arab media's bloody-shirt campaign was very effective. In Riyadh, Saudi Arabia, after watching the war for nine days on Arab satellite television, a well-to-do Saudi housewife and physician named Leila was seething with rage at the Americans. As Carol Morello of the *Washington Post* reported, Leila raged: "America is so unfair it makes people frustrated and they want to kill every American in the street." Morello offered a memorable portrait of Leila as a stylish woman in her forties, nervously smoking a cigarette, wearing jeans, a tight pink sweater, and stiletto heels. Leila lives in a beautiful home with her husband and children; her lifestyle is apparently luxurious enough that she was served snacks by a maid during Morell's interview. But the television and the war have made her furious. "If America wants to step over everybody, then we will fight. I will kill Americans in the street."

Of course Leila is unlikely to become a suicide bomber, and Morello's report makes clear that Leila and her husband Mohammad, an export-import businessman, are fairly new to this level of anger. They have simply been enraged by what they have seen on the television: the bloodied corpses in the morgues, the lifeless hands jutting out of the bombed rubble in Baghdad.

Mohammad is furious; his wife is even more passionate. "Bush should listen to this message: If you continue in this war, everyone in the Islamic world, out of frustration, everyone will become a suicide bomber and terrorist to show [that] you are wrong," she says angrily.

Most Arabs do not recognize what Mamoun Fandy reported about the "political pornography" of the Arab media. Most are unaware of the extent to which they were manipulated during the war. But some were, and some Arab commentators tried in vain to sound the warning.

Writing in the Saudi *Arab News* on May 9, 2003, for example, Sheikh Abd Al-Hamid Al-Ansari said: "The Arab media succeeded in deceiving the people. On the whole, the deception was worse than in 1967. Fatwas succeeded—'Rise up for Jihad!'—in burying some misguided volunteers and suicide bombers. The misguided Fatwas did nothing but confirm those who were already miserable in their misery while those responsible for the Fatwas continued to enjoy life." The writer was dean of faculty of Shariah Law at Qatar University, who takes a critical view of the Arab media and the activities of politicized clerics.

"The question is why did the Arab media consent to align itself with the Iraqi regime while at the same time pretending that it was with the people?" Ansari asked. "Our media attempted to increase the degree of hatred against the coalition by concentrating on the degree of the destruction and the number of civilian victims, without making clear that this was because the regime positioned its forces and tanks in civilian areas.

"The aim of the Arab satellite stations was to suggest that the allies were 'savage' in their treatment of civilians."

Why? Ansari suggested one answer. "It is my view that the answer was stated by the director of one of the satellite channels: 'It is competition. In such circumstances, either we win the viewers or others win them.' Their aim is to win the street at any price."

Ansari's was a rare voice of self-reflection in the Arab world. He was also rare in another way: He listened to actual Iraqis. "The musings of a simple Iraqi from a liberated area caught my attention. He said: 'The Arabs left us and did not liberate us. Why are they attacking the coalition which wants to liberate us?' Why is this simple fact not realized by our men of culture, our intellectuals?"

Ansari's question has been left unanswered, however, because with the rare exception of writers like Al-Mawari, Arabs don't want to face their own failures. It's easier for both governments and the people to blame America and Israel.

"We are going our own way. We are not against the American agenda, but nobody here trusts American policy," said Essam Erian, as T. Christian Miller reported in the *Los Angeles Times* in August 2003. Erian heads Egypt's Muslim Brotherhood, one of the leading fundamentalist movements. "We are struggling for our democracy, not American democracy."

What kind of democracy is that? A democracy of theocratic diktat that rides to power in a car bomb? Is it automatically an inferior democracy if it is an American democracy? What is "an American democracy," anyway?

Miller also quoted Mahmoud Abdul Karim, a Syrian filmmaker. "Nobody can be on America's side. We will be accused of being traitors," Karim said. "They are supporting the guys in Israel who are occupying our land. It's not acceptable."

There is another reason for all this hostility and bitterness: The Arab people are hungry for a target for their anger, since it can be illegal, difficult, and even deadly to criticize the Arab governments they live under. From the Gulf of Arabia to the Atlantic Ocean, not a single Arab country is governed democratically. Despotism and tyranny is the rule, from the Arab sunrise to the Arab sunset.

"One of the unexpected consequences of 'the war on terror' and the U.S. focus on the Arab element in the 'axis of evil' has been that Arab citizens find themselves feeling pity for their rulers for the first time," Lebanese political commentator Samir Qassir wrote in the Beirut daily *An-Nahar* shortly before the Iraq war.

"They all realize that they are also targets for a U.S. campaign that among other things, aims at 'reshaping the Middle East,'" wrote Qassir. "And pressuring Saddam Hussein is also something the fiercest opponents of the Baathist regime in Iraq do not want to do, for fear that this might set a precedent that would later be used against them."

Between these two unpalatable choices, Qassir continues, "the paralyzing extent of the confusion that has struck the Arab regimes is evident to all."

The build up to the war in Iraq, the U.N. Security Council debate and vote in late 2002, the return of weapons inspectors, President Bush's State of the Union address in early 2003 that set forth America's path to war: All these events engendered a sense of dread and loathing among Arabs everywhere. In Iraq itself, there appeared to be a strange group myopia among Arabs: Press accounts suggest that they saw nothing but terrible events besetting Arabs—but had become blind to the fact that the suffering of the Iraqis was ultimately the fault of Saddam Hussein, the ruler they suddenly rushed to defend.

"There's an unusual helplessness and sense of humiliation of Arabs and Muslims," social commentator Abdul Bari Atwan said on Al Jazeera in January 2003. Almost hopefully, he added, "The most important concern is that we have to remember during Operation Desert Fox [when the Clinton administration bombed Iraq in retaliation for Saddam Hussein's efforts to thwart U.N. weapons inspectors] the Arabs were up in arms and the Arab leaders begged Clinton to back down. If four days caused this explosion, imagine what a prolonged war would do. And what if Iraq meets these expectations and managed to resist? This could lead to an explosion, a real revolution in the Arab world."

In the end, this prediction was more hopeful than realistic.

Eight days before the fall of Baghdad, the Palestinian daily *Al-Quds* said in an editorial: "The apocalyptic images beamed around the world by Arab satellite TV showing Baghdad being pummeled from the air should have woken the consciences of Arab leaders," says the paper. "Pictures of the capital of Arabism and Islam—the city of Arab Caliphs al-Rashid, al-Ma'mun, al-Mu'tasim, and the citadel which absorbed the shock of the Mongol invasion so many centuries ago—being razed to the ground by American bombs and missiles should have at least moved those shameless Arab leaders who have chosen to stand with the Anglo-American invaders."

Taha Yassin Ramadan, the Iraqi vice president, put it more bluntly on the eve of the war: "Why are the Arabs supplying the aggressor with oil to operate their aggression? Why don't they decide to stop pumping oil to the aggressor states? Why don't they close their air spaces and land and waterways before any activity by the aggressor states?"

Worse, the Arabs saw several major states helping the Americans—some overtly, such as Kuwait, Qatar, and Bahrain; others quietly, such as Saudi Arabia. Unlike the aftermath of the 1973 Arab-Israeli War, when Saudi Arabia punished the United States and the western world with an oil embargo, this time the Saudis quietly stepped up production to smooth out world oil fluctuations and to make up for illicit Iraqi crude, which would soon disappear from the market.

Two days before the Iraq war began, President Bush withdrew his second war resolution from consideration by the U.N. Security Council before a vote had been taken. Since the French had already made it clear that they would veto the resolution, the other members of the Security Council saw no reason to vote yes. Without the requisite nine votes in favor, the vote would fail, and the French would be able to say that the proposal would not have passed regardless of their vote. American officials, frustrated, simply walked away. The United Nations would not have a voice in the war. America was going ahead, and leaving the United Nations behind.

President Bush issued an ultimatum for Saddam Hussein and his sons to leave the country, a demand widely expected to be ignored. American generals ordered huge openings cut in the enormous sand berms that protected Kuwait from an Iraqi invasion, opening a path for thousands of American tanks to stream north toward Basra, Nassarieh, Karbala, and Baghdad. The war was no longer merely a possibility. It was a fact.

The Arab response? A fifty-year-old unemployed Cairene told a Reuters reporter: "May God grant President Saddam victory."

The first bombs fell on March 19 in an attempt to end the whole enterprise abruptly by killing Saddam Hussein in one of his secret bunkers. When there was no evidence that the hastily mounted attack had been successful, the war officially began on the night of March 20. President Bush, Prime Minister Blair, and President Chirac all made televised announcements to their citizens. American and British troops poured over the border from Kuwait, while 350 miles north, American warplanes pounded Baghdad and other targets from the air.

The Arab response? A twenty-five-year-old graduate student from Beirut: "I hope the Iraqis stick it out just to humiliate the Americans and force a debate about whether the Iraqi people really wanted their so-called help anyway."

The Arab media had succeeded in convincing the Arabs on the street that there was no difference between George W. Bush and Saddam Hussein.

"I think the real war has started now. I hope the Iraqis inflict losses on the Americans and that the Americans and the government of Saddam Hussein both leave Iraq, because they are all evil," Ahmad Al-Tuwaijri, a student on the streets of Cairo, told Reuters.

Writing in the Saudis' *Arab News* in April 2003, Dr. Khaled M. Batarfi said: "I told some friends a few weeks before the war on Iraq started that I was optimistic things would end well. They asked: How could that be, when the invaders are banging on Hell's gate threatening to smash it open at any moment? I said: Because those who open the gates of Hell will be the first to be burned there . . . the U.S. and allies will only leave the swamp of Iraq after being taught a lesson like that of Vietnam."

Despite Saddam's cheering section in the Arab street and circles of elites, the war was much quicker than anyone expected. After a seemingly endless stream of continuous television images of American forces driving north, hour after hour of video of armored columns seen through green night-vision lenses, the taking of Baghdad airport was over in a blink.

Suddenly, on the morning of April 9, 2003, television viewers around the world were startled to see American tanks in the traffic circle of downtown Baghdad's *Firdos* (Paradise) Square. A man in Cairo said he was watching the war on television when he got out of his chair to go to the bathroom. When he came back, "Baghdad was gone."

The Arab world was caught gaping in disbelief and—once again—humiliation.

Adnan Abu Odeh, a Jordanian political commentator and former advisor to the late King Hussein, told the *Washington Post* after Baghdad crumbled: "We wonder now whether we'll ever be able to recover and be respected worldwide."

In the Arab world, a new equation entered common thinking: America equals Arab humiliation, which equals hate. As Saudi King Abdul Aziz once said: "Kill an Arab, but never humiliate him."

Amr Moussa, secretary general of the Arab League, said: "How can [the Iraqis] be happy with the destruction that has happened since the start of the war on Iraq last week to topple President Saddam Hussein?"

But they were. Joyous Iraqis pulled over Saddam's statues, even while Saddam's followers obeyed instructions issued before the war to loot and burn government offices.

As the lightning-fast war in Iraq came to a sharp conclusion, the Associated Press reported the words of the Arab street:

- "Our last walls of resistance fell in Baghdad," said Samia Megtouf, a twenty-year-old university student in Tunis. "I feel like an orphan now."
- "I am really very shocked and sad," said Ali Abbas, an employee at a company in Bahrain. "It's very bad and it's unfair to see foreign tanks in an Arab capital. I couldn't sleep for thinking of the people in Baghdad."
- "The Arab nation is tasting another defeat. I have a bitter taste in my mouth. It is difficult to think now," says Ali Findouli, a fifty-five-year-old Tunis shop owner.
- The *Arab News* fairly spit out the words in disgust on April 9 as Saddam's statue was pulled over by a U.S. Marine tank: "Less predictable, but equally devastating, was the passive betrayal of the Republican Guard. They betrayed their honor and dignity, which we are supposed to believe are the most important things to any Arab man, let alone an Arab fighter."

Some Arabs seemed equally angry that Saddam had failed to offer any resistance. When Baghdad fell, the Associated Press interviewed Adnan Hamed, a twenty-seven-year-old salesman at a store in a suburb of Amman, Jordan. "Where is the resistance Saddam promised us?" Hamed clenched his fists in anger and fumed. "Karbala and Basra put up stronger resistance. Baghdad has crumbled unbelievably quickly."

The *Washington Post* quoted a thirty-seven-year-old Jordanian architect: "In Baghdad, the Iraqis had weapons. They had an army. If you fought only with your hands, you could last two weeks. They didn't fight. It's humiliating."

"Baghdad means a lot to Muslims and Arabs," Abeer Bakel, in Amman, told the *Washington Post*. "We expected more from the Iraqi people."

The Arab audience had been convinced that the Iraqi army, the Republican Guard, and the Special Republican Guard would make it look good—not for Saddam Hussein, but for the Arabs. They prayed that the Americans would be defeated—or, short of that, bloodied or mired, bogged down. The sandstorm that briefly halted the American's northward advance, and the initial reports of resistance in Um Qasr and Basra, gave Arabs the sense that the war might go their way. Once the storm abated and the Americans made rapid forward progress, the Arabs still held out hope that the Iraqis would make a good showing.

In the Muslim world, pollsters found widespread discouragement among Muslims that Iraq failed to put up more of a fight against the United States and its allies. Overwhelming majorities in Morocco (93 percent), Jordan (91 percent), Lebanon (82 percent), Turkey (82 percent), Indonesia (82 percent), and the Palestinian Authority (81 percent) said they were disappointed the Iraqi military put up so little resistance. Many others around the world shared that view, including people in South Korea (58 percent), Brazil (50 percent), and Russia (45 percent), according to a June 3, 2003, poll by Pew Global Research. Why? The world was clearly hoping against hope that America would lose and Saddam Hussein would win. Yet, by what stretch of logic would it be better for Saddam Hussein to have won? The question was too painful to contemplate and was ignored by Arabs.

Instead, Arabs focused on the question: Why do we always lose?

"The invasion of Iraq is the first to reveal the extent to which the current Arab system is vulnerable, fragile, and disconnected in the face of the threats and challenges which it is facing," wrote Majid Al-Kayyali in the UAE daily *Al-Bayan*.

Labib Kamhawi, a Jordanian political analyst, shut off his television in disgust. "Enough. Whatever we do, we lose," he said. "Failure after failure after failure. There must be something wrong with us after all these defeats. We always defeat ourselves. We should look inside to see why and have the guts and courage to say why."

It was a trenchant question, for the Arabs' path through recent history is bereft of success. The newspapers so often list the defeats of the past fifty years that many readers can recite the long and sad litany with little effort. The creation of the state of Israel in 1948, the gravest sin in the Arabs' eyes—was followed by the 1967 war, in which the Arab forces were defeated in a week; a few years of discouraging skirmishing were followed by the 1973 war, which also ended in an Arab defeat (though 3,000 Israelis were killed; it was widely regarded as Israel's most embarrassing war); then came the 1982 Israeli invasion of Lebanon and siege of Beirut; the 1987 to 1993 *intifada,* the post-1991 peace process; the eight-year Iran-Iraq war; the Iraqi invasion of Kuwait; the subsequent Gulf War rout; the continuing *al-Aqsa intifada* of 2000; and the latest outrage, the American-led invasion of Iraq and toppling of Saddam Hussein.

"We can see that the Arab system has been unable to take the initiative to solve these issues, or manifest its ability to deter, because of its advanced state of petrifaction, decay, and dislocation," Al Kayyali wrote.

Modern Arabs also possess a cultural memory of history stretching back a thousand years. The rise of the Islamic civilization, and its collapse, are part of every Arab's inbred history. The collapse of the Muslim empire, from its beginnings in 1693 with the defeat of Ottoman armies at the gates of Vienna, Napoleon's invasion of Egypt, the subsequent centuries of European advancement, and the regression of Arab culture and political influence: Any Arab could recite the entire gaudy tale.

Of course, the Arabs tend to forget their own victories—much to the frustration of Osama bin Laden. After all, they did evict the

Soviets from Afghanistan, and arguably inflicted such a bloody defeat it spelled the end of both the Soviet Union and superpower communism (bin Laden has yet to say what exactly he plans for China). Among the Arabs, though, Afghanistan was old news—especially since it also represented a recent defeat. What Arabs wanted to focus on was Iraq, now in the crosshairs of the Crusader Americans. It made little difference to most Arab commentators that the United States was the only nation both willing and able to liberate the long-suffering Iraqi people from the murderous Saddam. To the Arab world, it was the Americans who posed the clear and present danger.

"Was this the only way for a political regime to be changed, through the American tanks? Couldn't we think of any other way to effect political change in the Arab world?" asked Al Jazeera commentator Qassem Jaa'far on the day Saddam's statue was pulled down in Paradise Square.

"We will hate America and will support from today every phrase or political speech that puts the black bull in its place," a seething Ali Saad Al-Moussa wrote in his column for *Al Watan Daily,* a newspaper in the Persian Gulf sultanate of Oman. He accused the United States of "leading humankind to a catastrophe."

The overblown language suggested a kind of intramural competition in the Arab world: Who could hate Americans most, loudest, hardest, most enthusiastically?

One main contender had to be the Egyptians, recipients of $2 billion a year from America and evidently very unhappy to be forced to take it. A well-known singer's latest hit—all the rage in Cairo— was "Better Saddam's Hell Than America's Paradise."

At one point, Ambassador David Welch complained that the Egyptian media were taking things too far after a newspaper columnist declared that American forces in Baghdad were cannibals, and another writer called for more "martyrdom" operations against Americans. That only earned Welch another round of public wrath.

"Egypt is not one of the American states which are ruled by the Pentagon," wrote columnist Gamal Bada in Egypt's *Al-Gumhuriya,* "and it is not subject to the influence of the Zionist gang that dominates the White House. Instead of frequenting coffee-houses and clubs, the American Ambassador should have analyzed the content of the Egyptian papers, because they accurately reflect the rage and fury that are simmering in the popular cauldron against America's policies. He should have related this missive back to his country."

For all their fulminations, though, the Egyptians did not finish first in this contest. That honor must go to Saudi Arabia. The clear superstars of anti-Americanism in the Arab world were the very Arabs who claim to be America's greatest friends: the Saudis.

It was, after all, the Saudis whose sons were fifteen of the terrorists who struck America on September 11 and sent up so many cheers in the Arab world. It was the Saudis who raised, and enriched, and taught Osama bin Laden, the terror leader who has targeted America. And it was the Saudis who have sent billions of dollars to an array of Muslim countries funding Islamic schools that teach hatred of the West, and particularly of the United States.

The Saudis's oil reserves have made them the richest of the Arabs, and they have been richer longer than any of their neighboring oil-rich Gulf States.

The Saudi–American relationship dates back more than half a century, cemented by Franklin Roosevelt in a 1945 meeting with King Ibn Saud, founder of the current Saudi Kingdom. Roosevelt traveled a great distance, to the Great Bitter Lake in Suez, toward the end of World War II to meet the king for a very important reason: The United States had run out of oil. World War II had depleted America's oil reserves in Texas, Oklahoma, Louisiana, and California, and we needed new and steady supplies.

Saud had a different problem. The Saudi Kingdom was fragile, beset by enemies and predators, and it needed protection. The United

States had just demonstrated that no power on earth could seriously challenge it, and Saud wanted U.S. protection.

An arrangement was made giving Americans access to Saudi oil fields and the Saudis the ongoing protection of U.S. forces. The arrangement worked well until 1973, when the Saudis—seething with rage over America's defense of Israel in the ill-conceived and losing war the Arabs launched against Israel—engineered a crippling oil embargo.

Why did the Saudis lash out at the West by withholding the very commodity that makes the world economy function smoothly? The very same reason those Saudi hijackers—and bin Laden, their fellow Saudi—executed the horrendous attacks of September 11: the virulent anti-Americanism and anti-Westernism of the official Saudi sect of Islam known as Wahhabism.

Muhammad ibn Abdul Wahhab was born at the dawn of the eighteenth century in a remote and isolated region of the Arabian peninsula, the son of a religious judge. As a young man, he moved to Medina, where he followed Hanbali Islamic scholars, admirers of the fourteenth-century Islamic writer Ibn Taymiyya. Taymiyya believed that outside influences had corrupted the religion of the Prophet Muhammad, and he denounced Muslims who had adopted certain practices of Christians and Jews.

Ibn Wahhab traveled to the major centers of Islamic thought— Iraq, Syria, and even Persia—and was well acquainted with the leading trends in Islamic practice. He returned to Arabia convinced that the branches of Islam practiced in the Ottoman Empire and Persia had been corrupted. The veneration of saints, and pilgrimage and prayer at their tombs, were practices borrowed from other religions, which Ibn Wahhab deplored and insisted must be driven from Islam. In his book, Ibn Wahhab wrote that true Islam is "a rejection of all gods except God," and that worship of anyone or anything except God "is evil, no matter what the object, whether it be 'king or prophet, or saint or tree or tomb.'"

Ibn Wahhab's wrath was directed at Shiites, literally "partisans" of Ali, the Prophet Muhammad's son-in-law, married to the prophet's daughter Fatima, who in turn was granted a saint-like status the Wahhabis label as religiously corrupt. The Shiites believed in a hereditary dynasty of spiritual leaders, an *imamate,* which would inevitably lead to the arrival of a savior or messiah, a so-called twelfth imam.

Ibn Wahhab fought this and other trends he considered to be deviations from true Islam, which he saw as the recreation of practices of seventh-century Arabia at the time of the Prophet Muhammad. Offending all the political and religious leaders of his time, Ibn Wahhab found protection in Muhammad Ibn Saud, the ruler of the region known today as Riyadh. Saud was subjugating Bedouin tribes into what became the first Saudi Kingdom; he and Wahhab made a covenant that Wahhab would grant Saud religious legitimacy for his rule as king, and Saud would grant Wahhab religious leadership to impose a puritanical form of Islam soon to be known as Wahhabism.

The Saudis have been Wahhabis ever since, and while Saudi Arabia is officially recognized as a moderate state aligned with America, it has also been the most successful and energetic purveyor of Muslim fundamentalism in the Islamic world.

Fifteen of the nineteen September 11 hijackers were Saudi Wahhabs. Osama bin Laden was a Saudi until the Saudi royal family stripped him of his citizenship for embarrassing the kingdom by declaring war on America and killing Americans in terrorist attacks— and for the crime of declaring the Saudi regime itself apostate and calling for its overthrow. In religious terms, he remains a Wahhabi, though he condemns the clerics on the Saudi payroll who issue *fatwas* supporting the regime. Bin Laden's philosophy is taken directly from the *jihad* philosophy of Ibn Wahhab: the imposition of the rightful path of Islam by the sword.

From the birth of Wahhabism, its greatest enemies have been fellow Muslims, who recognized its incendiary and deadly nature and have tried to stamp it out. An Egyptian Sultan even managed to capture and behead the second Saudi king.

"The Wahhabi rebellions of the nineteeth and twentieth centuries were very bloody because the Wahhabis indiscriminately slaughtered and terrorized Muslims and non-Muslims alike," wrote Khaled Abou El Fadl, Distinguished Fellow in Islamic Law at UCLA School of Law, in the Winter 2001 *Middle East Report*. "Mainstream [Islamic] jurists writing at the time, such as the Hanafi Ibn 'Avidin and Maliki al-Sawi, described the Wahhabis as a fanatic fringe group."

The Wahhabi code of violent opposition to any form of what Wahhabi clerics judged to be "polytheism," the worship of more than one god, has for centuries imposed on Wahhabi followers the absolute requirement of *jihad* against the unbelievers.

"The Wahhabi creed also considered any form of moral thought that was not entirely dependent on the text [of the Koran] as a form of self-idolatry, and treated humanistic fields of knowledge, especially philosophy, as 'the sciences of the devil,'" wrote El Fadl. "According to the Wahhabi creed, it was imperative to return to a presumed pristine, simple and straightforward Islam, which could be entirely reclaimed by literal implementation of the commands of the Prophet, and by strict adherence to correct ritual practice."

According to El Fadl, after the sharp rise in oil prices that occurred after the 1973 oil embargo, the Saudis aggressively promoted Wahhabi beliefs around the Muslim world, through the annual donation of hundreds of millions of dollars to Wahhabi schools known as *madrassas*. These fundamentalist academies have been established in Pakistan, Afghanistan, Indonesia, and even the United States, and have been lavishly funded by Saudi Arabia for more than a quarter century, to the tune of billions of dollars.

El Fadl, a scholar of Islamic law at UCLA, calls puritanical Wahhabism the driving force behind the righteousness of the modern terrorist. "One can easily locate an ethical discourse within the Islamic tradition that is uncompromisingly hostile to acts of terrorism. One can also locate a discourse that is tolerant toward the other, and mindful of the dignity and worth of all human beings. But one must also come to terms with the fact that supremacist Puritanism in contemporary Islam is dismissive of all moral norms or ethical values, regardless of the identity of their origins or foundations. The prime and nearly singular concern is power and its symbols. Somehow all other values are made subservient."

Donald Rumsfeld asked in his now-famous leaked memo of late October 2003: "Are we killing or capturing terrorists as fast as they are turned out by the Islamic fundamentalist schools?" The answer is no. Hundreds of Saudi-funded schools indoctrinate tens of thousands of young Muslims in Wahhabi *jihad* principles every year.

It was from those Saudi-sponsored *madrassas* that Osama bin Laden drew his *jihadis* for war against the Soviets in Afghanistan, and for the Taliban who succeeded them. And it is to those *madrassa*-educated fundamentalists that bin Laden has declared that American "crusader armies" must be expelled from Saudi Arabia, "the land of the two holy cities" Mecca and Medina. Bin Laden and his followers refuse to refer to the country of Mecca and Medina as Saudi Arabia because they also believe that the Saudi royal family and the Saudi government are apostate—heretics who must be overthrown.

In his book *Hatred's Kingdom*, Dore Gold writes, "Islam is not the problem. Rather, the problem is the extremists in the Middle East who have manipulated Friday sermons in the mosques, textbooks in the schools, and state-controlled television to one end: to systematically prepare young people to condone the cold-blooded murder of innocent civilians."

The Kingdom of Saudi Arabia employs 50,000 imams, or Muslim clerics, who preach Wahhabi sermons in the country's mosques. The kingdom is the custodian of Mecca and Medina and the facilitator of the *haj,* the pilgrimage to Mecca that is the duty of all the world's one and a half billion Muslims at least once in their lifetime.

The Kingdom of Saudi Arabia was a major sponsor of the war against the Soviets in Afghanistan, and it is the major sponsor of the Palestinian *al-Aqsa intifada* against Israeli occupation of the West Bank.

The Kingdom of Saudi Arabia, through its official sponsorship of the religious teachings of Wahhabism, is the major sponsor of hate against America in the Muslim world. In the Wahhabist view, America is polytheist, licentious, lewd, and immoral; America is modern, granting rights to women and allowing freedoms Wahhabism condemns; America is the world's prime, if not sole, sponsor of Israel, and therefore complicit in the murder of Palestinians.

America may have protected Saudi Arabia from its neighbors and from Soviet expansionism for fifty years and may have enriched the Saudi elites and government beyond the wildest dreams of the Bedouin nomads who founded the desert kingdom. But we have also come to be the object of intense hate and scorn.

"Why don't you all stay home? Stay in America. We don't need you, we don't want you. We don't need you to tell us what to do or where we want to live or why we should want to live in your land of the free. Take your ideas, your bombs, your threats, get out, go away. The world hates you? What a surprise. The world is retaliating to your evil." That e-mail was from a Saudi woman, sent to Fox News Channel's *The Big Story* well before the war.

Writing in the *Arab News* in May 2003, Amr Mohammed Al-Faisal, a stridently anti-American political commentator, said: "The U.S. has embarked on a campaign to both kill and humiliate Arabs, the consequence of which is that any and all U.S. citizens will be regarded by some as legitimate targets upon which to unleash their rage."

Al-Faisal is not just any political commentator: he is a member of the Saudi royal family, one of a few thousand Saudi princes who are entitled to a half-million-dollar annual income from Saudi Arabia's enormous oil revenues, largely derived from the automotive driving habits of ordinary Americans.

Al-Faisal likes to adopt a mocking tone toward America. In one column, in the July 27, 2003, edition of the *Arab News,* he described the siege, and ultimate deaths, of Uday and Qusay Hussein in Mosul, Iraq, as an American military failure. "As for you, the American people, you must start to worry that the performance of your military does not start to give ideas to your southern neighbors. If they continue to perform like they are doing in Iraq, then I for one believe the Mexican Army is a serious threat to your national security."

One of Al-Faisal's relatives, the late King Faisal's granddaughter Reem Al-Faisal, also has made ludicrous attempts to link our actions in Iraq to other events in American history. "It is time for the American nation to acknowledge its crimes and apologize and ask forgiveness from the many people it has harmed. Beginning with the Native Americans, followed by the Africans and South Americans, right through to the Japanese, who have suffered such horror by being the only race to know the true meaning of weapons of mass destruction."

In the *Wall Street Journal* in July 2002, James Taranto reported on a clever ploy that revealed something about our Saudi "allies." When the registration for al Qaeda's online site lapsed, an online pornographer named Jon David Messner took notice and moved quickly to set up a "decoy site" using the name. "We have all the IP [Internet Provider] addresses to the tune of 27,000 visitors a day seeking alneda.com from every hostile country imaginable," Messner said. "But interestingly enough, 90 percent were from Saudi Arabia."

Officially, Saudi Arabia was horrified and embarrassed by Osama bin Laden's *jihad* against America. His Saudi citizenship was stripped, his terrorist activities officially disavowed. But *Newsweek's* Christopher Dickey has reported that in a secret state-sponsored poll taken in October 2001, the Saudi royal family learned that *95 percent* of Saudi men between the ages of twenty-five and forty-one said they approved of bin Laden's cause.

In wondering why this might be, the Saudi government began by looking elsewhere. In the days and weeks after September 11, the Saudis were apparently in deep denial that their countrymen were involved in the attacks. When the hijackers' identities were clearly established as young Saudis—some of them from well-known families—many Saudis looked outside their borders for the origins of bin Laden's bloody religious philosophy. Jamal Khashoggi, deputy editor-in-chief of the *Arab News,* wrote in October 2001: "How did Bin Laden come to create this fantasyland of terror? In part, it was through the bad influence of a radical Egyptian Islamic group called Al-Jihad. This group crossed many boundaries of conduct and decency, which were agreed upon in the Islamic world." The Saudis blamed Egypt's Muslim Brotherhood, the radical group that spawned Al-Jihad and assassinated Anwar Sadat for making peace with Israel. But Egyptians blamed Saudi Arabia in return, charging that the Sadat assassins were all trained and indoctrinated in Wahhabi Saudi Arabia.

In the same column, written only a month after September 11, Khashoggi also blamed America itself for the attacks, a sentiment shared widely in Saudi Arabia: "Americans want unconditional condemnation of the horrible attacks that happened in their skies and on their land. They also want total cooperation in their fight against terror according to their own definition of what terrorism is and exactly who the terrorists are. But Saudi Arabia will not give in to such demands. Saudis tend to link the ugliness of what happened in New York and Washington with what has happened and continues to happen in Palestine. It is time that the United States comes to understand the effect of its foreign policy and the consequences of that policy."

This is a favorite theme of Saudi commentators and citizens: America's support for Israel is the root of the Arabs' hatred against Americans. It is repeated in the mosques, in televised fund-raisers for the Palestinian Authority, in newspaper columns and editorials, in the deep denial of an entire nation of its role in the birth of al Qaeda and its terror.

In November 2001, an editorial in *Business Week* asked: "Can the House of Saud Save Itself?" The magazine was pessimistic. "The fact that 15 of the 19 terrorists were Saudi was shocking. The revelation that Saudi money provided funding for bin Laden has left Washington deeply angered. The statements from the royal family implying that America brought the death of thousands on itself by not supporting the Palestinians were infuriating." A final dagger waited at the end of the article: "The policies that the House of Saud used to stay in power have become a threat not only to the royal family but to its chief ally, the United States."

What were those policies? Seeking to deflect political dissent by encouraging ultraconservative clerics to preach anti-Western, anti-American, and anti-Israel extremism, the House of Saud has poured billions of dollars into thousands of religious schools in Saudi Arabia, Pakistan, Afghanistan, and even the United States that do not, as *Business Week* observed, "teach science math or literature; they teach anti-Westernism, anti-Americanism, and anti-Semitism." Those are the very schools where young John Walker Lindh of Marin County, California, went to transform himself into Taliban Johnny, student of sharia law.

In the time since the al Qaeda bombings of Riyadh in May and November 2003, though, the Saudis have begun to recognize the true beliefs of bin Laden and his followers: America is their major target, because it is the center of the modern world's *unbelief*—but no less a target is Saudi Arabia itself, the land of the two holy cities now corrupted by an apostate regime that hosts "crusader" American armies and does the bidding of infidel America.

The Saudi ambassador to Britain, Prince Turki Al-Faysal, admitted as much in the June 11, 2003 edition of *Al-Quds Al-Arabi,* a Saudi-sponsored London newspaper. "A solution to the Palestinian-Israeli problem will not affect Al-Qaeda operations. This is because even if the Palestinian problem were to be solved this organization would continue to look for reasons to carry out terror operations."

And the news only gets worse for the Saudis: "The Voice of Jihad," an online magazine identified with al Qaeda, has revealed that the new debate within the terror organization is whether to fight the Americans in Iraq or stay in Saudi Arabia and fight to corrupt leaders, the House of Saud. And for those who do stay, the question is whether or not to bomb Saudi Arabian targets.

"It is also true that we must use this country [Saudi Arabia]," writer Abu Hajjer says, "because it is the primary source of funds for most *Jihad* movements, and it has some degree of security and freedom of movement. However, we must strike a balance between this and the American invasion of the Islamic world and its strangling of the *Jihad* movement."

President Bush redacted a critical twenty-eight pages from a voluminous congressional report on September 11—pages widely thought to contain specific information on Saudi involvement in the terror attacks. It was already widely known that the wife of the Saudi ambassador to the United States had made what she claimed she thought was a charitable contribution to a man who turned out to be one of the September 11 hijackers. And an employee of the Saudi Civil Aviation Authority helped secure housing for two of their hijackers upon their arrival in San Diego, where they lay in wait preparing for September 11.

The Saudi government went so far as to demand the release of the twenty-eight withheld pages, claiming that a hostile media was using the existence of the secret pages to malign the kingdom. But the *Washington Post*'s Susan Schmidt reported in October 2003, a fact about the September 11 attacks not previously known outside investigative and intelligence circles. It involved a Saudi minister named Saleh Ibn Abdul Rahman Hussayen, later given oversight of the mosques in Mecca and Medina—who arrived in the United States on August 20, 2001, for a visit with some of America's highest-ranking fundamentalist Sunni leaders.

According to Schmidt's intelligence sources, Hussayen met with "the creators of Islamic web sites that U.S. authorities contend promote the views of radical Saudi clerics tied to Osama bin Laden." The sources also told Schmidt that Hussayen's schedule included a stop to see the leader of a religious center located in Falls Church, Virginia. "On the night of Sept. 10, 2001," Schmidt reported, "Hussayen stayed at a Herndon [Virginia] hotel that also housed three of the Saudi hijackers who would slam an aircraft into the Pentagon the next day."

Schmidt also reported there was no evidence that Hussayen had contact with the hijackers during that fateful overnight. But the fact that investigators, months later, could not nail down the details— phone records, eyewitnesses—that would establish as indisputable fact there was a meeting, weighs only slightly against what is otherwise a startling and telling coincidence: A major Saudi Wahhabi imam was in the very same hotel as three Saudi Wahhabi al Qaeda terrorists the night before the most important operation against the United States ever mounted by an Islamist group. Here was the culmination of every America-hating sermon ever shouted out to the faithful in every Wahhabi mosque in Arabia—yet these men didn't speak, they didn't meet, they didn't confer, they didn't counsel? They were merely Wahhabi ships passing ever so close in the night, the tantalizing timing simply a coincidence?

Though investigators could not prove that Hussayen took the opportunity to speak to three Saudi *jihadis* about the attacks—or about their reward in the next life (Hussayen was, after all, a religious counselor), prosecutors and FBI agents did uncover a network of Wahhabi fundamentalist groups whose purpose, they suspected, was "to incite violent jihad, or holy war, and recruit people to fight it, according to sources familiar with aspects of the investigation," Schmidt reported. As of June 2003, charges had been lodged against nineteen people associated with the groups, and seven had pleaded guilty.

Sheikh Nasser Al-Najidi, a Wahhabi cleric, wrote this on the Voice of Jihad website on October 17, 2003: "The heresy of that infidel [America] and his rebellion against the religion of Allah requires the permitting of his blood and [sanctions] his humiliation . . . his blood is like the blood of a dog and nothing more." And this: "Bush, the son of Bush, is a dog and the son of a dog, his blood is the blood of a dog, his bark is the bark of a dog, and he has all the traits of a dog except for loyalty."

The focus on America never wanes, despite al Qaeda's renewed interest in the cleansing of the "land of the two holy cities."

Al Qaeda theorist Sheikh Yousef Al-Ayyeri, who was killed on June 3, 2003, in a gunfight with Saudi police near Riyadh, wrote on another, now-defunct al Qaeda website that the apostate Saudi leadership corrupted itself by its own subjugation to the United States. "The real ruler is Crusader America. The subjugation of these rulers to America is no different than the subjugation of district rulers to the king or president of their country. Anyone who fights them is in effect fighting the one who has given them authority and made them (the Americans) rulers over the Muslims. Jihad is a commandment that applies personally to every Muslim."

Al-Ayyeri explained why a beleaguered and hounded al Qaeda is on the ascendancy. "It must also be noted that in its war with America, the Al Qaeda organization adopted the strategy of expanding the battle arena. This strategy has priceless advantages; the enemy who had only his country to defend realized that he now must defend his enormous interests in every country." Referring to the Riyadh bombing of May 12, 2003—which killed Americans, but many more Saudis—al-Ayyeri said, "While this strategy might cause some damages to Muslims in the process of defending the nation, this happens all the time, and in every Jihad. It is better than some damage be caused to the people in the interests of religion than in the interests of establishing the thrones of the despots and agents."

Jihad warrior Suleiman al-Dosari wrote on the Voice of Jihad in October 2003: "One of the greatest places in which *jihad* is a commandment applying to each Muslim individually is the land of the two holy places [the Arabian peninsula]. In this land there is the occupying Crusader enemy who steals the land's treasures, determines its policy, and sets out from it to make war on the Muslims. It also has an apostate agent government, and it implements the plans of colonialism, supports the infidels, and rules by a law that is not the law of Allah."

Amir Taheri, the widely read expert on Islamism and al Qaeda, has offered a careful analysis of a book by al-Ayyeri, published by al Qaeda shortly before his death. "What al-Ayyeri sees now," wrote Taheri, "is a 'clean battlefield' in which Islam faces a few form of unbelief. This, he labels 'secularist democracy.' This threat is 'far more dangerous to Islam than all its predecessors combined.' The reasons, he explains in a whole chapter, must be sought in democracy's 'seductive capacities.'

"This form of 'unbelief' persuades the people that they are in charge of their destiny and that using their collective reasoning they can adopt policies and pass laws as they see fit. That leads them into ignoring the 'unalterable laws' promulgated by God for the whole of mankind and codified in the Islamic shariah [law] until the end of time.

"The goal of democracy according to al-Ayyeri is 'to make Muslims love this world, forget the next world and abandon *jihad*.'" *Jihad* (fighting for Islam), and martyrdom (dying in battle for the religion), are guarantees of passage into Paradise.

Where does America fit into these ancient and mystifying religious concepts?

The great Islamic scholar Bernard Lewis has reminded us of a phrase of the Ayatollah Khomeini: that America has long been considered the "Great Satan."

"In the Koran, Satan is described as 'the insidious tempter who whispers in the hearts of men.'" Satan is not a fearful demon roaming the earth as a conqueror; "he is, first and last, a tempter."

This, says Lewis, explains it all. "For the members of al-Qaeda it is the seduction of America that represents the greatest threat to the kind of Islam they wish to impose on their fellow Muslims."

What is America if not the freedom to be tempted . . . and occasionally, the strength and wisdom to resist?

THREE

THE BRITS' ANNOYING TENDENCY TO HATE THEMSELVES FOR NOT HATING AMERICA QUITE VICIOUSLY ENOUGH

On a trip back to Europe this summer I was struck by how angry, cynical and frightened people are about the United States. And that was just in Britain, America's staunchest ally. It is probably not much disputed, even among the most optimistic members of the Bush Administration, that the world hates America a bit more than it did on September 10, 2001, and a lot more than it did on September 12, 2001. The net effect of the past two years has been, on the face of it, to give a significant boost to the America-haters.

—Gerard Baker, Washington Bureau Chief,
Financial Times, August 2003

The fervently anti-American British poet and playwright Harold Pinter gave the degree speech at the University of Florence on September 10, 2001, mere hours before Mohammad Atta and his colleagues launched their attacks. In his speech, Pinter described the United States thus: "Arrogant, indifferent, contemptuous of International Law, both dismissive and manipulative of the United Nations—this is now the most dangerous power the world has ever known—the authentic 'rogue state'—but a 'rogue state' of colossal military and economic might."

Pinter concluded his speech to the gathered Italian graduates with a virtual call to arms: "I believe that this brutal and malignant world machine must be recognized for what it is and resisted." The very next day, Mohammad Atta and Osama bin Laden did precisely that.

Inasmuch as Pinter spoke only a day before the attacks, it's almost impossible that the hijackers heard his bitter anti-American words or took inspiration from them (not, of course, that it would have made a difference; they had charted their course years before). But Pinter could not help but be embarrassed by the horrifying coincidence of his speech and the attacks. On September 13, he issued a statement distancing himself from the terrorists who lived, died, and committed mass murder in the spirit of his hateful words.

"My speech at the University of Florence," Pinter said, "was highly critical of the NATO action in Serbia and other manifestations of U.S. foreign policy. Nowhere in this speech, however, did I advocate violence. I was not throwing bombs, I was using words. The atrocities in New York and Washington are horrific, appalling. No responsible person can regard them in any other light." Of course, Osama bin Laden, though seen in an al Qaeda video trying to fire a weapon, has never engaged in "throwing bombs" either. He uses words, only words, as Pinter would say. Yet those words are at the very core of bin Laden's terrorist projects.

And Pinter was not through. On his website, he added a post-script to his earlier disclaimer: "The remarks [in this speech] seem even more valid to me now than when I made them on September 10. The 'rogue state' [the United States] has—without thought, without pause for reflection, without a moment of doubt, *let alone shame* [emphasis added]—confirmed that it is a fully fledged, award-winning, gold-plated monster. It has effectively declared war on the world. It knows only one language—bombs and death."

While Pinter was in Italy issuing statements, his anti-American colleagues back home in Great Britain were busy as well, writing furiously to meet deadlines, in tones that could be fairly described as gloating.

On Thursday, September 13, 2001, Suemas Milne wrote in his regular space in London's *Guardian:* "Nearly two days after the horrific suicide attacks on civilian workers in New York and Washington, it has become painfully clear that most Americans simply don't get it."

Get what? Apparently, that the blame for those attacks should be laid at our own doorstep.

In fact, the *Guardian* had much to say about America getting what it deserved. John Pilger, the noted anti-American, weighed in the same day. "Far from being the terrorists of the world, the Islamic peoples have been its victims—principally the victims of U.S. fundamentalism, whose power, in all its forms, military, strategic and economic, is the greatest source of terrorism on earth."

Anti-Americanism, as an essential part of British life, made itself plain on the BBC on the night of September 14, 2001. *Question Time,* an important and popular BBC program, asked Phil Larder, the former U.S. ambassador to Britain, to join three British political figures on a panel to be questioned by a studio audience. Larder would have done well to stay home.

As Larder tried to explain his nation's pain, as well as his own—as a former banking executive, he lost friends and colleagues in the

World Trade Center—he was shouted and hooted down by a virulently anti-American studio audience. Larder was barely able to restrain his tears.

The BBC received hundreds of calls from British viewers complaining of the program's anti-American bias. A BBC spokeswoman said the program was designed to elicit "lively interchange," and a BBC senior manager issued a public apology for the tone of the program. In the dizzy rush of events, the incident was forgotten as soon as possible. It was, after all, a vicious attack on Britain's most important ally, and much attention to the anti-Americanism on display could not be helpful, except in a futile effort to further chastise the impiously anti-American BBC.

Yet, we Americans hardly heard a word of the story, busy as we were watching New York firemen and construction workers search in vain for survivors in the rubble—"the pile," as it was called—of the still-smoking World Trade Center.

Precisely one week after the terror attacks, the *Guardian*'s columnists were hitting their stride. Charlotte Raven, a self-described "literary journalist," titled her column "A bully with a bloody nose is still a bully."

"It is perfectly possible to condemn the terrorist action and dislike the U.S. just as much as you did before the WTC went down," Raven wrote. "If anti-Americanism has been seized, temporarily, by forces that have done dreadful things in its name, there is no reason for its adherents to retreat from its basic precepts."

It would be easy to dismiss these incidents as the outbursts of a minority of the British public because anti-Americanism is not the majority view in Great Britain—at least according to polls. The Pew Research Center's series of polls of Great Britain—has indicated a general downward trend in support for the United States among Britons from the end of the Clinton administration through the early days of the Bush administration, and continuing into the Iraq postwar period. Even setting aside the expected spike of sympathy that occurred immediately after the September 11 attacks, roughly half of the British populace supported the United States in the run-up to the war and held it in reasonably high esteem.

Yet the Brits have also shown a tendency "to go wobbly on us," to borrow the phrase Margaret Thatcher used to strengthen the determination of the first President Bush. Just before the terror attacks of September 11, the Pew polling also showed that Britons were highly suspicious of George W. Bush's new America. Where 66 percent had approved of Bill Clinton's international policies, only 17 percent approved of those of George W. Bush. By April 2002 (the period between the Afghanistan and Iraq wars), Britons' view of Bush's international policies had risen to a 40 percent approval, with 73 percent approving of the war in Afghanistan.

If Britain was "half-American" in the debate about the Iraq war, though, it was also "half-European"—and that was the problem half.

Writing in the antiwar *Daily Mirror,* Tony Parsons noted that Americans were finally realizing, "to Europe's eternal shame," that Europeans believed 9/11 was America's "comeuppance."

"Secretaries and waiters leaping from the top of the burning twin towers?" Parsons wrote, mocking the prevalent attitude of too many of his countrymen. "The fault of American arrogance." In one of the hijacked planes, a cowering four-year-old girl about to die? "Blame it on America's support for Israel." Flight attendants lying in the aisles with their throats slashed by Atta's box cutters? According to Parsons, the Euros—and many Brits among them—just grinned and thought, "One in the eye for American imperialism." And nearly 3,000 people murdered in plain sight? "Europe blames America."

Parsons said quite rightly that anyone might have expected to see the Palestinians dancing in the street. "But who would have expected the grim look of satisfaction on the faces of old Europe?"

Anybody could see the writing on the wall—if they were looking. The *Washington Post* noted on February 11, 2002: "Anti-Americanism, West European-style, is widespread, rising, and migrating from its traditional home among left-wing intellectuals, academics, and café society to the political mainstream, according to analysts, critics, and public opinion polls. Countries such as France, Germany and Britain, which for more than five decades have been the closest allies of the United States, are beginning to drift away, propelled by a popular wave of concern, alarm and resentment. The immediate focus might be U.S. policy toward Iraq, but the larger emerging theme is an abiding sense of fear and loathing of American power, policies and motives."

In France and Germany, the anti-American feelings of the general public were sustained and fanned by the national leadership. In Great Britain, Prime Minister Tony Blair pleaded with his countrymen to see how their national interests were linked closely to the United States. And Blair was pilloried for it.

"I can't understand how an intelligent man like Tony Blair can listen to a moron like George Bush," said Dennis Halliday, a British career diplomat with the United Nations, in a comment quoted by the fiercely antiwar London *Daily Mirror*. As intemperate as his words might have seemed, Halliday actually made a habit of it. A year earlier, in February 2002, he told Cairo's *Al-Ahram Weekly:* "We Europeans . . . think Mr. Bush is a moron. We know he's dangerous."

A campaign of scorn and derision such as Halliday's certainly didn't help either Bush or Blair. By March 18, 2003, on the eve of the Iraq war, the polling had taken a significant turn against the United States. Only 48 percent of British subjects polled held a favorable view of the United States; 51 percent opposed the war, and a minority 40 percent thought the United Kingdom should remain close to the United States.

As a general conclusion, then, it would be fair to say that support for the United States among the British teetered, but a major portion of the public maintained a favorable attitude. We might also conclude that a significant part of the British public—occasionally a majority, depending on the ebb and flow of the news—frequently harbored strong doubts about the United States, and a large number of people engaged in open and hostile anti-Americanism that was often described as hate.

Salman Rushdie, who knows well what it means to be hated, published an article on the subject in the *Guardian* on February 6, 2002. In the article, "Anti-Americanism Has Taken the World By Storm," Rushdie wrote: "America did, in Afghanistan, what had to be done and did it well. The bad news, however, is that none of these successes has won friends for the United States outside Afghanistan. In fact, the effectiveness of the American campaign may paradoxically have made the world hate American more than it did before.

"America finds itself facing an ideological enemy that may turn out to be harder to defeat than militant Islam: that is to say, anti-Americanism, which is presently taking the world by storm."

Rushdie noted that Muslim nations have a certain set of specific complaints—the plight of the Palestinians topping the list. Speaking of his fellow Britons, however, he wrote: "The main objection seems to be American people. Night after night, I have found myself listening to Londoners' diatribes against the strange weirdness of the American citizenry. The attacks on America are routinely discounted ('Americans only care about their own dead'). American patriotism, obesity, emotionality, self-centeredness: these are the crucial issues."

At the time Rushdie made these observations, the Afghanistan campaign had been completed, and President Bush had just given his January 2002 speech naming Iraq, Iran, and North Korea as the "Axis of Evil." The Bush administration had gone to the United Nations to organize a "multilateral" coalition to topple the Taliban in Afghanistan and crush al Qaeda, but the world was beginning to squirm with worry about America. The nations of the world weren't so certain that America's "internationalist" approach was genuine or would continue, especially when it came to Iraq.

The complaints about America were largely unfocused, reaching far back in history; in large part, they were propelled by factional griping about George W. Bush the "Toxic Texan," or about America's new tendency to make decisions on its own without consulting the world. There was griping about the Bush administration's withdrawal from the Kyoto Accords, the International Criminal Courts, and the 1972 Anti-Ballistic Missile treaty. But the "crucial issues" tended to shift depending on who was making observation and comment. In June 2002, British economics journalist Will Hutton used America's corporate crime scandals to attack our capitalist blueprint, arguing in a book that Britain should look to Europe ("across the Channel rather than across the Atlantic"), with its high taxes and high levels of government service, as a direction for the future. The American preference for lower taxes, deregulation, and a freewheeling capitalist marketplace was inherently abhorrent to Hutton, who reached back 150 years to find his reasons: "The states of the Confederacy remain the heartland of the distinct brand of American conservatism that combines Christian, market and America-first fundamentalism . . . reinforced in the South by a legacy of barely submerged racism."

Americans might be startled to see the long-dead ghost of the Civil War raised in contemporary what's-wrong-with-America discussions, but for Hutton those shadowy apparitions carried special relevance: "The rise of American conservatism has closely followed the rise in the economic fortunes of the Confederacy, together with its belief in a take-no-prisoners form of capitalism." In this analysis, the titans of Wall Street became logical heirs to Jefferson Davis's Confederate States of America—and the South actually won the Civil War by losing, thus remaining in the Union and making piles of money.

Such fanciful confabulations of history aside, events changed dramatically in the closing months of 2002—and the British were the first to react in horror and revulsion.

On September 12, 2002, President Bush addressed the opening of the U.N. General Assembly in New York, challenging the skeptical and restive world body to confront the "grave and gathering danger" in Iraq—or become, in his word, "irrelevant." The path to war was suddenly clear before the world.

Five days later, President Bush released his administration's National Security Strategy, an official document outlining a new national defense position providing for the possibility of first strikes to deal with threats to U.S. interests. It emphasized, darkly to some, that the United States would use its military and economic power to ensure there will never be a challenge to its military supremacy by any country in the world, friend or foe.

It took a while for this notion to sink in—especially among academics, who move and think at a subdued pace. In May 2003, long after both the military and rhetorical action, the *New Statesman* published a piece by David Marquand, a former principal of Mansfield College, Oxford, who cited the 350-year-old Mastrecht Agreement among European kings and potentates, in arguing that sovereign states—even Iraq—are entitled to run their domestic affairs as they wish and that interventions to change regimes are always illegitimate. "As Iraq has shown," Marquand wrote, American officials "think the U.S. is above the law which, with all its weaknesses and ambiguities, offers the only hope of developing any world order worthy of the name." In a tone surprisingly threatening for an Oxford don, Marquand warned that the world cannot indefinitely tolerate a "lawless hegemon," and called for some alternative power strong enough to challenge or balance the United States. Where such a power might emerge was left unclear.

The British government weighed in on September 24, issuing a "dossier" on Iraq's weapons of mass destruction. It was to prove a fateful document, not only leading Britain to join the Americans in the Iraq war, but plunging them into a virtual civil war between the government and the BBC after the death of a scientist who broke the rules by talking to a reporter. Blair was forced to assure his dovish Labour Party that he was not rushing to war, nor simply playing yes-man to the Americans. But he did remind his colleagues that to cede the debate to the Washington unilateralists would be self-defeating. "The danger of saying to the Americans, 'You are on your own,' is that they will say 'Well, we are fine with that.'"

Less than a month after announcing the new National Security Strategy, on October 10, 2002, the U.S. Congress adopted a joint resolution authorizing the use of force against Iraq, giving the president authority to take preemptive, unilateral military action against Iraq if necessary. And a month after that, on November 8, the U.N. Security Council adopted Resolution 1441, imposing tough inspections on Iraq, as well as unambiguous definitions of what would constitute a "material breach" on the part of Saddam Hussein's regime. Three weeks later, weapons inspections began anew in Iraq.

John Pilger, a London-based Australian journalist who writes for the antiwar *Guardian* and other publications, said in a November 2002 interview with the *Progressive* that the Bush administration had done the world a service by declaring a policy of preemptive attacks on security threats. "We're grateful to them because they've made it very clear to other people just how dangerous they are. Before, Clinton persuaded some people that he was really a civilized character and his Administration had the best interests of humanity at heart. These days we don't have to put up with that nonsense. It's very clear that the Bush Administration is out of control. It contains some truly dangerous people."

The "truly dangerous," of course, was a matter for the eye of the beholder—for those whose eyes hadn't already been gouged out. Just as Pilger was identifying the Bush administration as "out of control and dangerous," the British Foreign and Commonwealth Office issued a report on the torture, murder, and persecution record of the regime of Saddam Hussein. Among other horrifying details, it listed a few of Saddam's methods of torture: "eye gouging, piercing of hands with electric drill, suspension from ceiling, electric shock, rape, and acid baths." Apparently such outrages were of little consequence to America-haters like Pilger, Pinter, and the rest.

On December 2, 2002, the British government issued its report on Iraq's human rights abuses. The report was immediately attacked by Amnesty International, which complained that the suffering of Iraqis, long ignored, was now being used to sell a war.

On December 7, Iraq submitted a twelve-thousand-page declaration purporting to describe its chemical, biological, and nuclear weapons programs, blithely assuring the world it had no banned weapons. The United States quickly recognized that the Iraqi document was virtually worthless. On December 19, the president declared Iraqi in "material breach" of Resolution 1441 after the United Nations' chief weapons inspector, Hans Blix, concurred that Iraq's weapons declaration contained little that was new.

On December 21, 2002, two weeks after Iraq submitted its voluminous but vacant statement, President Bush approved the deployment of U.S. troops to the Gulf region, announcing that an estimated 200,000 troops would be on station by March. Exactly one year after America had moved against the Taliban, the United States resolved swiftly to mobilize against the defiant and dangerous regime in Iraq.

In the drama of alignments, it was becoming clear that the French were not going to come along with the Americans. Under Tony Blair's leadership, the British would join the coalition—though his decision would be made in the face of massive public disapproval.

On January 7, 2003, Blair made his annual speech to the gathered assemblage of Britain's ambassadors, making a clear and convincing case for sticking with the Americans and putting his country on notice that he himself was sticking regardless of whatever jeers and catcalls he could expect from his own people.

"We are the ally of the U.S. not because they are powerful, but because we share their values. I am not surprised by anti-Americanism; but it is a foolish indulgence," Blair said. "For all their faults and all nations have them, the U.S. are a force for good; they have liberal and democratic traditions of which any nation can be proud." Mindful of America's ongoing immigration challenge, Blair said, "I sometimes think it is a good rule of thumb to ask of a country: are people trying to get into it or out of it? It's not a bad guide to what sort of country it is."

Blair explained to his ambassadors, and to his nation, why he thought it important that the United Kingdom stay at America's side: to help ensure that the United Kingdom was in a position to influence America's policies, which have such great effect on the world.

"But the price of influence is that we do not leave the U.S. to face the tricky issues alone. By tricky, I mean the ones which people wish weren't there, don't want to deal with, and, if I can put it a little pejoratively, know the U.S. should confront, but want the luxury of criticising them for it." In two quick sentences, Tony Blair expressed precisely the position in which the United States found itself, in the new anti-American world.

January 13, 2003, was a key day for those keeping an eye on the details that make all the difference. The head of the International Atomic Energy Agency, Mohammed el-Baradei, announced that the upcoming January 27 weapons inspectors' report to the Security Council would only be an "update report," and that the inspectors would need a "few more months" to finish their work. But the White House made it clear that "months" were out of the question. In a televised briefing, Tony Blair insisted that Britain must join in acting against Saddam Hussein immediately, or face a future in which terrorists armed with weapons of mass destruction could act at will.

As the pieces began to fall into place for a late-winter war, the gasps from Britain were heard across the Atlantic in Washington, D.C., and New York.

"The United States Has Gone Mad," declared a London *Times* article by spy novelist John le Carre. "America has entered one of its periods of historical madness, but this is the worst I can remember," he wrote. "Worse than McCarthyism, worse than the Bay of Pigs, and in the long term potentially more disastrous than the Vietnam War."

John le Carre is the *nom de plume* of onetime British spy and university professor David Cornwell, who has published eighteen novels since 1961. Le Carre has engaged in several public debates during his long career as a novelist, most famously an angry exchange of letters with Salman Rushdie when the latter was under a death *fatwa* issued by the Ayatollah Khomeini in retaliation for perceived insults to Islam in Rushdie's novel *The Satanic Verses.*

This time le Carre felt compelled to attack George W. Bush himself, as an entity separate from American policy. "How Bush and his junta succeeded in deflecting America's anger from bin Laden to Saddam Hussein is one of the great public relations conjuring tricks of history. But they swung it."

Scenes of anti-American fervor were becoming a regular feature of the political landscape in Britain. At an antiwar rally at Ruskin College in Oxford, England, a packed audience cheered passionately as Ken Nichols O'Keefe, a former U.S. Marine, described the United States as "the most despicable and criminal nation in the world."

January 18 and 19 were crucial days. If Saddam Hussein had taken either offer made over those forty-eight hours, there would not have been a war.

First, it became known that the Saudis had floated a plan to whisk Saddam into exile if the U.N. Security Council passed a new resolution authorizing war. Other plans by the French and the Russians were also believed to have been in the works. The next day, President Bush offered Saddam Hussein immunity from prosecution if he would leave Iraq before war.

Saddam ignored both offers.

On January 24, the first use of an old and nearly forgotten military concept made a reappearance on the *CBS Evening News* with

Dan Rather and entered the international lexicon as the catch phrase of the early phase of the war.

CBS correspondent David Martin interviewed Harlan Ullman, co-author of a 1996 National Defense University Book called *Shock and Awe: Achieving Rapid Dominance.* In a forty-eight-hour period sometime in March, Ullman asserted, the U.S. military would launch 800 precision guided missiles into Baghdad. The phrase "shock and awe" entered common usage by early March, as the plans for the war gradually entered the public awareness through further print and broadcast interviews with military experts. "Shock and awe" would be to the Iraq war what "The Mother of All Battles" was to the first Gulf War: descriptive, frightening, and so overused it became a punch line.

By Sunday, January 26, the *Washington Post*'s Glenn Frankel was reporting that America's insistence on war with Iraq—and on British cooperation—was producing an ugly British reaction.

"The debate here," former U.S. Ambassador to Britain Raymond Seitz told Frankel, is "not about how you deal with weapons of mass destruction or how you combat the threat of terrorism in the world. It's about how do you constrain the United States. How do you tie down Gulliver[?]" As Frankel observed, the British thought America "a gluttonous society of large cars, fast food and environmental degradation seeking cheap Iraqi oil to feed its consumption habits."

Columnist Michael Grove of the *Times* said: "Anti-Americanism is a real force here and a growing one. It starts with tightly focused arguments but broadens into the crudest of caricatures." *The Madness of George W.* was packing the house at around this time, with its portrait of a childlike president in jammies hugging a teddy bear.

Hans Blix, the all-things-to-all-leaders Swedish diplomat who headed the U.N. weapons inspection agency, reported to the Security Council on Iraqi cooperation with weapons inspectors on January 27. While he said that the inspectors needed more time, he also said that "Iraq appears not to have come to true acceptance, not even today, of the disarmament that was demanded of it."

The following day, in his State of the Union address, President Bush reported that Saddam Hussein was not disarming, but in fact deceiving. Bush announced he was prepared to attack Iraq—even without a U.N. mandate.

In the *London Review of Books,* Perry Anderson wrote: "Cultural dislike of the Bush Presidency is widespread in Western Europe, where its rough affirmations of American primacy, and undiplomatic tendency to match word to deed, have become intensely resented by public opinion accustomed to a more decorous veil being drawn over the realities of relative power."

On February 5, the day Colin Powell made his make-or-break presentation to the Security Council urging a second resolution authorizing the use of force against Iraq, Britain's Channel 4 News gave equal weight to Saddam Hussein himself, who was interviewed by longtime left-wing British parliamentarian Tony Benn.

Powell told the Security Council: "The facts on Iraq's behavior demonstrate that Saddam Hussein and his regime have made no effort—no effort—to disarm as required by the international community."

But Saddam Hussein maintained his cooperative pose, trying to persuade the British public to take Iraq at its word. "Every fair-minded person knows that as far as resolution 1441 is concerned, the Iraqis have been fulfilling their obligations under the resolution."

Over the next five weeks, the United States took Britain along as America nudged the world toward war. Most days, the news revolved around our "allies" and their attempts to derail America's war timetable. On February 9, for example, the French and Germans offered a peace initiative that would have tripled the number of weapons inspectors in Iraq and given inspectors surveillance flights. The United States rejected the proposal, pointing out that Saddam was parceling out permission for tools the inspectors should have had from the beginning, stalling for time in the process.

The next day, France, Germany, and Belgium vetoed a request backed by the United States for NATO to protect Turkey if Saddam Hussein should attack. It was the first time NATO members had ever rejected a request for defensive assistance from a fellow NATO member—flying in the face of NATO's reason for existence. Donald Rumsfeld called the move "shameful," but the French, Germans, and Belgians responded by claiming that any such pledge would seem to suggest support for a war they opposed.

The issue festered for six days before the deadlock was broken and NATO agreed to extend the assistance in question. But the willingness of France, Germany, and Belgium to abrogate the NATO charter over a disagreement with America was a jaw-dropper.

The second half of February saw attempts from every quarter to break America's resolve. On February 14, Hans Blix surprised the U.N. Security Council with a rather upbeat report on compliance with Resolution 1441, refusing to give the United States and Britain a clear *casus belli*. The next day was International Peace Day, with over a million people marching in the streets of London, and perhaps millions more marching in protest of American policy in other world capitols. At the end of February, Saddam Hussein agreed to destroy his stockpile of Al Samoud missiles, which were illegal under the terms of the agreement he had signed at the end of the Gulf War.

Around this time, the United States began circulating the text of a draft resolution by which the Security Council would authorize war. The French, Germans, and Russians made their opposition clear and, as events unfolded, it seemed likely that the Americans and British might go to war alone.

Tony Blair and the British public—at least those who supported the war—may have known it was going to get lonely, but this level of unified opposition was shocking. In an essay that appeared in

February's *London Review of Books,* Conor Gearty exemplified the tone of the opposition. "If [such a war] has to be done in tandem with an unsavory Texan right-winger who cheated his way to his own election," he wrote, "then so be it: 'the hand of history' (another Blair phrase) should not be scorned just because of the company it means having to keep."

What happened to the longtime British gratitude for the aid America had shown an embattled Britain facing its worst hour? "The end of the cold war has robbed the trans-Atlantic alliance of an essential glue," Philip Stephens reflected in the *Financial Times* in late May 2003. "Aggressive U.S. power is anathema to a continent deeply scarred by a history of nationalism. Preventative war is an alien concept." Martin Wolf had written in the *Financial Times* two days earlier, "The U.S. believes in unbridled freedom of action. Europeans believe in international rules. The U.S. wants to transform the world. Europeans want to manage it."

It may not have been bloody, but in many ways America saw some of its toughest battles in this war of words before any boots were on the ground. On March 1, the Bush administration was surprised when the Turkish parliament rejected America's offer of a multibillion dollar aid package in exchange for access to move U.S. troops through Turkish territory on their way to Iraq's northern front.

American preparations for war continued. The next day it became known that the United States and Britain had stepped up their air strikes in the no-fly zones in an apparent attempt to "soften up" Iraqi defenses in preparation for full-scale war. On March 5, though, France, Germany, and Russia issued a joint declaration that they would not allow the American resolution authorizing military action to pass the Security Council.

The very next day, in a nationwide television address, President George W. Bush indicated that war was very close. But both France and Russia had indicated that they would veto any war resolution that comes before the U.N. Security Council.

The British government found itself moving away from Europe—even as its population continued to decry American leaders as blood-thirsty belligerents. As a *New York Times* correspondent wrote: "Whether they admit it or not, Britons have always felt ambivalent about the awesome strength and unvarnished self-regard of the United States, their country's closest ally."

On March 16, the British public watched Prime Minister Blair travel to an impromptu war summit in the Azores to meet with President Bush, as the only member of the "coalition of the willing" with any real power. (Spain also attended, apparently for moral support.) The coalition gave the United Nations a twenty-four-hour deadline to act on the second resolution. As expected, the next day, the United States and the United Kingdom officially withdrew the second resolution, blaming a veto threat from the French.

Sir Michael Howard, one of Britain's most eminent military historians, predicted in London's *Sunday Times* that more soldiers could die in the Arabian desert than perished in the trenches of the Somme in World War I. "It is," he said, "a vile gamble."

The run-up to the war culminated with President Bush's March 18 televised address, giving Saddam Hussein forty-eight hours to leave Iraq or face invasion. In London, Parliament debated the impending military action in Iraq, and passed a war resolution by a roughly three-to-one margin. With 40,000 British soldiers among the 170,000 coalition troops massed on the Kuwait border for an invasion, however, before the war began several of Tony Blair's cabinet ministers had resigned in protest.

Shortly after the forty-eight-hour period elapsed, on March 20, the war began. As American and British troops crossed the Kuwait border, coalition warplanes began pounding military targets in Baghdad and elsewhere in Iraq.

On that day, London's *Daily Mail* reported that a Church of England bishop had declared that God himself was not necessarily pulling for the U.S. in the war. The Right Reverend Jack Nicholls, Bishop of Sheffield, declared that "to claim that God is on our side would be arrogant in the extreme."

It was also on that day that this new wave of British hatred for America began in earnest. For at that moment a specific purpose came into focus: to enrage the British public over being brought along with the hateful Americans on such a terrible and deadly war. This hatred became the foundation of the protestors' case against Tony Blair, and for the war after the war, over whether the evidence presented to justify the war was perverted and twisted to bolster the Allies' case. If the war was built on a lie, then the question became, who did the lying? From day one, Blair was the principal suspect. Characterized by antiwar voices as Bush's all-too-willing tool, Blair was accused of engaging in willful exaggeration of Saddam Hussein's capabilities and intentions, in order to talk a skeptical public into war.

To be sure, Blair won some respect among his domestic opponents by his willingness to face any critics and travel to any venue to debate the war. As the *New York Times* observed, Blair appeared willing to take on all comers to make his case, speaking "forthrightly to mutiny-minded members" of his own party in Parliament, leading a ten-hour debate in the House of Commons, and bravely taking angry questions from an audience of sullen and suspicious young people "handpicked for their hostility to his hard-line stance" by MTV—"an exercise hard to imagine any other world leader undertaking," as Warren Hoge of the *New York Times* observed.

In that debate, the much-feared British television host Jeremy Paxman "sneeringly asked Mr. Blair whether he and Mr. Bush had prayed together." The audience mocked Blair openly, addressing him as "Mr. Vice President" and referring to him, in a burlesque of Parliamentary custom, as "the honorable member for Texas North."

Ignoring the insults—there and elsewhere—Blair made his case that Britain should act because it was the right thing to do and because Saddam Hussein posed a threat to Great Britain. It was on that last point the British people dug in their heels demanding considerably more proof than their cousins, the Americans.

Blair's unflinching responses earned him a quantity of respect. The *Independent,* a fearsome enemy of Blair's war stance, published an editorial praising his dogged determination, energy, and passion: "Despite all the doubts about this war, Mr. Blair has shown himself in the past few days to be at once the most formidable politician in the country and the right national leader for these deeply uncertain times."

Still, the deep thinkers kept returning to the question: Why did Blair do it? Why did he go along with Bush and the United States? Ross McKibbin, a fellow at St. John's College, Oxford, offered his theory in the *London Review of Books:* "We support America because the country's elites long ago concluded that what remains of British influence can be preserved only in alliance with the United States."

As deeply galling as that may be, McKibbin reasoned, it was nonetheless true. "America is widely admired, but also widely disliked; and the America whose chief ally we have become represents the America which is widely disliked. *It is faith* [emphasis added] which leads the Prime Minister to argue with immense force that challenges to America's freedom and way of life are also challenges to ours— something which is not true, though it might well become true."

Many Britons feared they would create animosity with Muslims around the world—particularly in Britain—by siding with America. September 11 was America's problem, not Britain's. So why not leave it that way? And eventually the attacks on Blair escalated once again.

The *Guardian* printed an opinion piece by David Hare, a playwright, screenwriter, and antiwar activist, attacking the logic behind the war. "The introduction of the doctrine of the right to the preemptive strike is an event in international history of infinitely more consequence and importance than anything that happened on September 11."

" . . . of infinitely more consequence and importance than anything that happened on September 11." Hare did not bother to explain why the attack on America, the deaths and the destruction did
not warrant preemptive response. He left his statement unexplained,
as if it were self-evident: as if America's demonstrated vulnerability
were a minor matter not worth his consideration.

Hare also took a shot that was a guaranteed applause line in
Britain: "George Bush is a born-again Christian and a recovering alcoholic. I see in him the uncontrollable anger of the alcoholic, once
directed at himself, sluiced away every night into his bloodstream and
out into the gutter, now, tragically, directed, via his amazingly aggressive, amazingly triumphant body language, onto whatever poor
soul comes into his sights."

From the other side, fellow Briton William Shawcross rebutted
Hare's argument in the *Los Angeles Times.* "The newly articulated
notion of preemption raises both fears and hackles in Europe," he
wrote. "But surely everyone would agree that it would have better if
the U.S. had preempted 9/11 by confronting al-Qaeda and the Taliban before September 2001. There was ample cause. Osama Bin
Laden had destroyed two U.S. embassies in Africa, killing hundreds of
people; he had blown up American barracks in Saudi Arabia; he had
declared jihad on the United States; he had blown up the U.S. de-
stroyer Cole, killing 17 Americans in Aden harbor. Was this not
enough?" It was a trenchant response to the British who wailed their
hatred for America's allegedly warlike ways: "If the U.S. had acted
earlier to destroy Bin Laden's bases in Afghanistan, the 3,000 people
who died on September 11 might still be alive."

The war itself lasted from March 20 to approximately April 9,
when Iraqi forces protecting Baghdad were either crushed in the on-
coming American assault or simply took off their uniforms and went
home.

More than any war that had come before, the Iraq war happened
on television. We watched it unfold in downtown Baghdad, where the

bombing campaign began in full view of the live cameras feeding the world from the journalists' hotel in next to Paradise Square, and on the road to Baghdad, in the grinding drive north by American troops—and "embedded reporters" whose green night-vision pictures held the world spellbound.

But the war also unfolded on the BBC, and Al-Jazeera, and Al-Arabia, and many other television networks, which approached the war from a very different premise: that it should never have happened, that Saddam Hussein should have been allowed to remain in charge in Iraq rather than being threatened by the naked aggression of the Americans.

"All we have now is America doing what it likes best: waging war on poor countries, never rich countries; and taking them over," forty-six-year-old Aurangzeb Durrani, a retired banker in East Renfrewshire, Great Britain, wrote to the *Guardian* in early April.

"Laser bombs beam down from the stratosphere, cluster bombs drop from the sky," Steve McPherson wrote to the editor of the *Sydney Morning Herald*. "On the ground the artillery fires shells containing 80 grenades. Dalek-like humans, cocooned in armored shells, roam the land crying 'exterminate!' And we're the ones frightened of weapons of mass destruction? You've got to be kidding."

Three weeks into the war, Piers Morgan, editor of Britain's *Daily Mirror,* conducted a series of exchanges on the war with Charles Moore, his counterpart at the *Daily Telegraph,* published in the *Guardian.* "What is clear is that there is a widening gulf between the way the Americans wish to conduct this war, and the way the British do. Their forces seem gung-ho, trigger-happy and rather arrogantly steaming to Baghdad in tanks emblazoned with graffiti like 'apocalypse.' Our troops seem more actively engaged in trying to win the hearts and minds of a suspicious, angry and terrified Iraqi population. The removal of British helmets for berets struck me as importantly symbolic and worth encouraging."

"The Americans should have gone in on their own," British land-scape gardener Ted Ferard told the *New York Times* on April 1. Ferard was embarrassed, he said, at seeing Tony Blair acting like "Bush's puppet," in thrall to an American president who seemed not to understand the consequences of his country's military might.

Another article, this one in the *Scotsman,* quoted Stuart Crawford, a retired lieutenant colonel in the British Army and now a military analyst, as saying that the Americans had "little history of dealing with civilian populations in the same way" as Britons. "At times," he told the paper, "American warfare can be characterized by an overwhelming arrogance."

The talk in Britain about uncontrollable American aggression had been bad enough before the war. But its tone intensified dramatically after the images of American tanks rolling into downtown Baghdad began to appear on television. It was bad enough that the Americans had gone to war without the permission of the infinitely more sophisticated and intelligent elites of Britain. Once it was clear that the Americans had prevailed, once the fighting had ceased without the disasters the British intellectuals had so confidently predicted—no refugee camps, no thousands upon thousands of civilian casualties—once all the predictions were proven wrong, the true depths of British anger at America were revealed in earnest.

"I Loathe America," crowed the headline over an article by English novelist Margaret Drabble in the *Daily Telegraph* on May 8, a month after the fall of Baghdad. "I now loathe the United States and what it has done to Iraq and the rest of the helpless world," Drabble wrote. "I detest Disneyfication, I detest Coca-Cola, I detest burgers, I detest sentimental and violent Hollywood movies that tell lies about history. I detest American imperialism, American infantilism, and American triumphalism about victories it didn't even win." Drabble didn't explain which victories America "didn't even win" she had in mind. Certainly she could not have meant World War II or World

War I, the two major conflicts of the last century, when America's power and its willingness to sacrifice the lives and treasure of its own people saved the lives of countless British subjects. (Six months later, when Drabble was in the United States promoting her latest book, her express hatred for America had either subsided considerably or was simply judiciously concealed. After all, no point in offending potential book buyers.)

Michael Bywater, a columnist whose published work includes reviews of video games and erotic art, was given space in the apoplectically antiwar *Independent* to make a peculiar complaint: He *hated* hating Americans, but he just couldn't help himself.

"I hate hating something which calls itself a peace-loving nation when I can't remember a time when it wasn't bombing people somewhere; something which mouths platitudes about a pluralism which in truth it hates; which claims belief in individual choice yet has an anti-abortion clause in its bidding conditions for companies which want to get rich rebuilding the things which it itself has destroyed. . . .

"I hate hating a religious fundamentalism as imbecilic as any Bedouin peasant's, complete with epiphenomena (they see angels; they see the embodiment of Death at the bed's foot; they plunder ancient cultures for the soft, sweet bits and call it New Age) incorporate[d] de facto (though never de jure) into the world's most powerful government, when in a civilized state a deeply held religious faith should act as an absolute bar to public office of any kind." Bywater was one of many anti-American voices who shared the peculiar European bias against any public profession of religion, a skepticism and suspicion that bordered on discrimination against the religious. It was clear that George W. Bush, with his public prayers and tendency to invoke God, had deeply rankled and infuriated the British.

"I hate hating the swaggering youths, fed to bull-size on burgers and Michelob, swaggering round Amsterdam's Walletjes seeing only whores ('You want her, go screw her, man!') while the ancient liberal civilities underpinning it go wholly unseen," Bywater wrote—and on he went for several more paragraphs before drawing his virulent column to a close.

Tony Blair seemed ashamed of such intemperate remarks from his countrymen. "I actually believe that some of the rhetoric I hear used about America is more savage than some of the rhetoric I hear about Saddam and the Iraqi regime," Blair observed ruefully.

The British seemed in particular to resent the fact that American policy had been shaped in part by representatives from regions unfamiliar to their commentators. It was bad enough that the U.N. Security Council had risked "becoming simply the instrument for Washington's will in the world," observed BBC world affairs editor John Simpson in the *Sunday Telegraph* in May 2003. If the British should fail to take the lead in turning the Security Council into a more effective organization, "What we will hear instead is unknown politicians from American states which are not much more than a large empty place on the map explaining that the UN has lost its value and credibility, and should be done away with."

Stewart Steven, writing in the *Mail on Sunday* just three days before the fall of Baghdad, cited three members of Parliament in particular as America haters of the first order. One was Glenda Jackson, the onetime actress whose ex-husband once said, "If she had gone into politics [originally], she'd have been prime minister; if she'd taken to crime she'd be Jack the Ripper." The others were George Galloway, who is married to a Palestinian and passionately supports Arab causes—he would later have to fight off charges that he was actually on Saddam's payroll—and Scotsman Alex Salmond. Each of them, Steven reported, quite simply hates Americans. "That hatred courses through their collective political consciousness. They hated the Americans enough to give moral support to the Soviet Union at the very time it was murdering or imprisoning its own citizens. They hated the Americans enough to champion the cause of

Communist China when millions of its citizens were dying from state induced starvation."

The *Mirror* was loudly antiwar ("Are We Still Anti-War? Bloody Right We Are," read one headline) until public sentiment in the United Kingdom began shifting after British troops were actually in harm's way. Before then, the *Mirror*'s Tommy Sheridan had sounded a typically hysterical note: "The World Health Organization estimates civilian casualties could range from 100,000 to 500,000. With half of Iraq's population under the age of 14, most of those killed and maimed will be children. This is not a war. This is a massacre. A massacre with the goal of building a twenty-first century American empire."

Two weeks into the war, the *New York Times*'s Sarah Lyall reported on the state of British public opinion. The newspapers in the United Kingdom "have portrayed the Americans as Godzilla-like invaders," she wrote, "stumbling clumsily through foreign terrain, ill-prepared to the point of helplessness to reach out to the population they have pledged to liberate."

The anti-American press eventually hurtled so far over the top that it provoked an opposite response in some British commentators. "The left-wing majority is wrong on this, and becomes more wrong the more it allows the anti-Americans to take the lead in the debate," John Lloyd wrote in the February 2003 *New Statesman.* "The impression now growing is that the left regards the U.S. as more of a threat than Saddam—or indeed, almost any other dictator with weapons of mass destruction. The route of reasoned disagreement on grounds that war would be more dangerous than continued surveillance is increasingly being eschewed in favor of denouncing 'Bush and Blair' as warmongers, set on invasion for the worst of reasons. In taking this route, the left is discrediting itself."

Writing in the May 5, 2003, *New Statesman,* Nick Cohen agreed with Lloyd. Noting that Britain had seen the largest street demonstrations in its history over the issue, Cohen noted, "However honorable the motives of some (if not all) of the anti-war protesters were, they ran into the problem that the only way to bring down Ba'athist tyranny was foreign invasion. To oppose the war was to agree that the Iraqis should continue to live in a prison state."

When British Cabinet member Robin Cook resigned in protest over Blair's cooperation with the American-led war on Iraq, he was interviewed by Will Hutton and Kamal Ahmed in the *Observer*; his comments were published in March 2003. "The events of September 11 created an entirely new sense, not only in America but around the world, of the priority and urgency of dealing with international terrorism," Cook said. "It had a particularly powerful effect on American society because they are not accustomed to war coming to them." Presumably, Cook had concluded that the Nazis' blitz of London sixty years ago, or the IRA terror bombings of twenty years ago, better equipped the British to make such judgments than the Americans, whose attack was only two years ago.

"If we are going to have a multilateral system," Cook continued, "we've all got to have ownership of what the priorities are going to be." In other words, Americans must never dare to claim ownership of their own priorities, even after suffering such grievous losses. The "priorities" could only be managed responsibly by others who had *not* been attacked, in Cook's view.

"We need to engage in an international community that can bring to international forums and state with clarity the type of European values that are certainly not shared by many of those in the Bush administration," Cook said.

Prime Minister Tony Blair generally—though not always, to his great distress later—made a point of underscoring two distinct reasons for going to war: the belief that Iraq possessed weapons of mass destruction, and the ongoing threat that the murderously repressive

Iraqi regime posed to the region and to its own people. "There are also horrendous consequences for the people of Iraq if we do not take action. This is not something we are making up."

As mass graves in Iraq were discovered after the major combat ended, revealing upwards of 300,000 murdered Iraqi citizens—a circumstance that only confirmed what most informed observers had assumed in advance of the war, even among the British public— Professor Norman Geras of the University of Manchester, a noted leftist, felt compelled to admonish his colleagues on the left.

What we had been seeing among the British populace, Geras wrote in the *Wall Street Journal,* was not reasoned opposition to war, but "opposition to the U.S., come what may."

Geras pointed out to his former colleagues that "opposition to the war—the marching, the petition signing, the oh-so-knowing derision of George W. Bush, and so forth—meant one thing very clearly. Had this campaign succeeded in its goal and actually prevented the war it was opposed to, the life of the Baathist regime would have been prolonged, with all that that entailed: years more of the rape rooms, the torture chambers, the children's jails and the mass graves recently uncovered."

Geras's words seemed to shout off the page: "This was the result that hundreds of thousands of people marched to secure. Well, speaking for myself, comrades, there I draw the line. Not one step."

The British needed the lecture. Before the war, American pastor Ken Joseph had traveled to Iraq with British antiwar organizers to act as a human shield. In a piece titled "I Was Wrong," he wrote about his eye-opening experiences talking to ordinary Iraqis out of the sight and earshot of Saddam's secret police and "minders." "One man told me, tears in his eyes: 'No matter how bad it is, we will not all die. We have hoped for some other way of change but nothing has worked. We cannot wait any more. We want the war and we want it now.' Ordinary Iraqis told me they would rather commit suicide than survive under Saddam. They were willing to see their homes demolished, livelihoods destroyed and even loved ones killed for freedom."

One elderly woman told Joseph: "The war is the only way we can escape our hell. Please tell them to hurry."

The British knew this all very well, from years of candid press accounts of Saddam's crimes; those who dismissed the arguments for invasion did so, most likely, because they simply did not want to go along with the Americans, with the despised George W. Bush. In the Sunday, May 11, 2003, *Independent,* columnist Adrian Hamilton put it succinctly: "The huge majority of people in Europe, east as much as west, opposed the war not because they didn't believe regime change was a good thing in Iraq, not even because they refused to believe that the majority of Iraqis wanted rid of Saddam Hussein. They opposed it because unilateral action by the world's hyperpower on preemptive grounds was the very opposite of the world they looked forward to after the fall of the wall."

On the eve of President Bush's postwar visit to Great Britain, the *New York Times*'s Warren Hoge quoted an academic on the problem Tony Blair created for himself by standing with the United States in Iraq.

"Bush's visit will remind people . . . of what Blair has done that they dislike most," said Anthony King, professor of government at Essex University, "namely, joining the United States in the war in Iraq." Bush may be "greeted with wary respect at 10 Downing Street, [but] his unilateralism and folksy Texas style don't go down well with the chattering classes, who regard him as exceedingly dangerous and something of a buffoon,"

For Tony Blair, the war *after* Iraq proved far more damaging than the war itself. Blair was regarded in the United States as America's best friend, a reliable partner who could be counted on when it was time to commit forces—but also as an eloquent and fluid speaker who helped an admittedly less fleet-footed American president make the case for war brilliantly. The British resented Blair enormously for that. If George Bush couldn't help but walk all over his own tongue trying to get a sentence out, if he could only manage to blurt out half a reason for war when the world was waiting to hear a dozen good reasons well-articulated, why should Tony Blair appear beside him to pick up every ball he dropped?

No institution in Great Britain embraced this attitude more than the British Broadcasting Corporation, which waged a tireless battle against the war, the United States, and thus against Tony Blair himself. The BBC's antiwar campaign, which began before the war, carried on even during the war's most dangerous stages—and reached its most dramatic impasse after the war.

The BBC's attitude was simple: (1) the Americans, as usual, were to blame for their own troubles, including the terror attacks against them; (2) the Americans had behaved outrageously in insisting on its right to go to war without the approval of the international community; (3) the prime minister had allowed himself to be swallowed whole by the hated Americans, resulting in a commitment of British resources to a war that was wrong and illegal; and (4) therefore the prime minister was to be punished.

As mentioned earlier, the ominous hints of the BBC's anti-American bias came as early as the first days after September 11. But the issue came most sharply into focus once the war had begun.

First came a series of disquieting reports that angry British naval crews had switched off the BBC and chosen another source of news while at sea. The reason? The BBC reporters' "pro-Iraqi bias." This news came from the warship HMS *Ark Royal,* the nation's flagship naval vessel, which was operating in the theater of war in support of British troops engaged on the ground and in the air. The ship received live television signals direct from Britain, but the crew said it had come to believe that the BBC "places more faith in Iraqi reports than information coming from British or Allied sources."

One crewman said: "The BBC always takes the Iraqis' side. It reports what they say as gospel but when it comes to us it questions and doubts everything the British and Americans are reporting. A lot of people on board are very unhappy."

Ark replaced the BBC feeds with rival broadcaster Sky News.

The BBC's troubles in this regard were not accidental. Three weeks before the first shots were fired in the Iraq war, the BBC instituted a policy that seemed to *ensure* that the broadcaster would take an antiwar line. Stephen Whittle, the controller of editorial policy, issued orders to his staff that even after a war is underway opposition voices should be given airtime. "We must reflect significant opposition in the U.K. (and elsewhere) to the military conflict and allow the arguments to be heard and tested. Those who speak and demonstrate against the war are to be reported as part of the national and international reality," Whittle said.

Noting the network's extended reach into 160 countries around the world, Whittle further instructed his staff that armed forces should be referred to as "British troops" and not "our troops."

At the time, Conservative "culture spokesman" John Whittingdale accused the BBC of antiwar bias. "People inside the BBC who are opposed to the conflict are imposing their own views," he told the *Times* of London. By mid-November 2003, the BBC was announcing the appointment of a special executive to monitor a "pro-Arab" bias at the broadcaster. The head of the BBC World Service's Arabic Service had been singled out by some critics as the most anti-Israel source of the corporation's news operations, but London's *Daily Telegraph* also noted "the BBC has been the target of Downing Street accusations that it toed a pro-Baghdad line over the Iraq war."

What happened to change BBC management policy between March 2003, when the war was still under way, and November, when its management finally started to rein in its anti-American coverage? The intervening months had seen not only a decisive victory in the major combat phase of the war, but accusations of government lies, countercharges that the BBC had lied, the suicide of the source for a scandalous broadcast, a government inquiry with far-reaching implications, and an ongoing debate over the prime minister's fitness for office and the BBC's continued existence as a news organization. In sum, a lot of trouble.

The BBC, of course, is no ordinary broadcaster. Nearly its entire $5.86 billion annual budget comes from a mandatory $192 annual fee or tax paid by the individual owner of every color television set in the nation. The BBC broadcasts into 160 countries to 150 million people in every major language from Arabic to Urdu, mainly through its World Service, whose annual budget runs to $370 million. BBC Television produces entertainment, documentaries, and news. Its power and reach far exceed any commercial television organization on the globe, including CNN or any of the behemoth American networks. It operates under a ten-year government charge, which doesn't come up for renewal until 2006. Though nominally supervised by a board of governors appointed by the prime minister, it insists on such a ferociously willful independence that its journalists are almost required to wake up every morning assuming their government (and the government of the United States) is wrong, and must be made to pay.

As the incident aboard the HMS *Ark* illustrates, the BBC's Iraq war coverage was problematic. "In English, Arabic or any of the other 43 languages used by the BBC World Service, attaching a virulently anti-American viewpoint to one of the most trusted brands in the world has a deep significance," wrote Denis Boyles, in the July 2003 *National Review.* "When the Iraqi leadership calls on suicide bombers to attack British and American soldiers, the call goes out over the BBC, without any attempt to deflate the accompanying rhetoric."

Noting that a German newspaper had recently described the BBC World Service as "U.N. radio," Boyles commented: "The newspaper meant this as flattery, but it might have added that the World Service resembles the U.N. in other ways too: it's unresponsive to critics, certain of its virtue, fascinated by radical governments, dependent entirely on taxpayers' handouts for its survival, and after a while, stupidly self-serious."

Boyles described one incident that highlighted the BBC's inherently biased reporting. On April 5, a column of American armor made a sweeping movement for the first time in Baghdad itself. The column turned near the university, drove out of the capital, and stopped at the new American base at the Baghdad airport. A Fox News Channel crew riding with the column provided virtually continuous taped coverage of the event, as American troops made their first foray into Baghdad after arriving on the city's doorstep a day or two before. Television viewers could see the wide boulevard the column was traveling on, as well as the sporadic resistance it encountered from Iraqi troops or irregulars. Burning tanks were visible, hidden among trees just off the road.

Boyles was watching more or less the same thing on television in France. But he was also listening to the BBC World Service's defense correspondent, Andrew Gilligan, in Baghdad. "I'm at the center of Baghdad . . . and I don't see anything," Gilligan sneered, "but then the Americans have a history of making these premature announcements.

"Gilligan was referring to a military communiqué from Qatar the day before saying Americans had taken control of most of Baghdad's airport," Boyles explained. "When that happened, Gilligan told World Service listeners that he was there, at the airport—but the Americans weren't. Gilligan inferred that the Americans were lying."

Gilligan and two of his BBC colleagues insisted the Americans weren't even in the city—and for confirmation they referred listeners to the Iraqi Minister of Information, Mohammed Saeed al-Sahaf, known in the United States as "Baghdad Bob" (and then, as his statements grew more and more outrageous, "Comical Ali"). Al-Sahaf called the American incursion a "hoax," claiming that the Iraqis had retaken the airport, and Republican Guards were "pounding" trapped American troops.

"This bizarre announcement was accepted at face value by the BBC," said Boyles.

"It was a startling multimedia event. I could listen to the BBC's Paul Wood telling me once again that there was no sign of the American incursion into Baghdad. Yet on the screen in front of me there was the 3rd Infantry. They were cruising through Baghdad. . . . Along the sidewalks there were waving children and adults, cheering them on. Men passed in trucks and cars crying out 'Saddam down!' "

On this day, the BBC wouldn't even accept the truth from its own people. Obviously flummoxed by the conflicting reports, one BBC anchor asked Jonathan Marcus, the BBC correspondent at coalition headquarters in Qatar, "Who should we believe?" Marcus answered straightforwardly: The Iraqis were obviously lying—the American incursion was real and it had gone deep into the capital. "Anybody who questions that can't see the forest for the trees," he said.

"The anchor instantly went to another, more trustworthy correspondent," Boyles noted.

Of course, the obvious soon became incontrovertible, even for the BBC. Four days after this incident, BBC correspondents looked up to find American tanks rolling unimpeded into Paradise Square, directly in front of the journalists' hotel. Some might have argued that this was a defeat for the BBC's own intrepid obfuscators. But the service merely moved its war against America and its allies in the British government back to Britain.

In the weeks after Baghdad fell, it became clear that weapons of mass destruction were either far better hidden than anyone had imagined or were no longer to be found in Iraq. For the BBC, this simply meant opening up a rearguard action against the Americans and those in the British government who supported them, namely Prime Minister Blair and his hard-nosed subordinates at 10 Downing Street.

In fairness, Blair had made his own bed in this area. In addition to the voluminous dossier released September 24, 2002, which detailed intelligence on Iraq's weapons of mass destruction, his government had issued a second report. Later called "the dodgy dossier," it was a ridiculous compendium of rehashed claims, the central of which turned out to be a doctoral dissertation Blair's people had lifted off the Internet, later discounted as a justification for war by its own author.

From the time the original weapons of mass destruction (WMD) dossier was released, though, Blair had settled on the existence of Iraqi WMD as the reason for war. "We have the evidence," he had announced conclusively before the war. And shortly after the war, on April 27, he sat down for an extended interview with two ranking editors of the *Financial Times*.

"Would you still say that depriving Saddam Hussein of his weapons of mass destruction was the main motivation of the war?" Blair was asked.

"Yes," he replied emphatically. "Because the United Nations' resolution made it clear that these weapons were a threat and that he had to be disarmed of them." Blair added that "the nature of the regime" also provided a "moral justification" for the war, and that it was "right" to get rid of a horrific regime that legalized murder and tortured and killed hundreds of thousands.

"You don't have to find weapons of mass destruction to morally justify the war?" he was asked again.

"The reason for our action was around the issue of weapons of mass destruction and the link with terrorism," Blair said.

Blair's unequivocal assertion—that Britain had acted with America on the basis of its own independent judgments about Saddam's weapons of mass destruction—led the BBC's Andrew Gilligan to step back and take another hard look at the British government's dossier on Iraq's weapons programs.

Buried in that report was a claim that was both crucial and questionable: that Iraq could deploy and fire chemical weapons on a mere forty-five minutes' notice from commanders to the field units.

If such weapons had not been readily discovered by invading American and British troops, which had specialized units looking for those particular weapons, how could the forty-five-minute claim possibly be true? Surely they could not be transported from undiscoverable bunkers—concealed so well that they had not been found weeks after the war—to field units in under an hour. So what was the origin of this claim, which had been a central pillar of the prime minister's conviction that Britain should go to war with the Americans?

On May 29, in an appearance on the highly popular radio program *Today,* Gilligan reported that the forty-five-minute deployment claim was tantamount to a lie perpetrated by the Blair government—created, his sources told him, by Blair's people to "sex up" the WMD dossier in an effort to bring Britain into the war with his new best friends, the Americans.

The reaction was furious. Number 10 Downing Street said that Gilligan's report was itself a lie. BBC executives stood by their reporter—but behind the scenes they scrambled to find corroborating evidence or another correspondent who could verify Gilligan's report.

After forcing Gilligan to name his source, they discovered another BBC reporter who was in contact with the same source—Dr. David Kelly, an expert in bio-weapons who had worked on part of the WMD dossier. The second correspondent, Susan Watts, was pressured to confirm Gilligan's report with the source—but resisted because she felt that Gilligan's characterization of Kelly's story was either incorrect or exaggerated.

Soon another worry arose within the BBC: Kelly wasn't quite the impeccable source Gilligan had claimed. Though Kelly had worked on one part of the WMD dossier—a section on the history of Iraq weapons inspections—he was not as high-placed in the government as Gilligan had claimed (or as the BBC would have liked).

Yet the BBC executives' concerns were not relayed to the BBC's on-air staff, which continued to treat the Gilligan story as true and damning. In an on-air spat between John Reid, the combative leader of the House of Commons, and BBC Radio 4's veteran "presenter" John Humphrys, a furious Reid snapped that the anonymous intelligence source of Gilligan's bombshell report could have been "a man in the pub" for all the public knew. With nothing to go on but faith in Gilligan, Humphrys hinted that the program's intelligence sources had been at the highest levels.

BBC executives knew otherwise. First of all, there were no "sources." There was merely a single source—and by no means was he a government official of the "highest levels."

Inevitably, Kelly himself noticed the storm that had been created by Gilligan's report. He notified his superiors that he had, in fact, spoken to Gilligan over lunch. Yet he couldn't imagine he was the source for Gilligan's story—because he had told Gilligan nothing of the sort.

Called before a committee of the House of Commons, Kelly admitted that he'd talked to Gilligan about the dossier, but disavowed the story: "I do not see how [Gilligan] could make the authoritative statement that he was making from comments that I made." Kelly said he never said definitively that he knew political pressure had caused the dossier to be "sexed up."

In its battle with the stridently antiwar, anti-American, and anti-Blair BBC, the government was delighted to have found Kelly. First, he cast serious doubt on Gilligan's reporting, suggesting that Gilligan was either an exaggerator or a liar. Second, he was simply never in a position to have known whether the Blair government had purposely inserted a falsehood into the dossier.

Three days later, Kelly walked out of his Oxfordshire home, took a pain pill, sat down near some trees overlooking a meadow, slit his wrists, and laid down to die.

Kelly's suicide shook both the BBC and the Blair government—and each blamed the other for the quiet scientist's death.

An investigating body called the Hutton Inquiry was quickly convened to determine where the fault for Kelly's death lay, and whether the government had in fact altered the truth to trick the British public into supporting the war. Even before the Inquiry issued its findings, though, damage on both sides was done. Blair's public approval ratings plummeted, and the BBC was forced to admit that Gilligan's journalistic standards and techniques fell below those of the BBC.

The *National Journal*'s William Powers put it this way: "The scandal has plunged the BBC into what some are calling the worst crisis of its history, as it fights for its own survival. Both Gilligan and the network have been charged with pursuing an antiwar agenda, and abusing a source so badly he was driven to suicide."

At this exact moment, the BBC dropped another anti-American bomb, almost as if to confirm that they were pursing a political agenda. On June 16, 2003, BBC Television aired a program called *What the World Thinks of America,* based on an eleven-country opinion poll of 11,000 people in the United States, Europe, the Middle East, and Australasia. According to the poll, 60 percent of non–Americans worldwide had an unfavorable attitude toward the United States. The program's host stood on a set dominated by maps of the world, each nation emblazoned with its one-word verdict on America: "ARROGANT."

As the *National Review*'s Dennis Boyles observed, "One way to mount a defense? Keep Spinning! According to the BBC, the investigation into Kelly's death really shouldn't be about Kelly's death at all. After all, he's dead. It should be about—what else?—the war in Iraq and the lack of legitimacy."

The BBC appeared determined to pursue its agenda, even when reporting on the Gilligan-Kelly affair. As Boyles reported, the BBC's own coverage of the story was framed as Blair's problem alone: "Political pressure is mounting for the inquiry into the death of weapons expert Dr. David Kelly to look at the way the government made its case for the war in Iraq."

The controversy eventually began to worry some of the BBC's staunchest supporters in Britain. The former culture minister Chris Smith published a plea in late July 2003: "The BBC Must Not Be a Casualty of War." With members of Parliament talking seriously about punishing the rogue broadcaster by eliminating its license fee income (the television set tax), Smith asserted the BBC had a *right* to be *wrong*. "The BBC is the most important of our public service broadcasters," he said. "It is a fundamentally important part of the life of the nation. It is of greater value than *any individual politician* [emphasis added]. . . . It does not always get everything right. But it cannot and should not become a victim to be threatened."

Ultimately, though, more than half the British population has no interest in threatening the BBC—for the simple reason that it has taken upon itself a service the public has come to see as valuable: attacking whatever pro-American position the government might take.

Thankfully, the madness does not appear to have infected everyone in Great Britain. William Shawcross, writing in the antiwar *Guardian,* noted that opponents of the war predicted "all manner" of disasters—refugees, starvation, thousands of deaths, and uprisings in the Arab street (including, it was argued, parts of London).

"None of these horrors happened," Shawcross pointed out. Instead, he said, it was obvious that the Americans and Brits had freed the Iraqis from a monster, ushering in a new age "which just might offer the region hope."

"All that is unbearable to those who preferred the Saddam status quo," Shawcross wrote in rising anger. "So they have used the missing weapons [of mass destruction] to turn on Mr. Blair with self-righteous fury. They declare that the war was 'a monumental blunder' and that we have been 'duped.' This is opportunistic, irresponsible and self serving rubbish."

Blair's pro-American stance may have cost him dearly, as he arguably might have foreseen. As British historian Paul Johnson wrote in a July 2003 column for *Forbes:* "Anti-Americanism is factually absurd, contradictory, racist, crude, childish, self-defeating and, at bottom, nonsensical. It is based on the powerful but irrational impulse of envy—an envy of American wealth, power, success, and determination. It is an envy made all the more poisonous because of a fearful European conviction that America's strength is rising while Europe's is falling."

Tony Blair tried to save his country from Europe's fate. He was not rewarded.

FOUR

GERMANS DELIGHTED: AT LAST SOMEONE ELSE IS HITLER

The legacy of the German election campaign last fall has complicated and harmed U.S.-German relations. Many of us . . . have
trouble understanding why a German chancellor would seek re-
election on a platform reduced to criticism of the United States,
assailing a friendship so many Americans and Germans have sworn
to protect. That said, we are still friends. . . . I believe many
Americans will put this issue behind them if Germany meets its
responsibilities in the Security Council on the matter of Iraq.

> —Senator John McCain, February 8, 2003, at the
> Munich Conference on Security Policy before
> European Parliament and defense ministers

G ERMANY DID NOT MEET its responsibilities on the matter of
Iraq, despite Senator McCain's imprecations. Instead the German government sided with the French, and told the United

States that it would never secure approval for military action against Iraq from the U.N. Security Council.

That, coupled with the shocking decision of the Germans, French, and Belgians to veto Turkey's petition for NATO defensive support, put relations between the United States and Germany on the worst footing since the end of World War II.

Admittedly, it may not have been realistic for McCain to expect Germany to join America and Britain in the war in Iraq. After all, at the moment when McCain spoke before European Parliament and defense ministers at the Conference on Security Policy in Munich, it had been five months since the chancellor of Germany and the president of the United States had spoken. And the reason they hadn't was precisely the issue to which McCain referred: the war in Iraq, and the campaign of stunning and reckless anti-Americanism that German Chancellor Gerhard Schroeder had mounted in his most recent and successful re-election bid.

Gerhard Schroeder had won re-election on September 29, 2002, just two weeks after President George W. Bush went before the United Nations to demand Iraq be disarmed—or the United Nations would become "irrelevant." But his campaign—originally waged largely on economic themes—had been reborn when Schroeder realized that the German electorate was ready for a large dose of anti-Americanism over the issue of Iraq. While Germany's European Union (EU) ally France was still maintaining the pretense that it might endorse a U.N. resolution authorizing war in Iraq, Schroeder loudly declared that Germany would not participate in a war, even with U.N. approval; that no German soldier would set foot in Iraq; that he would never be bullied by a rampaging, warmongering America.

Schroeder's hapless opponent, Edmund Stroiber, agreed that Germany should not participate the upcoming war, though he struggled in vain to point out that the 4.3 million Germans who would be unemployed the following winter were more important than whatever happened in Iraq.

But Schroeder's anti-Americanism had set him on a roll, and he was determined to stick with it and win. On campaign stop after campaign stop, Schroeder hammered home his message. "His stand has appealed to broad stretches of postwar German population bred to abhor war," the *New York Times* noted at the time, "but it has also brought charges of 'German unilateralism' and estrangement from its principal allies in the United States and Europe."

Across the Atlantic, the Bush White House fumed. And at least one German recognized Schroeder's campaign tactics as "a disaster." Friedbert Pfluger, a Christian Democrat opponent of Schroeder's party, observed: "In a matter of weeks, Schroeder was able to deprive Germany of its reputation of dependability which was developed over many years from Willy Brandt to Helmut Kohl."

Josef Joffe, the widely acclaimed German newspaper editor and author, said that it was all predictable—at least for anyone with a grasp of history. "It was only a matter of time before the First Law of Alliances would kick in for Nato: Alliances die when they win," Joffe said, referring to the West's defeat of communism and the Soviet empire. "This is the underlying reason for Chancellor Gerhard Schroeder's coldly calculated anti-American gambit in the run-up to . . . the German elections."

"No German chancellor would ever have dared to refuse a call from Washington, as Mr. Schroeder did," Joffe said, "while Moscow's armies were still poised at the gates of Hamburg and West Berlin. Nor would any German chancellor have deliberately pushed the button of anti-Americanism and pacifism for electoral gain."

In the the face of an election battle, Gerhard Schroeder let his anti-American impulses run wild. The reasons were plain: With the demise of the Soviet threat, Germany no longer felt it needed American strategic protection. For that matter, America no longer needed Germany's strategic geographic position.

A *BusinessWeek* editorial in December 2002 suggested further reasons for the fraying of the NATO fabric: "It's not a given that

Nato members are sailing by the same moral compass. Europeans reject the death penalty, fret about the treatment of al Qaeda prisoners, and regard U.S. President George W. Bush as dangerously warmongering. They are wary of globalization and the onslaught of U.S. culture to the point where some commentators veer into sympathy for terrorists."

The editorial described Schroeder as "flirting" with anti-Americanism; in retrospect, this seems almost absurdly short of the mark. In fact, Schroeder's America-bashing gambit appears to have been not only deliberate but entirely calculated. The late-September 2002 elections could not have dovetailed more perfectly with the debate over the war. Political analysts and the press had every reason to expect Schroeder to lose: The economy was in a shambles, the former East Germany was typically restive and angry, the jobless rate was through the roof, tax revenues through the floor, and thousands and thousands of businesses were teetering on the edge of bankruptcy.

With George W. Bush's designation of North Korea, Iran, and Iraq as an "Axis of Evil" early in 2002, however, Schroeder may have noticed a faint hint of light at the end of the tunnel. Certainly by the summer, as he contemplated the early fall campaign, Schroeder could see that George Bush was shaping a worldwide debate over an invasion of Iraq. On the issue of terrorism, Schroeder had promised unlimited solidarity to the United States after September 11, deploying 10,000 German troops to Afghanistan as peacekeepers. But Iraq was quite another matter.

Like many Europeans, Schroeder recognized that his fellow Germans did not see Iraq in the same light as the United States. For one thing, German companies did an enormous amount of business with Iraq. For another, the debate in Europe was framed early in terms of Saddam's possession of weapons of mass destruction—and in European eyes disarmament could and should be handled by U.N. weapons inspectors. So when the hawks in Washington, D.C. began to talk about "regime change," Schroeder watched his own electorate's wary reaction—and recognized an opportunity for his campaign.

The German people could hardly be blamed for casting a skeptical eye on the prospect of war. In the last century, after all, the German nation had caused two world wars, countless wartime deaths, the near-destruction of Europe twice in succession, not to mention the murder of six million Jews and countless other innocent Europeans. The postwar years have taught the German people nothing if not a basic rejection of war and embrace of pacifism. Everything the Americans were now talking about frightened the Germans—and only inflamed their long-term distrust of the United States.

The Pew Research Center for People and the Press had been conducting surveys of American and European opinion for a number of years. Tracking that polling from pre-9/11 through the months just before the German election campaign, their results trace exactly how the election eventually became an exercise in anti-Americanism.

A month before September 11, Pew polling showed that Germans were already alarmed about what appeared to be a very different president of the United States. Germans expressed a preference for Bill Clinton's international policies over those of George Bush by an 86-to-23 margin—better than three to one. They *disapproved* of Bush's policies over Clinton's by a 65-to-9 margin—better than seven to one.

Todd Richissin looked into this thinking for the *Baltimore Sun*. In early 2003, he reported on the German people's anger over Bush's withdrawal from international agreements such as Kyoto and the ABM treaty. As Richissin observed, the Germans and other Europeans were especially annoyed that their reasoned European arguments appeared to mean nothing to the unilateralist Americans.

Richissin quoted Christoph Bertram, director of the German Research Institute for International Affairs and Security, a think tank aligned with the German government. Bertram laid his criticism squarely at the feet of George W. Bush. "He didn't say, 'These have problems, let's try to fix them,' which was Clinton's approach—even if he never intended to go along with them. With Bush, he just said, 'No. We're not taking part.' How could Europeans not feel put down? How could resentment not grow?"

Bush's early rejection of the various international treaties was bound to cost him his standing with the European public. The Kyoto Accords were highly regarded in Europe—particularly in Germany, whose foreign minister, Joschka Fischer, was a Green Party member. Bush's revival of the idea of missile defense once again raised the possibility that the United States would withdraw from the ABM treaty, a traditional guarantor of German peace and mainstay of Cold War détente. And Bush's withdrawal from the treaty creating the International Criminal Court, yet another U.N. initiative highly regarded in Europe, only enhanced the impression of Bush as an unaccountable, lawless rogue.

In the summer of 2001, when the Pew polling was conducted, Germans were still giving Bush something of a chance: 51 percent "voiced at least some confidence in his abilities," the pollsters noted. Yet, the respondents disapproved of Bush's position on the Kyoto Accords by an eight-to-one margin. Sixty-eight percent of the Germans polled also disapproved of the death penalty; considering that Bush had most recently been the governor of the most-active American death-penalty state, that margin reflected a populace deeply out of sympathy with the American president. Perhaps most damningly, Germans concluded by a better than three-to-one margin that the Bush administration made decisions based *only* on U.S. interests, and that Bush personally understood Europe less than other presidents.

The next European tracking survey came in April 2002, shortly before Schroeder was gearing up for his re-election campaign. While Germans strongly disapproved of President Bush's Axis of Evil rhetoric, they gave him good approval ratings on the war in Afghanistan and the concept of tribunal trials for prisoners of war kept at Guantanamo,

Cuba. The good news for Schroeder (and bad news for the United States): 85 percent of Germans still thought America was acting entirely in its own interests, without consideration for others.

The war in Afghanistan, for many Germans, was a case in point. Although the German public generally supported the war, many viewed it as inherently wrong. And their voices were an early part of the public debate about America's ongoing plans overseas. "There are no universally valid values that allow one to justify one mass murder by another," wrote a group of 103 German intellectuals in an open letter published in the *Frankfurter Allgemeine* in response to a statement of principles by U.S. intellectuals who justified the war in Afghanistan. The German group further claimed that America had killed four thousand civilians in Afghanistan.

When later it became obvious (as Schroeder made certain it would) that the United States would come back wanting support for the war in Iraq, the Germans entirely rejected America's arguments. Karsten D. Voigt, coordinator for German-American cooperation in Germany's Foreign Ministry, told Richissin: "We've said Germany gives its unlimited solidarity in the stand against terrorism. The United States government says war with Iraq is an extension of the war on terrorism. We don't see the evidence of it. We don't buy it."

As it happened, Schroeder's campaign was perfectly timed, allowing the candidate to put anti-Americanism in play—especially in the former East Germany, where it had built-in appeal.

The strategy seemed to work well. Schroeder rejected the abrupt, high-handed way the Americans dealt with Germany over Afghanistan, complaining that a call from the Bush administration two hours beforehand to say "We're going in" hardly constituted "consultation." If the United States were going to take action against Iraq, acquiring the legitimacy of U.N. approval would be essential. Schroeder charged that the United States was threatening to destroy the world order of peace and security through "multilateralism" by going it alone (or nearly so).

And he promised that Germany would not allow its foreign policy decisions to be made in Washington, D.C.

There were ways, of course, to make such points without descending into virulent anti-Americanism. But Schroeder found it more strategically effective to oppose the United States in dramatic—even grandstanding—terms.

As Victor Davis Hanson pointed out in the *National Review* in October 2002, "The flurry of German anti-Americanism was *not* confined to Mr. Schroeder, but, in fact, was echoed by a variety of other politicians once considered to be more sober." Hanson cited Ludwig Stiegler, Schroeder's fellow socialist, who suggested that George W. Bush was similar to Julius Caesar, "the firebrand who destroyed centuries of republican government and sought to lay the foundations of Roman imperial rule."

Hanson also noted the incendiary rhetoric of Herta Daeubler-Gmelin, Germany's minister of justice, who famously declared that "Bush wants to divert attention from his domestic problems. It's a classic tactic. It's one Hitler also used." Hanson noted the irony: "Americans, who once rid Germany of Hitler, with very little help from Germans, are now to be properly slandered by Germans for being Hitler-like." Though Schroeder was embarrassed by his minister's remarks, he pointedly chose not to dismiss Daeubler-Gmelin until the polls closed on election day.

Schroeder himself had used subtler language to make the same points himself. Germany would not "click its heels," he charged, on orders from the United States. He talked of the "German way," a phrase reminiscent of the Nazi rhetoric of the 1930s. And he spoke constantly of Germany as a "modern" country. In the *Weekly Standard,* Christopher Caldwell queried: "Ask yourself what other leader of an advanced Western country would speak of an aspiration to be modern, and it becomes clear that what 'modern' means is free of hang-ups over World War II."

Hanson expressed the concern that Schroeder could be launching a Weimar Germany redux, "with all the attendant extreme reactions to it looming on the horizon," including the sobering possibility of a rise of German nationalism and militarism. Caldwell offered a more cautious, but still alarming, explanation: "A good case can be made that constant looking backwards has deprived Germany of both optimism and dynamism. The locking of the country's politics into atonement for World War II, necessary though it was for many decades, deserves some of the blame for the adolescent, consumerist, hedonistic, pornographic society that Germany has turned into."

When confronted directly on the issue, Schroeder pointed to Vice President Dick Cheney's August 28 speech outlining the case for preemptive war. Schroeder claimed he was simply responding to Cheney's speech, with its escalation American rhetoric for war in Iraq.

But the real purpose of the chancellor's Iraq offensive was to make all of Germany's other problems disappear—just as the justice minister had charged about Bush. Forty thousand German businesses were expected to go bankrupt that year, and no solution for the nation's high unemployment was presenting itself. Schroeder's only solution was to distract the populace from their own problems by "going negative" with an attack on the American president and his allegedly corrupt motives.

As Caldwell pointed out, taken as a whole Schroeder's position toward the United States made no sense. "If America was such a menace to world peace, why had Schroeder pledged his 'unconditional solidarity' to the United States in the days after September 11? Why, in fact, had Schroeder risked a no-confidence vote to send German troops to Afghanistan? If an okay from the United Nations was of the essence, then why had Schroeder chosen NATO's Kosovo operation, which had no U.N. sanction, as the occasion of Germany's first participation in a military attack since World War II? If unilateralism was such a problem, why was he insisting all Germany's decisions be made in Berlin?"

Schroeder's position was founded on another faulty premise: He was also making the assumption that Germany would be asked to participate in an American-led war. In fact, no such request had been made. As Caldwell noted, "Germany's defection from the Western alliance was of little military importance. The country's potential contribution to an attack on Iraq consisted of AWACS planes, a handful of medical units, and exactly six tanks . . . that can monitor biological and chemical weapons." Schroeder was right in assuming the Americans would want German support in the United Nations, but when it came to actual military support, it was a nonissue.

But such distinctions were meaningless on the German campaign trail, where Schroeder worked the angry, sullen, and underemployed former East Germans for votes with an anti-American fervor that must have had a nostalgic appeal for his audience. This was a people, after all, who had lived under a Soviet regime that had effectively de-monized the West—and especially the United States—for decades. Schroeder was merely the latest leader to make America his convenient scapegoat.

As Peter Ross Range noted, "By the time of the German election, bad will toward Bush was so rampant in the German public that tapping into it on the Iraq issue was a no-brainer for Schroeder." Schroeder campaigned hard, feeding the Germans more and more anti-American sausage. When his pollsters told him that Iraq had become the most important issue for undecided voters Schroeder upped the ante, pledging that Germany would neither help in any war against Iraq, nor help pay for one.

As the campaign unfolded, the White House complained that the German politicians' efforts to provoke anti-Americanism were "excessive."

Schroeder's opponents also accused him of "cheap anti-Americanism," but the charge did them no good. Schroeder found his narrow margin of victory in East Germany, and mined the old soil of Soviet anti-American propaganda to win by a nose.

President George W. Bush conspicuously neglected to call to congratulate Schroeder on his re-election, and administration officials began discussing Germany in cold-day-in-hell terms, even angrily promising it would be a very long time before the Germans would be forgiven. National Security Advisor Condoleezza Rice charged that the Schroeder campaign had turned relations between the United States and Germany "poisonous."

But veteran European reporter William Pfaff sounded a cautionary note for the Americans. Writing in the *International Herald Tribune,* Pfaff said: "Chancellor Schroeder did not whip up anti-Americanism in Germany. It was there already. That is what should worry Washington."

In his remarks in Munich months later, Senator John McCain addressed that point in a different way, issuing a warning to Berlin as well. "Some European politicians speak of pressure from their 'street' for peaceful solutions to international conflict and for resisting American power regardless of its purpose," McCain said, referring to several leaders, but Schroeder especially. "There is an American 'street' too," McCain said firmly, "and it strongly supports disarming Iraq, accepts the necessity of an expansive American role in the world to ensure we never wake up to another September 11, is perplexed that nations with whom we have long enjoyed common cause do not share our urgency and sense of threat in time of war, and considers reflexive hostility toward Israel as the root of all problems in the Middle East as irrational as it is morally offensive."

McCain spoke on February 8, 2003, exactly one week before millions of Europeans, especially Germans, took to the streets for massive demonstrations against the war. It was a day, many European commentators said, when Europe finally showed unity and became one. It was a day many hoped would be powerful enough to stop what they perceived as an unjust American war.

The day of protest may have failed to stop the war, but the sight of millions of Europeans marching on their national capitals did have the effect of galvanizing their leaders. If any were inclined before February 15 to hesitate in resisting the war, there was little such hesitation thereafter. That march crystallized the European consensus against the war, leaving only the leaders of Britain and Spain to join George W. Bush in the face of popular opposition.

It was astonishing how much trans-Atlantic relations had shifted in just a few years. In September 1997, Josef Joffe had ruminated in *Foreign Affairs* on what he called "the principal paradox of the post-Cold War era": how America, as the last remaining superpower, could have gone seven years since the fall of the Soviets, and "no nation has flung down the gauntlet. None has unleashed an arms race, none has tried to engineer a hostile coalition. The United States faces neither an existential enemy nor the threat of encirclement as far as the eye can see."

As Joffe observed, things don't usually happen this way. "History and theory tell us that the international system abhors primacy. Hence the United States should have become the object of mistrust, fear, and containment. Its Cold War alliance system should have collapsed, and its members should have defected to aggregate their power against the United States. The signal from Nos. 2, 3, 4, etc., should have been: We shall draw a new line in the sand; you shall not enjoy the fruits of your exalted position."

Joffe was right about the theory; only his timing was off. The United States managed to move forward thirteen years before the coalitions of allies began to form against it. When the issue of Iraq presented itself, one of the first to stand against the United States was Germany.

To many Americans, it was a truly shocking development. The *Germans,* of all people? Hadn't we saved Germany from itself twice? Hadn't we kept Berlin alive with an airlift? Hadn't we spent billions of dollars and sixty years in Germany protecting it from the Soviet threat? Hadn't we come in with the Marshall Plan to help Germany recover from the war, and become one of the great economic success stories of the world? Hadn't we helped the Germans establish a civil democracy that was one of the most successful in the world? Hadn't we wholeheartedly supported the expensive, often painful, and potentially threatening German reunification?

Even those Germans who recognized that American pressure had helped liberate the Eastern bloc nations from Soviet domination, easing the suffering of millions of Europeans, now lined up against their American protectors. Their own former Eastern-bloc colleagues, the Vilnius Ten, broke with the Berlin-Paris axis and announced support for the American position on Iraq. Having recently emerged from political repression themselves, their sympathies lay with the Iraqi people, violently oppressed by Saddam for decades. So what was the East Germans' problem?

Americans tended to forget that half of the German Republic of today was on the front lines of the Cold War for the past fifty years. To former residents of East Germany, America was a voracious power poised to sweep across the frontiers at a moment's notice with waves of tanks and attack helicopters and troops. The America of their imaginations was ready for decades to annihilate East Germany with battlefield nuclear weapons, just as it had fire-bombed Dresden to ceramic dust. When Gerhard Schroeder hit the campaign trail in the former East Germany, he found an audience ready and willing to believe the Americans were not simply wrong; we were warmongers, ready to launch troops at our whim, illegally and virtually without provocation.

The German politicians understood this deeply skeptical streak within the East German people, and exploited it shamelessly. They also saw an opportunity to appeal to a wide seam of subterranean German sentiment holding that Americans are coarse, vulgar, unsophisticated, unread if not illiterate, uncultured, ill-advised and intemperate— inferior to Europe in general, and Germans in particular.

Henry Kissinger warned in late 2002 that such anti-Americanism may have become a permanent feature of German politics. "This is especially painful for those of us," Kissinger wrote, "who actively nurtured what we consider one of the proudest achievements of American postwar foreign policy: the return of Germany to the community of nations as an equal, respected and indispensable member."

It was a proud achievement indeed. Centuries of world disruption by German warmaking had been ended in one fifty-year period by successive American administrations that shared a common goal: a permanently pacified Germany. Now all that work seemed to be in jeopardy.

Former Chancellor Helmut Kohl, who worked closely with a succession of American presidents, lamented in an interview a month after Schroeder's victory: "Memories of the United States' generous help for us Germans have faded. Many have no memories of the Marshall Plan, the Berlin airlift, the help and support during the Cold War and reunification."

"In this atmosphere," Kissinger wrote, "the word 'American' occasionally turned into an epithet, even when applied to American domestic economic policies. The comparison of Bush's domestic methods to those of Hitler by a cabinet minister was an aberration, but it grew out of a mood that had been deliberately fostered."

"Deliberately fostered" indeed, by Gerhard Schroeder, who was willing to torch his nation's relationship with America to ensure his own reelection.

And it didn't end when the votes were counted. "The tone deafness vis-a-vis American sensitivities continued after the election," Kissinger wrote, "when the newly designated state secretary in the German Foreign Ministry, Klaus Scharioth, described the new American strategic doctrine released by the White House as reminiscent of the Brezhnev Doctrine."

The Bush administration proceeded apace. In November 2002 the Security Council approved Resolution 1441, but when the weapons inspectors returned to Iraq they were largely unsuccessful in convincing Saddam that it was his responsibility to cooperate fully by taking inspectors to his weapons facilities. Instead, a familiar cat-and-mouse game ensued between Saddam's regime and the inspectors; though the Iraqis made an occasional show of cooperating, most observers recognized that it was purely for the public relations value. By the end of 2002, the calendar was clearly dictating events: A likely date for war was set for mid-March by military and political analysts, before Iraq's fearsome summer rendered conditions prohibitive.

Even Germans friendly to the United States somehow managed to question America's behavior. "Sept. 11 changed America," German legislator and NATO Parliament member Karl A. Lamers told the *New York Times.* "I remember 40 years ago, when John F. Kennedy came to this country and said that a Soviet attack on Cologne or Frankfurt was an attack on the United States. But he never imagined something like that could happen in America. It has happened, and everything has changed."

In some ways, the Germans' behavior during the run-up to the war wasn't the most disheartening turn of events. Some observers took the long view, and found themselves pleased to see that German pacifism had been so thoroughly and permanently ingrained. The Bush administration itself seemed not to have lost much sleep over the matter: Where France would be punished (and Russia accommodated) for straying from the fold, Germany was merely ignored.

As James W. Davis, a professor of international relations at the University of Munich, wrote in the *Los Angeles Times,* in Germany debates over international conflicts are first and foremost confrontations with history.

"Germans of Foreign Minister Joschka Fischer's generation define themselves through their opposition to the political values of their parents and grandparents," Davis wrote. "Theirs is the generation that asked, What did you know? Their pacifist reflexes flow from an acceptance of historical guilt."

When the war commenced on March 20, 2003, the Germans took solace in their righteous antiwar stance, and decried American impatience and unilateralism.

During the war, the Nobel Prize-winning German author Gunter Grass authored a series of columns for the *Los Angeles Times,* America's most determined antiwar newspaper. "No, it is not anti-Americanism that is damaging the image of the United States; nor do the dictator Saddam Hussein and his extensively disarmed country endanger the most powerful country in the world," Grass wrote. "It is President Bush and his government that are diminishing democratic values, bringing sure disaster to their own country, ignoring the United Nations, and that are now terrifying the world with a war in violation of international law."

Setting aside for a moment the debatable contention that Saddam posed no threat to the United States, what were the "democratic values" Bush and his administration were diminishing? Did he honestly believe what he seemed to be saying, that through the February antiwar demonstrations the "world" had somehow "voted" democratically against this war?

What was the "sure disaster" that would be brought to America in the wake of this war? Grass may have seen in Iraq the makings of another Dresden and feared a guilt-ridden future for America. But he seems to have been wrong on each count.

And how, exactly, was America "ignoring the United Nations?" Bush had made his appeal to the United Nations; the result was Resolution 1441, which promised "serious consequences" if Iraq remained in breach of its post-Gulf War obligations. If America was now ignoring the United Nations, it was only after the Security Council nations—Germany foremost among them—had made it clear that they would never approve a war to disarm Saddam Hussein. The process America was accused of ignoring had long ago been short-circuited by the Germans themselves.

Arguments like those Grass mounted in the *Los Angeles Times* raised a far more discomfiting question: What was a diehard antifascist doing taking any position that protected a murderer and torturer like Saddam Hussein?

In his strident protests, though, Grass had apparently found something precious to any Germans suffering under his nation's mantle of collective guilt. "We Germans often are asked if we are proud of our country," he wrote. "To answer this question has always been a burden. There were reasons for our doubts. But now I can say that the rejection of this preemptive war on the part of a majority in my country has made me proud of Germany. After having been largely responsible for two world wars and their criminal consequences, we seem to have made a difficult step. We seem to have learned from history."

Three days after the war began, Great Britain's minister for Europe, Denis McShane, proclaimed that, in general, Europe supported a tough line against Iraq at the United Nations. (McShane must have been counting different noses than the Bush administration.) As he admitted, though, "the one big exception is Germany."

In Germany, McShane said, "a strong anti-militarist politics stretching from the Right, via the politically influential German churches, to the activist Left is locked into a 'Nie Wieder' (Never again) politics. This is a historical reality."

As McShane observed, this hard fact about Germany was reflected in the course of the recent campaign season: By the time of the election, all of the candidates had fallen in line behind Schroeder, all promising the voters that Germany would not participate in war in Iraq.

"To us, war means Dresden," one German politician told writer Peter Ross Range in April 2003.

Wars went badly—always. One European might have been speaking for the Germans when he glumly explained to an American, "We don't have the same confidence as you."

In rejecting the prospect of war, though, the Germans were also choosing to abstain from the new century's first emphatic stand against murderous tyranny. The American show of force against Iraq was clearly recognized by others around the world, including Kim Jong Il, the lunatic despot of North Korea. But the Germans wanted none of it.

As David Pryce-Jones pointed out in the *National Review*, the Germans preferred to see Saddam Hussein as a business partner, not a despot. As Pryce-Jones reports, "Something like 200 German firms, large and small, have contributed in one way or another to Iraq's programs of mass-destruction weapons." Prosecutors in Germany have investigated one businessman accused of selling Iraq equipment for its supergun project; another German businessman who stole plans for an advanced centrifuge for making nuclear weapons—and sold them to Iraq—got a five-year suspended sentence from the German courts. To Pryce-Jones, such incidents of German collusion with Saddam go hand-in-hand with the growing wave of German anti-Americanism.

Stern magazine columnist Hans-Ulrich Joerges has asked whether "Germany is becoming a combatant on the side of Saddam." Marching with thousands of anti-war protestors at a Berlin peace event, Joerges noticed a young father with a small child telling a reporter, "I hope Bush not only loses the war on the ground but also in the hearts of the world community."

Joerges was alarmed at his own fellow Germans. "Up and down this nation Bush is being equated with Hitler . . . and when the 'invaders' suffer a slight setback, we Germans settle back in our armchairs and smile self-satisfiedly and say: 'It serves those Amis right.'"

It wasn't until April 4, 2003—two full weeks into the war, and five days before Baghdad fell—that Gerhard Schroeder was even willing to concede that he hoped the American and British forces would actually win the war. But it was hardly a resounding endorsement of the effort to overthrow Saddam. "Naturally, it will end with a victory for the allies," Schroeder said in a German television interview. "One must wish for this as a reasonable person because every additional day the war lasts is a day in which there are victims. Even one who was so against this war must wish for a swift end."

During the interview, Schroeder did allow that he might consider sending German troops into postwar Iraq to help in reconstruction, but it was a very tentative promise. More revealingly, Schroeder admitted that he had had no telephone contact with President Bush—that his office was communicating with the White House by letter. The chancellor of Germany was waiting by the mailbox.

The punishment of isolation didn't seem to faze most average Germans, their chests still swelled with the realization that after decades in the wilderness they had finally settled upon an international role they were proud of: They would stand against America, and the world would applaud and admire them at last. For the first time in modern history, they had taken what they believed to be the moral high ground.

The German press agency reported the newest round of America-bashing sweeping Germany. "Americans are basically aggressive and always have been," an older woman from East Berlin told a television crew. An elderly man agreed with her: "The Brits and the Yanks have committed atrocities in the past, the English set up the first concentration camps in the Boer War and the Brits bombed Dresden though it was not a military target," he said. "And don't forget the black slaves and the Indians. So much for democracy in America."

Even the forces of Newspeak got into the act. A group of linguists from a university in the former East Germany called for a purging of English words from everyday German usage, advising Germans who felt the need to use foreign words, to use "pro-peace French words."

Writing in *Foreign Policy* just before Schroeder's re-election, Josef Joffe raised another, far more alarming undercurrent within the wave of anti-American sentiment: the specter of anti-Semitism. "Pick a peace-minded demonstration in Europe these days or a publication of the extreme left or right, and you'll find anti-Israeli and anti-American resentments side by side—in the tradition first invented by the Khomeinists of Iran, whose demonology abounds with references to the 'small' and 'great Satan.'"

As Joffe noted, "there is an element of bad old anti-Semitism" in this thinking, updated to suit the times. "The Jews, so the lore goes, finally achieved global domination by having conquered the United States: Jews control the media, the U.S. Congress and the economy."

There it was: *Blame the Jews.* On the German *strasse,* anti-American sentiment had overlapped with ancient teutonic anti-Semitism. The war in Iraq, after all, was viewed as America doing Israel's dirty business. And besides, from the press to Congress, the Jews ran America, didn't they? "The British do whatever the Americans want and vested interests control Hollywood and the media," one young woman told Berlin TV. Few listeners had reason to doubt what "vested interests" she had in mind.

And who had the ear of Donald Rumsfeld? The so called neo-conservatives—or, as many Europeans saw them, the Jews (Paul Wolfowitz conspicuous among them) who had captured American foreign policy.

More than one writer has observed that anti-Semitism sometimes seems to be a default position for the German mind, an irresistible recourse whenever pressure or problems arise. Victor Davis Hanson noticed the undercurrents of anti-Semitism had once again begun to infect German politics: "Jurgen Mollemann of the Free Democrats spoke of the 'intolerant, spiteful style' of some prominent Jews—an anti-Semitism voiced earlier by former defense minister Rudolf Scharping, who complained that Mr. Bush was trying to please 'a powerful, perhaps overly powerful, Jewish lobby.'

"We sadly expect residual anti-Semitism in Germany, but when ex-officials there complain of the power of the American Jewish constituencies in New York and Miami, the awful subtext is, of course, that there is no such problem now in Germany, because . . ."

What Hanson left dangling in the air was for many people an ugly but undeniable truth: in a sense, the Nazi vision had ultimately prevailed in Germany. Hitler may not have survived to enjoy it, but the clever German people ("I had no idea what was going on") did, and all it cost them was two or three decades. Germany today is an economic power to be reckoned with—and its population is almost entirely free of Jews. The Jewish population, moreover, has been replaced with anti-Zionist Muslim immigrants, who provide the Germans with perfect camouflage: with the Arabs there to do the Jew-bashing for them, the Germans can safely nod their approval from the sidelines.

From time to time, of course, a troublesome note would rise to the surface. In November 2003, Defense Minister Peter Struck was forced to fire a career general who had served in Afghanistan after it emerged that he had written a letter praising a German politician's recent anti-Semitic speech. The general had urged the politician to continue speaking the truth.

Some commentators, such as Victor Davis Hanson, have expressed the fear that the Germans of today may not be as thoroughly pacifist as we'd like to believe—and that old-fashioned German nationalism may be peeking out of the grave. "If I were a Frenchman, Pole, Greek, or Czech," Hanson wrote, "I would reexamine very carefully the fashionable anti-Americanism of the continent, dissect it, and determine what, in fact, are its real undercurrents and repercussions—before the spooky German rhetoric is turned on them, and we, in our disgust, are long gone from the scene."

The great danger is that the twin strains of anti-Semitism and anti-Americanism will feed off each other. And by all evidence there's plenty of food to go around. "A vitriolic form of anti-Americanism is raising its ugly head in a country that for decades has been one of America's staunchest allies in Europe," wrote Toni Heinzl for the *Fort Worth Star-Telegram* just after the fall of Baghdad. Cruising the postings on the *Der Spiegel* website, Heinzl found ample evidence of anti-American sentiment. "In essence, America is depicted as a decadent, self-absorbed nation that worships unrestrained capitalism, with a culture lacking any redeeming qualities. And that's textbook anti-Americanism."

In a post that read more like a threat than an observation, one e-mailer promised, "The World Trade Center and the 3,000 dead were only an advance. War will return to America." It's hard to read a line like that without remembering that the 9/11 hijackers plotted as a cell in Hamburg, Germany.

What the German people resent most, according to Heinzl, is the fact that the Americans seem willing and able to do whatever they want in the world—precisely the kind of power the Germans lost after World War II. "The tone and scope of the seething and bubbling criticism of America amounts to a wholesale defamation of that nation's culture, political thinking, policies and its global role as the sole remaining superpower."

"Look," said one German political analyst, "what we hear is, 'Don't worry about what Europeans think, because they'll follow.' That may be true. . . . But Europeans don't want to hear that. We don't need our noses rubbed into it. Eventually, that works against the United States."

In May 2003, Schroeder accepted an invitation to speak to the American Chamber of Commerce in Berlin, at a ceremony marking the organization's centennial. Schroeder was philosophical about the icy relations between his chancery and the White House: "Never explain; never complain," he said, defending his antiwar stance.

In his speech, Schroeder tried to explain German unwillingness to use force arises out of the collective memory of defeat in both world wars, which turned most Germans into pacifists. Citing opinion polls showing that 80 percent of Germans opposed the Iraq war, Schroeder cautioned: "The German public will have to be very carefully and intensively convinced if military force is to be used as a final and inescapable means to resolve conflict."

And he admitted there were some aspects of the American world-view that befuddled Germans, and which they ultimately could not accept. "American pioneer spirit, the readiness for permanent mobility, the belief that even the most daring projects can be realized swiftly hit up against their limits in our country," Schroeder said.

While Germany refused to send soldiers to Iraq—and its politicians have pledged that Germany will not engage in the sort of "blank check" diplomacy that led the Kohl government to contribute $9.7 billion to America's first Gulf War—eventually the Germans did consider offering certain kinds of aid to the postwar effort in Iraq, such as contributing German law enforcement expertise to train Iraqi policemen, perhaps even at facilities in Germany.

When the Iraq Donors Conference convened in Spain in October 2003, though, Schroeder's government kept its promise that Germany would not contribute to rebuilding Iraq unless it were under U.N. auspices. Germany offered no funds for reconstruction at the conference.

The German-American impasse has had some odd consequences among the German public. Among them is a strange willingness to accept outlandish claims about America, its government, and its people.

"Somewhere between Kabul and Baghdad, we lost each other," said Ron Asmus, a senior fellow of the German Marshall Fund, of the German and American people. "At the end of the day, we didn't just disagree on the policy but on the facts of what happened, and from that there was a jump to the conspiracy theories."

And it was quite a leap. During the summer of 2003, a poll conducted for the weekly *Die Zeit* showed that 31 percent of Germans under thirty years of age believed that the U.S. government may have sponsored the September 11, 2001, attacks. Worse, 20 percent of people in all age groups held the same view.

Twenty percent may not sound like a threatening number. But think of it this way: In 1992, Ross Perot persuaded 19 percent of American voters to throw their vote his way—and in doing so managed to hand the election to Bill Clinton. One-fifth of a nation, in other words, can be enough to tip the balance in any close election.

What accounts for the startling willingness of Germans to believe such an obscene idea? In part, the German media is to blame, for entertaining demonstrably ludicrous theories, thus promoting them in the German consciousness. Among the ideas that have been deemed fit for discussion in Germany:

- No planes crashed in Pennsylvania or the Pentagon;
- Detonations, not plane crashes, caused the World Trade Center to collapse;
- U.S. intelligence either planned the attacks, or at least knew they were coming and opted to do nothing.

The motive for all this? Perhaps, the conspiracy theorists, to persuade isolationist Americans to intervene in world affairs—just as they contend President Franklin Roosevelt used the Pearl Harbor attacks in 1941 to persuade Americans to enter World War II.

"We are fighting a war on the basis of this attack, so we should get some answers," said television producer Gerhard Wisnewski, whose *Unsolved Case 9.11* appeared on ARD, a publicly run German broadcast network. The *Wall Street Journal* quoted Wisnewski, along with several other "documentary" producers, on the subject. "We don't claim to know what happened," said Ekkehard Sieker, producer of another program alleging that America had manipulated the facts about 9/11; Sieker's program ran on *Monitor,* one of Germany's leading television news shows. "But we demand that those who claim to know answer these questions. Otherwise, we can't believe them."

One of the most prominent of these theorists is Andreas von Bulow, a well-respected former member of the German parliament whose book *The CIA and the 11th of September: International Terror and the Role of the Secret Services* sold more than 90,000 copies, hitting #3 on *Der Spiegel's* nonfiction bestseller list.

His theory is that the U.S. government staged the 9/11 attacks to justify wars in Afghanistan and Iraq. Even von Bulow calls his theory "tentative," conceding that it was based mostly on his doubt that Osama bin Laden's al Qaeda terrorist group could have launched the attacks. "That's something that is simply 99 percent false," he reportedly claimed at a reading he gave on the second anniversary of the attacks.

In an interview with the German newspaper *Tagesspiel,* von Bulow charged that the American government needed to replace the threat of communism with something equally threatening, and they picked Islam. "They are accused of having given birth to suicidal terrorism."

Ignoring massive evidence within the Arab world—from the Palestinians to the Saudis and al Qaeda—that "suicidal terrorism" was a longtime Islamist specialty, von Bulow pointed to his twenty-five-year government career (including some exposure to secret agencies) and concluded that the 9/11 attacks were the work of professionals in government. "I can state: the planning of the attacks was technically and organizationally a master achievement. To hijack four huge airplanes within a few minutes and within one hour, to drive them into their targets, with complicated flight maneuvers! This is unthinkable, without years-long support from secret apparatuses of the state and industry."

After a von Bulow book signing, the *Journal* spoke with one Daniel Feifal, a twenty-four-year-old architecture student and a member of the extraordinary percentage of German young people who believe such conspiracy claims. "That they knew about the attacks and let them happen because it could further their foreign-policy aims, yes, I'm prepared to believe that."

As America learned in the wake of the Kennedy assassination, no society is immune to conspiracy theories when events seem to defy easy explanation. But the German openness to absurd theories about 9/11 bespeaks a basic willingness to deny the plainest common sense. Untold millions of viewers watched on television as the hijacked airliners flew into the World Trade Center towers; thousands upon thousands of New Yorkers witnessed the events firsthand. Millions have watched Osama bin Laden claim credit for the plan. The hijackers' pictures and life stories are all a matter of public record; the evidence of their training for the mission is detailed and thoroughly corroborated. Who can look at all that and reject the idea that those nineteen Arab *jihadis* set out to strike at the symbolic heart of America?

Likewise, how could anyone believe there was not an airliner hijacked that crashed into the Pentagon? Or deny that the hole in the ground at Shanksville, Pennsylvania, was not caused by the crash of United Airlines Flight 93? Where are all the passengers and crew? Where is Barbara Olson, the wife of U.S. Solicitor General Theodore Olson, if her plane did not crash into the Pentagon? Hiding in Tahiti, in some strange government plot to drag Americans into wars overseas they would otherwise have refused to fight?

Even as Germans were focusing on ridiculous theories about the American government, however, there is evidence that they were also ignoring ominous facts about their own.

On February 14, 2003, National Review Online published an article by Ion Mihai Pacepa, the former chief of intelligence for Soviet-aligned Romania, and the highest-ranking intelligence officer to have ever defected from the Soviet bloc.

Based on his own firsthand knowledge, Pacepa leveled serious and credible charges against the second-highest ranking official of the German government, Foreign Minister Joschka Fischer. According to

Pacepa, terrorist Illich Ramirez Sanchez—aka "Carlos the Jackal"—had told authorities that the weapons for a deadly terrorist takeover of an OPEC meeting in Vienna in 1975 had come from the Frankfurt/Main apartment where German terrorist Hans-Joachim Klein had been living with two other "red revolutionaries": Daniel Cohn-Bendit and Joschka Fischer. According to Pacepa, the claim was corroborated by none other than Muammar Qaddafi [as per *NYTimes*], the dictator and terrorist plotter of Libya, who also knew of the plot.

Fischer characterized the charge as "grotesque," but Pacepa pointed to a 1976 thank-you note from Qaddafi to Romanian dictator Nikolai Ceausecu—sent through Pacepa—in which "Qaddafi had emphasized that Carlos' OPEC operation would not have been possible without the help [of Romanian intelligence] and a 'West German revolutionary group in Frankfurt/Main.'"

After Carlos was arrested by French Intelligence in 1997 at his hideout in the Sudan, German journalist Bettina Roehl—daughter of the late Ulrike Meinhof, co-leader of the infamous Baader-Meinhof terror gang—revealed that Fischer did indeed belong to a Frankfurt/Main terrorist group in the 1970s. She provided pictures showing Fischer, wearing a beard and a helmet, beating a German police officer during a violent demonstration in Frankfurt/Main on April 7, 1973. "The pictures show Fischer fighting side by side with Klein, Carlos' deputy in the 1975 attack on the OPEC headquarters in Vienna," in which Klein killed two security guards, Pacepa reported.

The pictures, at least, were confirmed by Fischer himself. In late 2001—after the pictures had been authenticated, and there was no further room for denial—Fischer publicly apologized to the beaten police officer. But in October 2002, when Fischer was asked by a German prosecutor about veteran German terrorist Margrit Schiller's statement that she had stayed at the apartment of "Herr Fischer and Daniel Cohn-Bendit," Fischer sidestepped the question, denying that his apartment had been "a hostel for terrorists."

Whatever became of Daniel Cohn-Bendit, the other terrorist abettor? "Danny the Red," as he was once known, is now a member of the German parliament.

Pacepa also said Fischer has indirectly confirmed he participated in demonstrations in which he hurled stones at West German authorities. "These were not spontaneous demonstrations—they were all financed by the Soviet bloc foreign-intelligence community, including my own DIE when I was at its helm."

"It may never be possible to prove 'beyond the shadow of a doubt' Joschka Fischer's connection with the Soviet KGB," Pacepa wrote, "but I do know that the KGB—and my DIE—was financing West Germany's anti-American terrorist movements in the 1970s, while I was still in Romania."

Pacepa said that Fischer's "evidently ingrained anti-Americanism" is now spreading through the German government. And press reports suggest that Fischer has even loftier political ambitions. He is eyeing the position of foreign minister of the European Union, under a new constitution designed to make the EU a kind of United States of Europe, an entity of 600 million people that could someday develop a unified military capability and an economy that could challenge any power in the world—including the United States of America.

One year after the Munich International Security Conference in which John McCain expressed hope that Germany would come to its senses, Secretary of Defense Donald Rumsfeld addressed the same group. The tenor of his words reflected the lingering bitterness of the Iraq war debate, still festering a year later. "Think about what was going on in Iraq a year ago with people being tortured, rape rooms, mass graves," Rumsfeld said in what the *New York Times* described as an "emotional" tone. "There were prominent people from representative countries in this room that opined that they really didn't think it made a hell of a lot of difference who won," Rumsfeld said in a raised voice. "Shocking. Absolutely shocking."

Rumsfeld's stern lecture was met with the guilty silence of constrained fury. Later German participants said they were "stunned by
Rumsfeld's arrogance," according to the *New York Times.*

Even as the Germans choose to believe that the American government is capable of sending airliners loaded with passengers to crash into
its own Pentagon and office towers in New York, they ignore credible
public evidence that an old predatory force, thought to have been defeated, is rising within their ranks.

They have evidently been blinded by their anti-Americanism—
by the pure, addictive pleasure of hating America.

THE AXIS OF ENVY
Belgium, South Korea, and Canada

I N THE AFTERMATH OF September 11, Americans were mystified by the hostile sounds coming out of countries that had long enjoyed a good relationship with the United States—nations that, in their own best interests, should have been eager to protect such relationships.

Why would Belgium be picking a fight with the United States?

What was South Korea's problem?

And perhaps most obviously, why was Canada sounding so bitter and spiteful?

George W. Bush cobbled together the Axis of Evil from an unlikely threesome of malevolence: Iran, Iraq, and North Korea. But there's another odd collection of anti-American nations, who shared nothing more than their frequent declarations of hating America and the fact they were entirely inconsequential to Americans.

This Axis of Envy included three of the world's most ignored countries—three nations Americans look to for beer, chocolate, and kim chee, but not often in matters of foreign policy: Belgium, South Korea, and Canada.

BELGIUM: IF IT WERE GONE, WOULD ANYBODY NOTICE?

On June 19, 2003, the Associated Press (AP) reported the following: "Defense Secretary Donald H. Rumsfeld warned last week that the United States may encourage NATO to move its headquarters out of Belgium unless the country changes the newly amended law to rule out complaints against Americans." Rumsfeld's "encouragement," in fact, involved a promise to rescind funding for a new NATO headquarters complex, along with an investment of half a billion dollars, if Belgian authorities did not immediately invalidate a Belgian law that would have allowed local prosecutors to bring war crimes charges against American government officials.

This tempest in a teapot had begun a few weeks earlier, when a Belgian attorney announced that he would be seeking a war crimes indictment against General Tommy Franks, the U.S. Centcom commander and architect of America's winning military strategy in Iraq. After more than a year spent loudly insisting that its courts could try and convict anyone anywhere on the globe for war crimes under the concept of "universal jurisdiction," however, Belgium backed off in the face of one simple threat from Defense Secretary Rumsfeld. That same day, the AP reported, Belgium moved quickly to "dismiss war crimes complaints against President Bush and British Prime Minister Tony Blair, anxious not to create more tension with Washington over the Belgian war crimes law." The problem never even rose to the level of the president: In one quick aside ("We may want to move NATO Headquarters"), the Belgian "situation" was over.

When it came to war with the United States, Belgium simply folded at the sound of the first shot. Even the Iraqi Republican Guard in Baghdad put up more of a fight.

It was an odd and pathetic end to a strange war Belgium had been waging against the United States since President Bush stood before the United Nations in September 2002 and warned the international body that it must do something about Iraq.

Belgium had decided the United States could not be allowed to act in its own best interests, to do what it wanted, and it set out to stop America as a mouse might set out to halt an elephant. Belgium conducted a futile little war against America that ended as anyone might have predicted: in complete collapse.

"Belgium, for once, was totally coherent," explained Belgium's quixotic foreign minister, Louis Michel, in a postwar interview with *La Libre Belgique*. The tiny nation of 10 million had spent the run-up to the Iraq war trying to talk itself into believing its voice was loud enough to be heard.

"We said there was no cause to attack Iraq as long as the diplomatic avenues had not been exhausted. What would have been said if we had not gone to the limit in the NATO framework?" Belgium had vetoed Turkey's NATO request for defensive assistance. Belgium's move—made on the argument that helping Turkey was, in effect, helping the United States with a war Belgium sternly opposed—caught the fifty-year-old NATO alliance by surprise.

"We used all the means available to any member state to press home our point," Michel argued. "Unexpectedly, it is true. But if Belgium had not adopted this stance, France and Germany may have shifted direction earlier. The role we played is more important than people think." Of course, it's unclear how France and Germany had "shifted direction," exactly, when their opposition to the war remained steady throughout the prewar debate. But that was not the point.

The newspaper interviewers objected: Didn't Belgium actually go farther in its opposition than even its bigger partners, Germany and France? "In the prewar rhetoric, we wanted to apply maximum pressure for the United States not to attack," Michel boasted, referring to Belgium's series of futile demands and ultimatums.

During the run-up to the Iraq war, Americans became accustomed to hearing criticism from French and German leaders, and from some factions within the British populace. After Belgium repeatedly popped up in news reports about the European opposition, however, Americans were left scratching their heads. After all, in this debate between the world's big dogs, Belgium's minuscule economic power rendered it a lap dog with a yap instead of a bark.

But Belgium was opposed to the war, and it spent much of the run-up complaining that the United States and Britain were not listening to its constant antiwar arguments. Belgium seemed unable to believe it might have to take no for an answer. Belgium wanted what it wanted, and it lacked the good sense to simply say its piece and stand aside.

After the smoke had cleared and the tanks were rolling, the postgame show in Belgium centered on another question: Why did we choose a losing position and pursue it with such vigor?

In a lengthy interview with the newspaper *De Standaard* a month after the war ended, Foreign Minister Michel was asked why Belgium had gone so far in opposing the United States—why it had let itself be carried away with antiwar fervor, despite its own best interests.

"We were consistent," Michel replied. "As long as the war had not yet begun, we took the most deterrent position possible." This included threats both to evict what few U.S. troops were in Belgium, and to bar the entry of more. "But once the war began, I signed the transport agreements."

It was a revealing admission: Michel and the Belgian administration had threatened to prevent American troops leaving Germany to travel through Belgium on their way to board troop ships in the port of Antwerp; they had even threatened to refuse U.S. troops the right to fly through Belgian airspace.

The *De Standaard* reporters were incredulous. "Prohibiting the transport of materiel across our territory when there is no war going on and then allowing it once the war is underway—how logical is that?" they asked.

"I repeat," Michel calmly replied, "we were consistent."

The reporters from *De Standaard* pressed their point: "And were France and Germany, which never prohibited American flights and transport, thus *not* consistent?"

At this point, Michel exploded into a tirade, dropping any pretense of the diplomatic dignity of his office. "But who dragged me into this mess?" Michel blurted out. "I cannot break solidarity with [Defense Minister] Flahaut. If I am sitting on a TV soundstage with Flahaut, and he jumps in and says that he is going to say 'niet' to the United States, what do I do? Say that I do not agree and trigger a crisis in the government? No, I am obliged to go along with him like some kind of big idiot, and do whatever I can to avoid looking like a complete ass. Do you think I agree with his policy? But I cannot say that."

Trading solidarity for courage: It was a devil's bargain repeated throughout the sorry narrative of Belgium's single-minded—or mindless—opposition to the Iraq war.

One member of parliament—also a member of Belgium's left-wing Live Differently party—went so far as to demand that U.S. diplomats be expelled from Belgium, and U.S. troops blockaded as they tried to move through Antwerp if America chose to go to war without U.N. support. When Deputy Peter Vanhoutte was informed that this would have the effect of declaring war on the United States, the legislator saw nothing wrong with that: "If the United States starts a unilateral war, we should respond with a proportionate penalty."

Belgium was also one of the few countries to refuse an American request to expel Iraqi diplomats in the week before the war. The United States believed that many of Iraq's foreign diplomats were actually intelligence agents with orders to facilitate terror strikes overseas if America attacked, and dozens of countries expelled scores of so-called Iraqi diplomats. But Belgium sided with the Iraqis. "We feel there were no elements which would justify an expulsion," a spokesman for the Belgian Foreign Ministry said.

Belgium fell in behind France and Germany in its basic stance against the war, but led the way for others in important ways that made Belgians swell with anti-American pride. Belgium was especially vocal in railing against American policy: It accused America of imperialism, threatened U.S. diplomats, and refused to cooperate with America in matters of security and intelligence. It insisted that its status as a member of the European Union (EU) gave it the right to speak for the entire continent, and its politicians empowered Belgians with a sense of righteousness that far outstripped its ability to effect any change in its favor.

To top it all off, Belgium called its own mini-summit of EU members (only France, Germany, and Luxembourg attended) at the end of April, after the successful conclusion of the U.S.-led war. Europeans dubbed it "the Praline Summit," after Belgium's celebrated cream-filled chocolate trifle—the nation's real reason for being. Prime Minister Guy Verhofstadt had envisioned bringing the EU members together to organize a European military capability that could counter America's unmatched power to act alone, and force the United States to grant some "hard power" respect to "soft power" Europe.

The summit busied itself with a discussion of building a new European defense force headquarters in Brussels, not far from NATO headquarters. As Secretary of State Colin Powell pointed out, however, any discussion that failed to account for the costs of developing actual joint military capability was "irrelevant." The summit was a dismal failure, its two dubious accomplishments being to effectively split (and very possibly wreck) NATO, the very organization that ensured Belgium's freedom and independence for fifty years; and thrust Belgium into the front ranks of international anti-Americanism.

When questioned about the wisdom of taking on the United States, Verhofstadt sniffed: "There is no benefit to NATO in remaining a group with one superpower and 18 bigger and smaller dwarfs chasing behind it." NATO's sin was that it was just too American; having its headquarters in the Belgian capital of Brussels was just too potent a daily reminder that the Belgians play permanent host to a power they cannot control and increasingly loathe: the United States of America.

What was little Belgium up to in challenging the United States? Americans would be smart to think the worst—that Belgium was preening its anti-American feathers in a bid to assume a world leadership role.

Jean-Paul Marthoz, editor-in-chief of *La Libre Belgique* and European director of Human Rights Watch (no conflict there, we would undoubtedly be assured), offered an explanation to Reuters that inadvertently confirmed the impression of a growing Belgian anti-Americanism. "It may look a bit weird that Belgium is taking such a tough position and joining France and Germany," he said. "But Belgium has a tendency to be afraid of very strong states and so relies on multinational organizations to safeguard the interests of small countries, hence its insistence on UN involvement." Hence its insistence on favoring the opinion of a group Belgium has a voice in, such as the United Nations, over the right of the powerful United States to pursue its own national interest.

For Belgium, the only threads available that might serve to tie down the American colossus were the ties of internationalism, exemplified and codified in the internationalist structure of the United

Nations. If Belgium could not make the will of the United Nations stick, it would have to face the fact that it had no power at all.

And it's not as though Belgians were unaware of the precariousness of their position. In the election campaign that followed the war, opposition party leaders called Prime Minister Verhofstadt's policies "slapstick foreign relations." And when *La Libre Belgique* asked Foreign Minister Michel if the future of the United Nations had been put at risk by his nation's confrontation with the United States, Michel— the same man who earlier blamed others for his own lack of courage in an intramural dispute with another government official—calmly replied in the negative.

"If the international community had simply ratified U.S. military action," he argued, "one would not even be asking whether or not the United Nations must play a part in the reconstruction of Iraq."

At the moment Michel spoke, of course, the United Nations was emphatically *not* playing a role in the reconstruction of Iraq; its prospective role appeared to be limited to providing humanitarian aid, helping organize elections, and possibly deploying peacekeepers. But Michel was still convinced that Belgium could somehow oblige the unilateral power that actually controlled postwar Iraq to seek its permission to proceed: "The very question of the future of multilateralism would not even be asked because it would be no more than a tool to cover U.S. unilateralism. We saved the honor of multilateralism."

"With the United States outside it?" *La Libre Belgique* asked, astounded that its own foreign minister could conceive of a world where the United Nations wielded effective power without the cooperation of the United States.

Michel replied, perhaps a bit smugly, "But the Americans will have to return to [the United Nations]. *Because I do not have the impression they will be able to pull the same stunt twice.*" [Emphasis added.]

The display of denial was breathtaking, but there was even more. "Of course I regret that these efforts proved fruitless," Michel added. "There were moments when I had the feeling we were succeeding. When Bush was victorious at the [2004 Congressional] elections, I said: 'If I were him, I would build on this victory with a view to the next presidential elections and would not run the risk of a war.' But I am a better politician than Bush."

Any survey of European leaders and their worldviews would demonstrate that their sense of superiority of judgment is remarkably consistent; we might begin to wonder whether some psychiatric consortium is available to put entire national leaderships on the couch.

"Do you still have contacts with Colin Powell?" *La Libre Belgique* asked.

"By letter," Michel replied. Another "world leader" waiting for a letter from abroad.

All of this, it should be said, was nothing new. Belgium had also opposed the 1991 Gulf War, evidently preferring Saddam's military takeover of its neighbor to any international military response. In that conflict, Belgium actually refused to resupply the British with ammunition because of its political opposition to the war. And what would have been an international embarrassment for any other nation, became for Belgium a point of pride. Whatever the United States wants, Belgium opposes—no matter the legitimacy of the question.

What was the Belgians' problem? Belgium was the battleground for much of World War I, and the doormat for the Nazis' march to Paris in the opening days of World War II. Like the Dutch, the Germans, and the French, the Belgians believe they understand war better than the Americans, and have insisted on trying to shout down the very country that saved them from the Nazis and provided the capital and markets to rebuild their battered economies.

Veteran European reporter William Pfaff, writing in the *International Herald Examiner,* explained European attitudes as the war in

Iraq loomed. The Europeans, he wrote, "are interested in a slow development of civilized and tolerant international relations, compromising on problems while avoiding catastrophes along the way. They have themselves only recently recovered from the catastrophes of the first and second world wars, when tens of millions of people were destroyed. They don't want more."

Pfaff typified the anger and bitterness about the coming war among the Dutch (though the government of the Netherlands supported the United States), Germans, French, and Belgians. Reflecting the willful blindness to Saddam's brutal killing machine, the misery caused by his torture-addicted sons and secret police, he commented that "West European governments have seen the Iraqi dictator as a minor international problem."

In their refusal to see what was actually happening in Iraq, Pfaff and his fellow Europeans could not resist low blows and false charges. "American commentators like to think that the 'Jacksonian' frontier spirit equips America to dominate, reform, and democratize other civilizations," he wrote. "They do not appreciate that America's indefatigable confidence comes largely from never having had anything very bad happen to it."

But what was it that made the Belgians believe *they* could somehow teach us the lessons we so direly needed? Belgium is a nation of 10 million people, a little less than half the population of Iraq; a motorist would have to drive no more than two hundred and fifty miles to cover the distance between its most distant points. It is a dark and dreary place. Of the nearly nine thousand hours in a year, Belgium gets only about 16 percent—just under fourteen hundred hours—in sunshine. Belgians live through a lot of rain. As a nation, it is gloomy, pessimistic, introspective, highly traumatized by war, and deeply suspicious of everyone, including its own people.

Belgium does take pride in the fruits of its glum interior life. It has,a long and glorious cultural history: Belgium is rightly proud of the brilliant painters it has introduced to the world. Belgians are proud of their pralines, of their lace-makers, of their three hundred beers and nearly four hundred types of gin. They are also proud of the guarantees of their social welfare system, which places a near-zero priority on military power. Belgians are proud of their higher consciousness, their at-all-costs pacifism, of a sense of world morality they cling to regardless of the circumstances or risks.

It should come as no surprise that the Belgians are also the world's leading cranks; after all, there is so much the Belgians oppose and resent about *each other,* starting with language. The country is made up of three principal language and ethnic groups: the Dutch-speaking Flemish, the French-speaking Walloons, and a small German-speaking population. The Belgian constitution is an extremely lengthy and detailed document that spells out how Belgians live in sullen competition with each other, scrupulously protecting the territory and the rights of each major group.

It may be exactly that history of managing internal squabbles that has made Belgium the bureaucratic center for European aspirations for union, for a common currency, for open borders, and for multilateralism. Belgium is the headquarters for the European Union and NATO. It is home to the European Commission; the Economic and Social Commission (which controls labor rules and relations), important subsets of the European Parliament; and the European Council (the principal decision-making body of the EU). (Its even more diminutive neighbor, Luxembourg, is home to the European Investment Bank and the European Court of Justice.) Despite the vast national bureaucracies of Britain, France, and Germany, Belgium has taken the lead in promoting the idea that a united Europe can compete directly with the United States for world dominance.

In asserting themselves this way, the Belgians seemed to have in mind more than a simple interest in European solidarity. In a world accustomed to mocking Belgian aspirations, the prospect of a

Belgium-based EU gave the tiny nation a reason to feel better about itself. When your homeland is consistently described in the world press as "postage stamp-sized," "microscopic," "gallant little Belgium," it's hard to resist looking for ways to puff yourself up. In Belgium's case, that meant becoming the bustling host country for a cadre of EU bureaucrats and lawmakers, running back and forth between Brussels and the other European capitals, dotting i's and crossing t's, opening borders to trade, establishing rules that protect small states—and seizing every opportunity to nip at the larger states' heels.

The *Financial Times*'s George Parker, watchdog of the EU's antics in Brussels, reported a startling but typical incident in October 2002. At a summit of EU finance ministers, the bureaucrats of Brussels accused none other than France of violating the spirit of internationalism, characterizing its behavior in terms usually reserved for the United States: arrogant, unilateral, acting in its own interests. What event caused such indignation? A simple disagreement over tax policy. To the headmasters of Brussels, however, the issue was of less consequence than the behavior. France, wrote Parker, had committed the ultimate sin, when its finance minister "refused point-blank to bow to peer pressure to change his policy."

Whatever their problems with France, on a far deeper level the Belgians recognize that their tenuous claim to power rests entirely on the willingness of states to abide by international agreements, regardless of changing circumstances or their own national interest. And in that respect only one nation is strong and independent enough to pose a threat to the Belgians' throne: the United States.

The EU, in simple terms, is designed to amalgamate the power of (now) twenty-five states in order to balance the power between Europe and the United States. But this attempt has only thrown into relief the stark contrast between the American military and the atrophied forces of Europe. Throughout the Cold War and post-Cold War years, while America has been spending trillions of dollars on its ability to meet threats anywhere on the planet—not to mention protecting Western Europe from Soviet domination for half a century—the Europeans allowed their military to lie fallow. Instead, they talked themselves into believing that the soft powers of diplomacy, economic agreement, integration of states, and common currency could somehow be as effective as the threat (or use) of force. The Iraq war revealed that this was simply not true, and Europeans were shocked into recognizing a reality they had long tried to ignore: A nation's military actually matters.

Belgium, you might be surprised to know, *does* have an army. But it is more a job and retirement opportunity than a fighting force, with soldiers who are older on average than those of any other nation in the western alliance. The Belgians have apparently shelved any serious intention of marshaling a credible military presence, choosing instead to focus their national efforts on an attempt to bring evildoers to heel through judicial, not military, means.

All of which casts a new light on Belgian Prime Minister Verhofstadt's eagerness to denigrate the United States as "a deeply wounded power that has now become very dangerous" after September 11. As humiliating as it is, the Europeans realize that they are utterly helpless to defend themselves—yet all they can do is strike out at the only nation with the power to protect them. Pride goeth before a fall.

Shortly after the Belgians attempted to redress this imbalance with their ill-fated Praline Summit, former British Ambassador to Belgium David Colvin observed, "It is hard not to conclude that European defense union has less to do with improving Europe's defense capabilities than with buttressing Belgium's European Union federalist agenda. It was repeatedly explained to me as ambassador that a federally structured European Union is the natural, logical and necessary conclusion of the ceaseless process of constitutional revision which is a feature of Belgian political life and which has resulted in a complex, expensive and, some Belgians say, dysfunctional structure."

Pointing to the Belgians' recent history of foolhardy foreign-policy decisions—refusing to supply the British with ammunition during the 1991 Gulf War, defying NATO in 2003—Ambassador Colvin decried the nation's willingness to let its own EU agenda get in the way of international stability. "Belgium has many merits," he observed. "But serving as some kind of model for the enlarged European Union of 25 is not one of them."

The most reckless of Belgium's attempts to step onto the world stage, however, was a statute passed in 1993 known as the Universal Jurisdiction or Anti-Atrocity law. The Belgian Parliament intended to use this oddly presumptuous law to assume the role of international judge and jury, claiming the right to indict and try anyone on earth for alleged war crimes or crimes against humanity, regardless of where the alleged crimes were committed.

By their way of thinking, any nation that chose not to recognize Belgium's claim to control international justice should be branded an international outlaw, a renegade, a rogue. It was astonishing: a nation only a third of the size of California had attempted to assume for itself the power of world condemnation—as a substitute for the military, economic, and diplomatic power it could never otherwise muster.

The Universal Jurisdiction Law would allow Belgian courts to hold and try government officials on a whole array of charges for actions committed anywhere in the world—including war crimes, crimes against humanity, and violations of the laws of war. If you are an indicted prime minister or president of a state whose military actions have attracted the ire of the Belgian court, your counterpart inside the Belgian government would have no power to bail you out. Ally of Belgium? So sorry: the judges must judge. Under Belgian law, diplomatic immunity is piffle. "That's the peculiarity of the law," said Professor Eric David of the University of Brussels in a CNN report. "Immunity, which is traditionally recognized to foreign members of a government, to foreign heads of state . . . can't be an obstacle to the exercise of justice."

Speaking to CNN, Belgian Foreign Affairs Minister Koln Vervaeke tried to impart a sense of solemnity and dignity to a law that was transparently absurd. "The basic principle in Belgium is the separation of powers between the judiciary and the political level. And from the moment that the judiciary takes up a case against someone, a foreign head of state or foreign minister, on the basis of this law, the political field can't intervene. That's a basic principle in Belgium."

Such a role would have been breathtakingly presumptuous for any state to claim, but for a state that has no enforcement powers anywhere on the planet it rang especially hollow. Belgian appellate courts later acted to reduce the jurisdiction of the law in small but significant ways: under the amended rules, an indicted prime minister or president cannot be prosecuted until he or she is out of office, and must be taken into custody while on Belgian soil before a trial can proceed. Before canceling the law altogether, the Belgians attempted to mollify the United States by stipulating that any indicted American would be allowed to transfer his or her case back to the United States for trial. (American officials rejected this compromise, insisting on a complete rescinding of the law.) Overall, however, the breadth and the depth of the Belgians' claims to be the arbiters of world justice was stunning—and bemusing.

It's easy to understand what attracted the Belgians to the idea. In the business of war crimes there is never a shortage of offenses, of potential plaintiffs or defendants. It is a growth industry, with a global sweep and an endless time frame. And for a society like Belgium that mandates lifetime employment, setting up shop as a capital of international justice was like instituting a full employment act for ambitious lawyers and arrogant judges—both of which Belgium has in abundance.

Without the reins of international justice, Belgium is no more than Nova Scotia: pleasant, cold, and completely irrelevant. The Universal Jurisdiction Law promised to reposition Belgium as a permanent player on the international scene.

But it also threatened to make Belgium the fulcrum point for international anti-Americanism. It soon became clear that the Universal Jurisdiction Law would be open to abuse of the first order—as Belgium began using it as an opportunity to level high-profile accusations against the United States, Israel, and other nations.

As the war in Iraq was wrapping up, Belgium launched a determined effort to conduct an international show trial of Ariel Sharon for his alleged complicity in the massacre of Palestinians in two refugee camps in Lebanon in the 1980s. If the Belgians would pursue a twenty-year-old case with such vigor, one was left to wonder, what could be expected of them when they turned their attention to more recent events in Jenin, Bethlehem, or for that matter Baghdad?

This was no small issue: more than a few world leaders who have ordered armies into war have already felt the threat of war-crimes charges. Sharon and Henry Kissinger, among many others, have elected not to travel to Belgium out of concern that the nation's citizen's-arrest laws would theoretically allow any security guard or even flight attendant to take them into custody as soon as they set foot in Belgium. George W. Bush and Tommy Franks won't be stopping for gin and pralines in Belgium. And yet Robert Mugabe, the bloodthirsty African leader who was welcomed in Paris, might even find himself unmolested in Belgium as well; the Belgians appear to be fixated on perceived offenses of the first world, in particular the Americans. The outlook of the Belgian do-gooders seems to exempt third world killers from their wrath.

Mark Urban, diplomatic editor of the BBC's *Newsnight,* has described the complications created by the profusion of international criminal courts, with Belgium leading the way. "Former world leaders, including Margaret Thatcher," Urban writes, found themselves by the year 2000 "seriously assessing whether they, too, could face [such a] fate when travelling abroad. Tony Blair and U.S. President Bill Clinton could also be at risk."

Margaret Thatcher worried about Belgian courts over the sinking of the *Belgrano* during the Falklands war; Bill Clinton worried about his bombing in Serbia. "The fear of landing in a country that has unexpected extradition treaties with unlikely countries has also led top American statesmen to consult their lawyers before travelling. Henry Kissinger and George H. W. Bush are among them. After all, Dr. Kissinger ordered the bombing of Cambodia while keeping Congress in the dark. And President [George H. W.] Bush's invasion of Panama in 1989 might not meet stringent legal tests," Urban wrote in 2000.

By 2002, the potential for unwarranted trouble from these courts led the United States to take steps to rein in the international criminal courts, by using the authority of the U.N. Security Council—where the United States holds veto power—to quietly insist on time limits for the International Criminal Tribunals on cases such as Kosovo and Rwanda. The United States also made it clear it would not accept the jurisdiction of the U.N. International Criminal Court at The Hague. The Belgian initiative, meanwhile, was singled out as "a serious problem" by U.S. Secretary of State Colin Powell. "We have cautioned our Belgian colleagues that they need to be very careful about this kind of effort, this kind of legislation, because it makes it hard for us to go to places, it puts you at such easy risk," Powell said.

Powell also pointed out the law's obvious potential to backfire, isolating Belgium just when it was trying to assert itself as a major player. "It affects the ability of people to travel in Belgium without being subject to this kind of threat," he warned. "For a place that is an international center, they should be a little bit concerned about this."

Apparently, though, the only thing that really concerned the Belgians was using their courts to punish America for daring to use its military muscle in Iraq—not just in the past, but in the present.

The day before the Iraq war started, a lawsuit was filed in the Belgian court system naming the U.S. leaders of the 1991 Gulf War—George H. W. Bush, then-Secretary of Defense Dick Cheney, and Generals Colin Powell and H. Norman Schwarzkopf—as war criminals. As socialist lawmaker Patrick Moriau admitted, the suit was explicitly filed to curb the actions of the current Bush Administration in Iraq: "We are convinced that mistakes will be made again," he said, "and we want to signal that all legal means will be taken so that justice is done."

Within a week or two of the end of the Iraq war, Belgian judges entertained an indictment of General Tommy Franks, the American leader of coalition forces and the principal architect of the war. In the Belgian indictment, General Franks was accused of the indiscriminate use of cluster bombs, the killing of unintended victims, and the criminal negligence of bombing a public market with misguided missiles.

It was the height of absurdity, as Colin Powell's warnings about Belgium's presumptuousness signaled. And shortly after he made his remarks Belgium folded, deciding that it would forward the prosecution of General Franks to the United States to pursue (or not) as it saw fit, in its own judicial judgment. Having ventured into deeper waters than it could handle, Belgium bid a hasty retreat, exercising a trap-door loophole in its own law that provided for the prosecution to be handed over to the national courts of the accused if those courts were found by Belgian judges to be "competent."

When the law was finally rescinded in its entirety under the American threat to move NATO Headquarters out of Belgium, Secretary of Defense Donald Rumsfeld said, "Belgium has learned its lesson; there are consequences to its actions."

For a country starved for international respect, it was a monumental overrreach—and a comeuppance of the first order.

SOUTH KOREA: ABUSING ITS SAVIOR

America fought the Korean War to keep the people of South Korea free from communist conquerors. We defended South Korea at great expense in American lives, and have spent half a century guarding the nation's fragile position.

And yet, when it comes to hatred for America and Americans, South Korea takes a place at the front of the class.

Many of the pertinent facts have been lost to common memory here in the United States, in a mire of twisted and sometimes hostile U.S.-Korea relations. But the allegations in a U.S. military press release from September 15, 2002, tell the story of precisely how bad America-hating had become in South Korea.

It was just a year and a few days after the September 11 attacks: Three American soldiers were assaulted and kidnapped by demonstrators protesting the deaths of two teenage Korean girls in a road accident involving a U.S. heavy military vehicle on its way to a training exercise. The incident began on the train from Yongsan Station in Seoul, the nation's capital.

As the incident was reported in Western newspapers and by the military itself, John Murphy, Eric Owens, and Shane Tucker, three privates, were en route to their base camp from Seoul when demonstrators boarded their train and began handing out Korean-language flyers insisting that a group of American soldiers who had accidentally killed two South Korean teenagers in a road accident should be tried by South Korean authorities, not the American military. When Murphy refused to accept a flyer about the accident shoved at him by an older Korean man, Murphy said he was punched in the face by the man. He was then attacked by at least four of the demonstrators. When Murphy and his fellow soldiers decided to get off and wait for another train, the crowd of demonstrators blocked them from leaving the train station, and ended up pummeling them.

"According to the soldiers' initial statements, they were pulled, punched, kicked, and spat upon by demonstrators while a crowd of some 200 demonstrators watched," the American military said in its official statement on the incident. Two of the soldiers were taken to a nearby hospital by police, but Murphy was hauled away by the angry crowd to the local university stadium, where a memorial demonstration was being held for the accident victims. Forced to watch the demonstration, "he was photographed, videotaped, and allegedly forced to make a public statement about the incident on the train and in support of the demonstrator's demand[s]." When he was finally taken to the hospital, he was forced to apologize to the elderly man who had punched him in the first place.

The incident sounds like something from the era of the 1950s Soviets or Maoists. The fact that it happened to an American soldier in 2002, in a place that quite literally would not be on the map if it weren't for American soldiers who gave their lives, lent the story breathtaking power.

If an American soldier had been captured by the *North* Koreans, made to listen to a Kim Jong Il "Dear Leader" rally, and dragged around to hospitals to apologize to old men who had fought the Americans, the U.S. government would lodge a protest, diplomatic consequences would follow—but no one would be all that surprised. But this happened within the capital city of a close ally and allegedly reliable friend.

And yet the U.S. government knows the truth: South Korea is gripped by periodic waves of anti-American sentiment, a phenomenon that apparently rises and falls in lockstep with relations with North Korea, and what the United States is doing around the globe.

In the South Korea of 2003, where thirty-seven thousand Americans were still stationed—as a human tripwire that would bring the United States into war if the North were to attack—anti-Americanism was as predictable and as foreseeable as the weather.

Under South Korea's National Security Law of 1948, anti-Americanism was an official crime; violators were subject to arrest and jail. To be anti-American was tantamount to being a Soviet Communist, and therefore a security risk to South Korea. Anti-Americanism was, consequently, a highly marginalized political view.

Successive democratization movements changed the character of anti-Americanism, according to Jeffrey S. Robertson, a researcher for the Australian Parliament and one of the many academics who have studied and written about anti-Americanism in South Korea.

Writing in 2002, Robertson reminded readers that in two documented and infamous cases the American military had supported particularly repressive South Korean governments in their efforts to put down riotous anti-government protests (the latest being the particularly deadly Kwangju Massacre of 1980). It was a fact not lost on the South Korean people. "The hands-off attitude of the United States in South Korean politics," Robertson wrote, "amounted to tacit support for the unpopular repressive regimes opening the United States to accusations of complicity in the repression of democracy."

In the wake of such missteps, Robertson observes, anti-Americanism has changed over the past fifty years, and in the current period has become accepted as a part of South Korean life: "no longer unpatriotic, seditious, or radical, [anti-Americanism] had become, like the democracy movement, both worthy of respect and legitimate."

Added to that, of course, was the resentment over the usual issues—trade, jobs, and the ubiquitous American popular culture of music, movies, and fast-food franchises that has spread throughout the world. A spate of trade wars in the 1980s left Koreans feeling put-upon by an onslaught of American commerce, according to

Robertson; that led to a groundswell of cultural anti-Americanism, and a "Buy Korea" movement that may have actually worked too well. Later governments were forced to actually encourage Koreans to buy "foreign" or American products in order to reduce its growing trade deficit.

The incident may not have made a permanent impression on most Americans, but the Koreans' disappointment at the [2002] Winter Olympics only exacerbated bad feelings between the two countries. The Ohno Affair, in which an American skater won the gold medal after a South Korean skater was disqualified, sticks hard and bitter in the mind of the Korean public. To Koreans it was yet another example of their humiliation at the hands of the self-righteous Americans, who take whatever they want and glory in it. As evidence of the widespread anger at America that loss created, Robertson quotes the pop hit "F$&#ing United States" by Park Sung Hwan:

> Did you see the short-track [skating] race?
> Are you so happy over a gold medal?
> A nasty country, F$&#ing United States.
> Such as you are, can you claim that the United States is a nation of justice?
> Why on earth don't we say what we have to?
> Are we slaves of a colonial [imperialist] nation?
> Now we will shout: No to the United States . . .

South Koreans still support an American presence on the peninsula in large numbers—70 percent, according to a recent poll. But they also see the Americans as an obstacle to reuniting with the North.

A South Korean effort launched during the Clinton administration to open relations with the North culminated in July 2000 with a spectacular meeting between the leaders of the two Koreas, and a cooperative strategy that came to be known as the Sunshine Policy.

But with the arrival of George W. Bush in the White House, a series of events—the shock of September 11, the National Missile Defense project of the United States, the naming of North Korea as a point on the Axis of Evil, and the National Security Strategy, in which the Bush Administration announced a policy of global preemptive strikes—changed things dramatically in the minds of South Koreans.

Early in 2001, a Harris Poll found that 73 percent of South Koreans considered unification of the two Koreas likely in the near future (compared to only 28 percent in the United States). Once George W. Bush began drawing attention to the rogue behavior of North Korea, however, many Koreans felt that their chance to reunite with their northern neighbor was slipping away. A fresh round of Korean anger and resentment ensued.

It did not go unnoticed in the United States, especially among Korean Americans. "As a 29-year-old Korean-American born and raised in Philadelphia," Jennifer Oh of Exton, Pennsylvania, wrote to *Newsweek* in early 2003, "I am dismayed by the widespread hostility that a growing majority of young Koreans have toward the United States and its troops stationed along the DMZ. . . . I am appalled that many Koreans now view the United States as the enemy. I do not understand why they want to make peace with a manipulative, ruthless, egomaniacal communist dictator. Are they really that naive and ignorant?"

In the same *Newsweek* letters column, an answer came from Seoul. "Kim Jong Il is not a 'dear leader,' but a despot who has committed hideous crimes such as the killing of 115 innocent people by bombing a KAL airliner in 1987. He has also let 2 million North Koreans die of starvation over the past decade," wrote Kim Bo June of Seoul. "The day will come when a reunified Korea will bring him to justice."

If so, it will be a surprise to Mr. Kim, who seems to feel he is one of the most popular leaders of South Korea. Kim Jong Il's constant baiting of the United States has slowly but certainly created in a significant number of South Koreans an attitude that the United States is the problem—and that reuniting with the North and Dear Leader Kim Jong Il is the answer.

On the American side of the argument, there has been an institutional attempt to keep the resentments tamped down in Korea and covered up at home. American presidents never say, "We have to stay in Korea despite the fact the bastards hate us." Instead, American officials stress the half-century of friendship and cooperation between the two nations, the great strides in Korean democracy (those particularly violent televised riots and protests come to mind) and the Korean economy (after all, aren't Americans buying Gold Star televisions and Hyundai automobiles in droves?).

Anyone with firsthand knowledge of South Korea, however, knows that hating America is as intractable as the lunacies of the Dear Leader in the North.

Academic and government thinkers have been studying Korean anti-Americanism for years, and have linked its rise and fall directly to the perceived chances of reunification with the North. Irrespective of his hostile, bellicose, and often unpredictable relations with the United States, Kim the loony hermit has staged major diplomatic and public relations coups in recent years. He has held highly visible summit meetings with leaders of both South Korea and Japan and signed agreements that held out the promise of easing military tensions with South Korea, facilitating reunification of long-separated families, and extracting an apology for the brutal excesses of the Japanese occupation of Korea and the murder and enslavement of many thousands of people.

Are the South Koreans right to be twitchy and paranoid about the outbreak of a war with the North? Certainly. Seoul is in close proximity to the DMZ; the number of North Korean artillery shells that would rain down per minute if hostilities were to break out is well known. The oft-imagined scenes of thousands of North Korean troops suddenly popping up from hidden tunnels in downtown Seoul is less paranoia than reality. The North's missile tests—lobbing a few over Japan—have proven its ability to strike Seoul, Tokyo, and (American experts fear) perhaps even Los Angeles. Everybody knows that Kim's minions could roll a crude but deadly nuclear device up to the DMZ in a donkey cart.

Despite all that, by 2002 it was clear that the two Koreas were on a course for reunification—as long as no external forces intervened to effect unwanted changes. Those changes were seen looming on the horizon in the figure of George W. Bush.

Writing at the end of 2002, Robertson speculated on how the situation might go bad; his comments turned out to be uncannily prescient. "The preliminary stages would involve isolating the North Korean regime politically and economically, thereby forcing more desperate regime survival measures by the North. This could initially involve statements confirming recommencement of nuclear arms production, and the export of missiles and/or technology for hard currency, while later it would include direct threats, increased skirmishes in maritime zones and along the DMZ, and an eventual mobilisation along the DMZ. This would precipitate a conflict with the moral justification for preemptive American action."

The fact that these events have actually come to pass is not lost on the Koreans, and the fear of a preemptive strike by the United States— only heightened by a similar strike on Iraq—stokes the fires of Korean anti-Americanism. "The divergent views on North Korea policy between the United States and South Korea has been intensified by the fear that the preemptive strike policy may extend to North Korea, particularly in the wake of the nuclear revelation," Robertson concluded.

This up-and-down cycle of South Korean anti-Americanism is consistent, if not constant. To the American mind, though, it can often appear irrational.

In 2003, alone, the press office of the United States Forces Korea (USFK) has been obliged to issue repeated denials after Korean newspapers spread erroneous rumors that were apparently designed to stoke the fires of South Korean anti-Americanism.

In January, the press reported that the USFK had secretly and illegally placed great numbers of landmines around bases. Koreans feared that the Americans were secretly fortifying their own bases for an attack on the North. In February, a newspaper reported that USFK forces had quietly increased their readiness to a near-war footing; the American press office had to deny that troops were snapping bayonets into place on their firearms in anticipation of hand-to-hand combat.

And more recently, the American military press office was forced to deny Korean newspaper reports that the American general in charge of the Combined Forces Command (United States Forces Korea and the United Nations Command) had hinted at a preemptive strike on the North in a speech to the National Assembly. What the General had actually described was $11 billion worth of improvements to American *defensive* capabilities in and around Korea (including high-speed ships which could move a battle battalion into place from Okinawa in twenty-four hours), but the South Korean newspapers raised the alarm that the Americans were set to launch.

In fact, a pattern of such Korean newspaper reports goes back years, suggesting either an extreme paranoia about American military activity or a willful attempt to engender fears about American policy.

Korean suspicions about America's intentions are deeply ingrained. Many young South Koreans actually believe that the United States started the war with the North in 1950, and that Kim Jong Il's efforts to build nuclear weapons today (breaking his agreements to refrain) are a completely understandable result of a hostile and provocative United States policy. To the Americans who fought a horrendously difficult war to keep South Korea from being overrun by the North fifty years ago, this is a bitter pill indeed. But that fact is completely lost on the South Koreans. They are content to believe that their problems are America's fault, losing sight of the greater truth—that their freedom is America's gift.

CANADA: INVENTOR OF THE BAD NEIGHBOR POLICY

On September 11, Canada's prime minister, Jean Chretien, did not rush to show solidarity with the United States. He went instead to a fund-raiser in Toronto. When the first anniversary of the attacks came around—after a year sullied by his testy and often hostile relationship with the president of the United States—he sat down for an extended interview with CBC, Canada's national television network, and blamed America's "arrogance" for the attack. Though he avoided mentioning the United States by name, Chretien made himself abundantly clear: "I do think the Western world is getting too rich in relation to the poor world. We're looked upon as being arrogant, self-satisfied, greedy, and with no limits."

Chretien may have tried to hide behind the pronoun "we," but it was a thin veil for his real message. No one listening to Chretien mistook his words as a characterization of his own country. He was talking about the United States.

"You cannot exercise your power to the point of humiliation for the others," Chretien said.

Accusations of arrogance, of bullying on a planetary scale, of careless exploitation of the non-American peoples of the world—this was heady stuff, considering it was coming from the prime minister of a country that shares three thousand miles of border with the United States, boasts only one-tenth its population, and is almost entirely dependent on the United States for both economic and military support. Canada's government officials have also been alarmed to watch as about 2 percent of the population decamped for America to seek better opportunities.

All this denigration might seem like petty jealousy, then—except for the fact that it was also coming from a country where associates of al Qaeda have operated for years, if not openly then at least without fear. Ahmed Ressam, the Algerian who was on a mission to blow up LAX, was caught when he tried to enter the United States from Canada, where he had been living and plotting against America after immigrating from Tunisia. In the annals of terrorism, Ressam's case was a close call indeed. If he hadn't been sweating profusely from malaria, the sharp-eyed American customs officer might not have taken a second look at Ressam's explosives-laden car.

In a bid to reduce his 140-year sentence, Ressam has been telling authorities about the extensive web of al Qaeda "sleeper" cells in the United States and Canada.

On the second anniversary of September 11, American counter-terrorism agents were searching for four men who were suspected of planning a new terror attack. One of them, a Canadian named Abderraouf Jdey, was a former refugee claimant from Tunisia who promptly disappeared after being granted admission under Canada's generous asylum policies. Jdey's last known address was a Montreal apartment: after that it was anybody's guess. He could be living in America as we speak.

Adnan El Shukrijumah, a key North American al Qaeda member, was spotted in 2002 on the campus at McMaster University in Hamilton, Ontario, Canada. McMaster has a five-megawatt nuclear research reactor, and U.S. officials believe Shukrijumah was in Hamilton trying to obtain nuclear material for a radiological explosive device, also known as a "dirty bomb."

An informant told the FBI that three other al Qaeda suspects in addition to Shukrijumah were seen in Hamilton that same year.

They included Anas Al-Liby, one of the FBI's most wanted terrorists, Jaber Elbaneh, and Amer El-Maati.

Al-Liby had been linked to the 1998 bombings of U.S. embassies in Tanzania and Kenya. Elbaneh was wanted on charges of providing support to an al Qaeda cell in Lackawanna, New York, near Buffalo.

"Under our laws we presume they [Islamic immigrants] are here in good faith," Chretien said. "That's the system under which we operate." This despite the fact that as many as seventy Canadian citizens died in the collapse of the World Trade Center. Canada, clearly, was in denial about the terror threat—apparently on the slender premise that the specific target of the terror threat was not Canada but the United States.

As of the second anniversary of September 11, Canada reckoned there were 36,000 foreign-born non-Canadians on the loose in the country—fugitives who had been ordered deported but were dodging authorities attempting to remove them from the country. In a nation whose population is smaller than California's, this is a significant number.

And yet Jean Chretien wasn't the only Canadian official who was blind to the problem. The denial—and anti-American sentiment—appears to have affected other Canadian officials as well.

At the hour of the September 11 attacks, Canadian Foreign Minister John Manley received the news aboard a commercial flight from Frankfurt to Toronto. As he later told the CBC, after he was informed of the attacks by Lufthansa flight attendants, he admitted that his "first fear" was the possibility that terrorists had entered the United States from Canada.

Two weeks after the attack, though, Manley had quieted his personal fears (or resigned himself to Canada's powerlessness over the terrorist problem within its borders) enough to proclaim loudly that Canada would not bow to pressure to curb its liberal immigration policies. He urged U.S. politicians to abandon any thoughts they might have about increasing controls on the nations' unprotected mutual border.

A week after Manley went whistling in the dark, Canada's immigration minister, Elinor Caplan, chimed in, insisting that Canada's immigration system was "a model for the world" and that those who want to tighten it (members of the United States Congress, for instance) were "anti-immigrant, anti-everything."

David Jones, a former U.S. diplomat stationed in Ottawa, wrote in the Canadian foreign policy journal *Policy Options* that while none of the 9/11 terrorists entered the United States through Canada, "it would strain credulity to believe that Ahmed Ressam . . . was *a solitary clot of manure in a field of flowers*" [emphasis added].

And, then, as if in unison, a host of other Canadian officials stuck their heads in the sand. Joel Connelly of the *Seattle Post-Intelligencer* reported that Canadian Multiculturalism Minister Hedy Fry sat on a dais at a women's conference in Ottawa next to a female Islamic activist named Sunera Tobani who accused the United States of pursuing a foreign policy "soaked in blood." As Fry listened, apparently unperturbed, Tobani conceded that the victims of September 11 deserved sympathy, but asked "Do we feel any pain for the victims of U.S. aggression?"

In addition, while Prime Minister Chretien complained of American pressure to tighten up border controls, he must also have hoped to downplay his personal complicity in the spread of terrorism in Canada—specifically terrorism directed at the United States.

In 1995, Chretien had personally interceded with Pakistan on behalf of an Egyptian-born Canadian citizen named Ahmed Khadr. Apparently assuming he was innocent, Chretien stepped in after Khadr was arrested in connection with a terror bombing of the Egyptian embassy in Pakistan that killed sixteen. Chretien's pleas to Benazir Bhutto were, surprisingly, quite effective: As a consequence of his urgings, Pakistan released the man from custody. Unfortunately, though, the Canadian leader failed to perform an adequate background search on the man: Khadr, it turned out, was an al Qaeda founding member (and close associate of Osama bin Laden). After returning to Canada, he later traveled back to Afghanistan (after recovering from injuries—presumably sustained during the bombing—at Canadian government expense) to plot against Americans.

Until Canada's intervention, Khadr—known in terror circles as al-Kanadi ("the Canadian")—had been locked up securely in a Pakistani jail. But Chretien, bowing to pressure from Islamist groups in Canada, personally vouched for him as a father of six and an innocent "aid worker" whose Canadian rights should be respected.

After his release, Canadian intelligence later reported, Khadr promptly returned to his work for al Qaeda, and resumed his close association with Osama bin Laden as fund raiser and terror planner. In his role as a field worker for a Canada-based Islamic charity, Khadr directed Canadian government funds into "refugee camps" and other projects in Pakistan—or so went his cover story. The "refugee camps" and "schools" and "hospitals," it later emerged, were in fact al Qaeda terror training camps. Al-Kanadi later moved his family from suburban Ontario to the front lines of al Qaeda training in Peshawar and Jalalabad, Pakistan. He indoctrinated three of his sons, and brought them with him on *jihad.*

On October 2, 2003, in a raid on a suspected al Qaeda camp in Afghanistan, Khadr and his fourteen-year-old son were killed in a vicious firefight—or so authorities thought. Later it was learned that the fifty-year-old Khadr had escaped during the gun battle, leaving the body of his son behind. Khadr had already given two other sons to *jihad,* though neither had been killed, both were under lock and key in an American prison.

One of those sons, Abdurahman Khadr, was released from the U.S. prison camp in Guantanomo Bay, Cuba, in December 2003, insisting that neither he nor any member of his family was a terrorist. He did admit he spent three months with would-be millennium bomber Ahmed Ressam in an Afghan training camp—one of several that U.S. authorities charge was financed by Osama bin Laden, with the help of the elder Khadr.

The other son was Omar Khadr, only fifteen years old when he was captured in Afghanistan in July 2002. Surrounded by American troops, Omar and a group of Arab fighters put up a ferocious struggle to beat back the Americans. But the U.S. soldiers called in air strikes and pounded the compound where the al Qaeda fighters and young Omar were making a stand. When the smoke cleared, an American military medic rushed inside the compound to look for wounded. A stick-like figure rose from the pile of bodies, a pistol in one hand and a grenade in the other. It was fifteen-year-old Omar, born in Canada, raised in Ontario's suburbs, brought to *jihad* by a father who had been personally saved from jail by the Canadian prime minister. Omar threw the grenade, killing the American medic and wounding another American soldier so seriously he lost an eye. Wounded by American troops returning fire, and bleeding from chest wounds, Omar begged to be finished off.

"This was no teenage kid from the suburbs," one of the wounded Americans said. "That was a trained al Qaeda terrorist who was determined to kill an American as his last act on earth."

Omar's bleeding chest wounds were stanched; he was kept alive, and eventually recovered to take his place with other Taliban and al Qaeda fighters at the American prison camp in Guantanamo Bay, Cuba. He claimed the distinction of being the youngest prisoner at Guantanamo—one of a number of teenage suspected terrorists held there by the United States after 9/11.

Chretien later made a halfhearted effort to effect Omar's release, but the Americans denied even a consular visit. Chretien's reputation for misjudging terror suspects had preceded him; Chretien's government wisely chose not even to challenge the American decision on young Omar Khadr, the pubescent *jihadi*.

In fact, Chretien's eagerness to effect the release of a man like Khadr, whose identity as a terrorist was already known in intelligence circles, could well have been the reason American authorities deported another Canadian citizen—*not* back to his home in Canada, this time, but to Syria, his place of birth.

Maher Arar had first come to the attention of authorities in Canada and Syria for his association with a terror suspect already imprisoned in Syria. He was first taken into custody on September 26, 2002, while traveling through JFK International Airport in New York, en route to Canada from a trip abroad. The fact that he was whisked off to Syria, instead of simply being returned to Canada, suggests that the American authorities considered sending another terrorist back to roam free in Canada as good as setting him free in the United States. Canada's record on terror was so miserable that Americans couldn't even be certain Canada recognized its own problem.

Arar was held in a Syrian prison for ten months, where he says he was systematically tortured; he was finally returned to Canada only after the Syrians became upset over their deteriorating relations with the United States. "It is completely unacceptable and deplorable what happened to this gentleman, who is a Canadian and who was sent to Syria rather than to his country of Canada," Chretien said. "We have protested."

Chretien may have protested, but he could not have been under any illusions about how far his plea might have gotten him with the United States. After all, the United States was hardly Benazir

Bhutto's Pakistan, which had so readily acceded to Chretien's pleas for Khadr's release.

In fact, American authorities might have noticed that while Chretien went to some significant lengths to effect the release of the Muslim "aid worker" Khadr, *al-Kanadi,* he made little or no effort to force Saudi Arabia to release a Canadian it held in solitary confinement and tortured for two and a half years.

William Sampson, a Canadian contract worker in Saudi Arabia, was picked up in December 2000 by Saudi police who were determined to extract a confession that Sampson was responsible for a fatal terrorist bombing. Considering what the world later discovered about the activities of al Qaeda in Saudi Arabia, and its efforts to overthrow the Saudi royal family, it became obvious that the Saudis were trying to scapegoat a foreigner—preferably a westerner such as a white Canadian—and that the Saudis knew full well their Canadian victim was innocent.

After almost a full year of intermittent torture, and several forced confessions, Sampson was forcibly dressed, handcuffed, blindfolded, and driven to a Saudi courtroom for his trial. On September 4, 2001—a week before fifteen Saudi youths attacked the United States at the behest of a disaffected Saudi multimillionaire—Sampson was convicted in a Saudi kangaroo court. The next day he was driven to his execution, which he expected would be a public beheading. But after being driven around for a period of time, he found himself back at his prison and was told his execution had been postponed.

In his isolation, Sampson knew nothing of the September 11 terror attacks. The Saudis stepped up pressure on Sampson, hoping to divert attention from their own massive complicity in the terror attacks on America.

Sampson, of course, became irrelevant. But this pattern of torture and terror against him continued for two years and seven months before the Saudis finally released Sampson. He later described his ordeal in a five-part series in the *National Post,* one of Canada's premier dailies. "On three occasions, I told Canadian officials that I had been tortured," Sampson wrote (his visitors had included a Canadian psychiatrist and two members of the Canadian Parliament). "I felt that the statements I made to Canadian officials about torture had fallen on deaf ears."

The Canadian government had allowed Sampson to suffer at the hands of Saudi torturers, who accused him of an absurd plot to bomb and kill a rival in a expat guest-worker turf war over bootleg liquor. The Saudis were clearly trying to hide the extent of their problems with al Qaeda, which had vowed to destroy not only the United States but the "apostate" royal family.

The speed with which Chretien managed to effect the release of a man who turned out to be an authentic al Qaeda bomber, Ahmed Khadr, stands in stark contrast to Canadian William Sampson's two and a half years of imprisonment and torture.

Such erratic and willful behavior, flying in the face of the realities of terrorism, dogged Canada throughout the year-long runup to the war in Iraq, and the quick war itself.

In truth, the war went badly for Canada. It sat on the fence much too long, and eventually allowed a decision to be made by the passage of time rather than the wisdom of its of leaders. In late 2002, as America was making the case for war, Canada talked about joining the United States, as it always has; it debated endlessly whether its old friend the United States was right to head into the war. Eventually, though, the calendar dictated Canada's direction, and in a spasm of conscience and idealism, Canada set terms for cooperation with the United States that ensured it would sit this war out.

The result? In trying desperately to avoid becoming America's "Mini-me," Canada stumbled disastrously, and became France's

Mini-moi. In doing so, it turned its back not only on its best friend, the United States, but also on its brethren in Great Britain. To lose two allies was one thing, but to end up with France as the consolation prize for its antiwar stance was confusing, demoralizing, and demeaning. *What a mistake,* many Canadians must have thought, while they waited and wondered whether their U.S. meal ticket was still good.

After the war, Canadian historian J. L. Granatstein wrote: "Let us be very clear: the Americans are furious at Canada now, as angry as they have ever been and, as soon as the dust in Iraq settles, they will exact their revenge."

How did this happen? In part, the answer has to do with attitude. The Canadians have an old saying about their American neighbors: "You're bigger, but we're better." Once again, pride may have gotten the better of our newly gun-shy allies.

The war in Iraq provided focus and a reason to voice what many Canadians consider a state secret: that anti-Americanism is the default position of the Canadian mind-set. This despite the fact that Canada and the United States are the world's largest trading partners, with two-way trade pushing past $1.3 billion *per day.* Canada is America's largest supplier of natural gas, and second only to Saudi Arabia as a supplier of crude oil. Any businessperson or economist would express immediate alarm if an otherwise avoidable dispute were to disrupt that economic relationship. Yet, the Iraq war seemed to inspire among Canadians a need to tell the United States off, to make a childish statement of defiance: *We can't be bought.*

When Canadians try to explain the obvious rift between themselves and the United States, they look not to themselves, but to America and in particular to George W. Bush. "When you get the right-wing hordes in power, with their war-mongering, the rhetoric rubs up against Canadians," said Lawrence Martin, an author and former journalist who covered Washington, D.C., for Canadian newspapers.

As Martin has observed, Canadians prefer Democrats, who fit better with Canadians' liberal outlook. In fact, just before the 2000 American presidential election, the Canadian ambassador to the United States, Raymond Chretien (the prime minister's nephew), felt completely comfortable saying in a speech in the United States that Canada was pulling for Gore over George W. Bush. "We know Vice President Gore," he said. "He knows us. He's a friend of Canada."

The fact that the prime minister's nephew and ambassador to the United States felt empowered to take such a position on an important neighbor's election—and that he was in no way chastised for his remarks—only confirmed for candidate George W. Bush's camp that the Chretien administration would be no friend to a Bush White House.

With Canada suddenly facing a new President Bush shortly thereafter, Canadians characteristically reverted to the role of innocent victim. They groused about Bush's policies, in a litany of complaints parallel to those of the Europeans. Prime Minister Jean Chretien said the U.S. Congress suffered from a "democratic deficit"; he attacked U.S. agricultural policies as "stupid"; as we've seen, he made the hurtful charge, on the anniversary of 9/11, that American "arrogance" was to blame.

And yet, when a sudden surge of anti-Canuck rhetoric occurred in the United States during the debate on the Iraq war (such as Pat Buchanan's jibe that Canada had become a "Soviet style Canuckistan"), the Canadians professed to be appalled. The Canadians seemed strangely unable to understand that Americans had no reason to take umbrage—until that Canada took up near-permanent residence on the fence, dangling the prospect of help in the war for months before ultimately siding with France and denying support to America.

Why would a neighbor and erstwhile friend behave in such self-destructive fashion? Canada is one of many countries that seem permanently convinced that it could run America better than the Americans do. To the Canadians, it was obvious America had stumbled into the hands of the forces of darkness; the only thing that mystified them was that we Americans ourselves couldn't see it.

To many Americans, of course, there's little evidence to support such an odd notion. It's worth noting that Canadians come to America in large numbers (700,000 Canadians work and live in the United States), where their socialist worldview inevitably creeps into American life. Peter Jennings, Morley Safer, Robin McNeil, the producers and much of the cast of *Saturday Night Live,* and several thousand working in Hollywood: Need we say more?

Canada has long been a friend of the United States, but the nations' relationship has often been prickly, owing in part to their disparity in size. One is a giant that dominates world economies and walks the globe with confidence in its own judgments. The other, with only one-tenth the population, is a free-spending comfort state that has ceded its defense to its neighbor. Canada is permanently anxious about its place in the world, and consequently willing to surrender its independent judgment to fellow comfort states half a world away—even when their agenda is explicitly anti-American.

The few Canadian voices who spoke up to defend the Americans—to argue that they were right about Iraq and a number of other issues the so-called "world community" considered crucial—made the same observation about their fellow countrymen: by and large, most Canadians failed to grasp just how much 9/11 had changed the thinking of Americans.

From the fall of 2002 through the spring of 2003, the international press bristled with a remarkable display of Canadian anti-Americanism, following the now-familiar pattern: rising public outrage, bubbling up in sudden, telling outbursts from the nation's leaders and opinion makers.

"Damn Americans. Hate those bastards." In the entire international debate over the Iraq war, not even the French managed to distill the essence of anti-Americanism more pungently than Canada's Carolyn Parrish, a liberal member of parliament, as she walked away from the reporter/camera scrum in Ottawa in late February 2003. At that very moment, her leader, Jean Chretien, was trying to broker an alternative U.N. resolution, offering Saddam Hussein yet another deadline to comply with the U.N.'s disarmament demands. The United States had rejected the proposal, and Canadian antiwar politicians like Parrish were angry. Once again, America had refused to listen to Canadian good sense. What was the use of being so smart if the dummy next door wouldn't listen to your back-fence advice?

Excoriated for her blatant and inflammatory remark, Parrish issued an apology within hours in a letter to the U.S. Ambassador Paul Celluci. By all appearances, it was a rote apology, lacking both sincerity and plausibility; Parrish claimed that her outburst did not reflect her true opinions of America. (Upon hearing this, a *Wall Street Journal* columnist asked: If Parrish calls Americans "bastards" but says that doesn't represent her "personal opinion," then "What's she saying? If it's not her opinion, it's a fact?") The slander was nothing more than a slip of the tongue, she claimed, the heat-of-the-battle muttering of a frustrated peacemaker faced with the prospect of war. Outraged Canadians eager to preserve decent relations with the United States (even those who might not have agreed to be described as "pro-American") predicted that the slip would spell the end of her career.

In the Op-Ed pages of the *Montreal Gazette,* L. Ian MacDonald observed that "Canadians seem to have developed an unhealthy and insufferable air of moral superiority regarding Americans."

MacDonald underscored the hypocrisy of Parrish and her anti-war colleagues by pointing out that if Parrish's remark had been directed at any particular ethnic group in Canada, it would have constituted illegal hate speech. "Hate mongering is a crime in this country," Mac-Donald wrote. "The dissemination of hatred is defined in the Criminal Code as 'the promotion of hatred against identifiable groups.'" Such as Americans.

His point was obvious: Carolyn Parrish would not be prosecuted under the laws governing hate speech—laws she would so vigorously support in another context—because hating America is both acceptable and common in Canadian culture.

MacDonald also offered a trenchant condemnation of other Ottawa politicians: "Nor was Parrish's outburst an isolated occurrence. For several weeks, she and fellow MPs Colleen Beaumier and Bonnie Brown, all from the western Toronto suburbs, have been making stridently anti-American statements in the Liberal caucus, while Prime Minister Jean Chretien looked on in silence."

Well, not quite complete silence. Chretien issued no rebukes of his lip-flapping liberal caucus members—but he did come to the United States to get right in the face of Americans and warn them that Canada doesn't trust them.

Chretien gave a speech in Chicago on Valentine's Day 2003, but it was no love note to George W. Bush. Indeed, it was more like a brass-knuckled slap across the face. "The price of being the world's only superpower is that its motives are sometimes questioned by others," Chretien said, bluntly warning Americans that Canada no longer believed the Bush administration's stated reasons for war.

"Great strength is not always perceived by others as benign," the prime minister warned. "Not everyone around the world is prepared to take the word of the United States on faith." Translation: America is a lying bully.

These words were spoken on American soil, in a speech to an American audience.

Correspondent Robert Russo, writing for the Canadian Press Service, noted that Chretien's speech marked the first time the Canadian government had publicly expressed suspicion of the Bush administration's motives for going to war in Iraq.

The speech to the Council on Foreign Relations, a premiere forum for discussions on international affairs, was "likely to be perceived by some in the Bush administration as a lecture," noted reporter Mike Trickey in the *Montreal Gazette.*

Officially, Canada was still holding out the possibility that it would decide to join an American "coalition of the willing." As of Valentine's Day, though, no prudent person would take that bet. If there were any remaining doubt in Washington, D.C., on the question of Canadan support, Chretien's trip to Chicago set it to rest.

Chretien gave his speech on the very day that Hans Blix had returned to the Security Council and announced that his inspectors had discovered evidence of Saddam Hussein's violations of U.N.-imposed weapons bans (in the form of a small number of Al Samoud missiles). In an editorial, the *Montreal Gazette* expressed disbelief that certain Security Council members found this news comforting, that the discovery of such "technical" violations gave hope for progress in the inspection effort, and even that the Security Council could now trust that Iraq will come clean eventually. "What nonsense," the *Gazette* said.

Chretien had been demanding that the United States fight this war through the United Nations; as the *Gazette* noted, that was precisely what the United States was trying to do. Yet "what this UN jaw-jawing amounts to," the paper observed, was "an effort by a swarm of Lilliputians to tie up the United States in a web of words, for their own various purposes."

Americans could take some comfort from Canada's Western provinces, which tended to side with the United States. But the historically French eastern region was wholly aligned with France. The premier of Quebec, Bernard Landry, used the occasion of a minus-twenty-degree day, with 150,000 antiwar protestors marching in Montreal, to announce that opposition to the war was so strong in Quebec that any move by the national government to join the United States would revive the lagging independence movement in Quebec.

Later in the summer, while the elderly were dying and stacking up in mortuaries during France's heat wave, Jacques Chirac was holidaying in Quebec, refusing to disrupt his vacation, unmoved by as many as fifteen thousand heat-induced deaths.

Some Canadians began to think that anti-Americanism had turned into a semi-official government policy. Carolyn Parrish wasn't the only Chretien administration official who made public intemperate remarks; earlier, the prime minister's press aide Francoise Ducros had called George Bush a "moron" and was allowed to resign rather than be fired. Chretien's own comments about American arrogance and greed only lent further support to Peter Worthington's assertion in the *Toronto Sun*'s Op-Ed pages: "all these anti-American sentiments emerging from the Liberal party are not individual indiscretions, but a depiction of what the government feels."

David Jones, the former American diplomat, also saw Parrish's remark as a peek behind the scenes. "Does anyone, no matter if they are now being spun like gyroscopes, believe that if senior 'Chretienites' were speaking of Bush, Cheney, Rumsfeld, Powell and Rice as smart, focused, directed, organized and effective, Ms. Ducros would venture forth to label the president a moron?" Obviously not: just as obviously, her remark was a mirror of Chretien's opinion.

But hating America wasn't the exclusive province of Chretien and his team. In a letter to the *Ottawa Citizen* seventeen-year-old

Samantha Fex of "Kanata" wrote: "Canada is free of terrorists not due to being 'insignificant' but because we simply don't stick our noses into issues that are none of our concern and make loud-mouth comments. That's why Americans have to take all the heat: because you are the ones who caused it."

Excusing for the moment young Ms. Fex's errors of fact (her homeland may have many virtues, but it's hardly "free of terrorists"), she showed how dangerous Chretien et al.'s America-bashing comments were. With the prime minister suggesting broadly that America should look to its own behavior to explain 9/11, why shouldn't a Canadian teenager say the same thing?

Canadian musician and singer Carole Pope, who led a group called Rough Trade, had been well-disposed toward Canada's southern neighbor as late as January 2001. "I love living in America," she said. "I don't think I'm going to live in L.A. forever, but I love the whole American thing. The Americans are very amazing, don't you find?"

By mid-April 2003, though, she was frightened and alarmed about the new "American thing." Writing in the *Ottawa Citizen,* Pope asked: "What was it like to be a Canadian living in the U.S. in the middle of a preemptive attack on Iraq? Even with the inevitable regime change, we felt jumpy, conflicted, and completely impotent."

Pope tried to explain what life as a Canadian in America during the Iraq war: "We're sick of hearing about what traitors Canadians are on FOX and CNN. As one Canadian tells me 'The U.S. is mad at us because we didn't want to help them kill babies.'" Amazingly, no one came to haul Pope away, back to Canada.

Other Canadian writers made similar complaints. "When you're the biggest bully on the playground, it doesn't matter if nobody likes you and everyone's afraid," wrote Catherine Ford in the *Calgary Herald*. "In fact, that works to your advantage." With such rhetoric on the rise in Canada ever since 9/11, is it any wonder that the America-baiting eventually extended to the abuse of average American citizens?

That the American national anthem was booed at an NHL hockey game? That at a peewee hockey game on the northern side of the border the little visiting U.S. players—*children*—were subjected to outright abuse by their Canadian hosts? The *Toronto Globe and Mail* reported that youngsters from Massachusetts, who came to Canada to play youth hockey, had to watch the American flag burned; ordinary Canadians on the street flashed the kids a familiar obscene gesture.

Chretien couldn't bring himself to get out front and disavow the America bashers, but somebody in the government had to. The thankless task was left to Defense Minister John McCallum, who used a speech at the Conference of Defense Associates to issue the pay-no-attention-to the-loonies statement: "Never must we be smug and superior vis-à-vis the United States," he said firmly, if ineffectually.

Yet, even as he seemed to reject the anti-American element within Canadian culture, McCallum precipitated a telling moment, completely overlooked in the United States, in which the Canadian public was forced to confront its own inferiority complex about the United States. During the question-and-answer session, a high school student visiting the conference with her history class asked the minister of defense how the government could urge Canadian citizens to think well of the United States—when its own ruling party officials could not manage to keep anti-America sentiments out of their own words and thoughts?

Seventeen-year-old Rebecca Williams, the daughter of an American diplomat and a Canadian public servant, told the *National Post* that she was tired of hearing Canadians make disparaging remarks about Americans. "I just feel that Canadians have this inferiority complex when it comes to the United States. I don't know what we are afraid of."

Williams, who has lived in Canada since she was two, received a standing ovation for her courage in confronting the minister of defense with her question, which appears to have caught him off guard.

He could only stammer out a halfhearted response: "solidarity . . . is a core covenant that we have with the United States, our greatest friends, our greatest allies."

The ovation Williams received demonstrated the truth of her accusation. The Canadians themselves are well aware of this quiet vein of hatred within their culture, and do their best to cover it up, like an embarrassing uncle only allowed out of the basement once the company has gone. Scour the Canadian press, and it won't be long before you come across one columnist or another admitting that once upon a time they were rabidly anti-American—though now they inevitably see things differently.

A poll of Canadian citizens taken at the end of 2002 showed that although almost half of those surveyed agreed that the United States, as the world's sole superpower, has a responsibility to intervene in the affairs of other countries to protect global security, almost seven in ten believed that the United States was "starting to act like a bully." Not surprisingly, the poll also confirmed that more than half of Canadians opposed sending Canadian fighting units to help the United States in Iraq. The 69 percent antiwar vote was so large that any political observer would call it a mandate, a portion of political real estate so unassailable that any politician—Jean Chretien, for example—would be more than happy to plant his feet on that very spot, as long as the ground holds.

As the maddening behind-the-scenes betrayals of France demonstrate, the hand of the puppeteer is never far from the action. Chretien and a host of other Canadian politicians were not only slave to the polling numbers—they helped to drive the public in the direction they wanted, helping to unify their nation to rise up and say no to America.

A day or two after the "hate the bastards" comment, while the imbroglio was still in full flap, Chretien traveled to Mexico and complained that the Bush administration's call for "regime change" in Iraq was "dangerous."

"If you start changing regimes, where do you stop?" Chretien said, according to the *National Post*. "This is the problem. Who is next? Give me the list. . . . I'm surprised to hear now we want to get rid of Saddam Hussein." The *National Post* reporter described Chretien as "visibly agitated" in his exchange with reporters.

What was Chretien worried about? That Bush's "regime change" policy might one day extend to him? Worse yet, how on earth could he have been "surprised" by the idea that Iraq would be better off without Saddam Hussein? The *National Post*, which has shown consistent incredulity toward the America-bashers, went on to quote several prominent Canadian defense experts who maintain that disarmament and regime change were the only solution to the problem of Saddam Hussein, and that Chretien knew it. One was quoted as saying that "disarming Iraq without ousting Saddam would be like disarming Nazi Germany but keeping Adolf Hitler in power."

For a while, Defense Minister McCallum seemed to be stepping on landmines wherever he went. In another speech after the incident with the schoolgirl, he suggested that there were two scenarios in which Canada would enter the war without U.N. approval—including a situation in which there was good cause for military action, but U.N. action was blocked by the irrational position of one country (France, for example). Chretien's spokesman immediately let it be known that the defense minister was not speaking for the government: That was the prime minister's job, and he did not agree with McCallum. And before long, Chretien's liberal party soldiers emerged in lockstep to agree, like cuckoo clocks set in sync. Liberal caucus chairman Stan Keyes set the tone: "If the United Nations says we go then we will go. If the United Nations does not decide that we are going, than it's a given for most of us that we will not participate."

The mere idea that Canada would even consider joining America in its go-it-nearly alone rogue operations was horrifying to a great number of Canadians. "My constituents are very worried about the possibility of a unilateral move by the United States against Iraq and they don't want Canada to have any part of that. They want us to go in with the United Nations if we're going to do it at all," said John Godfrey, a Toronto MP.

Carolyn Bennett, another Toronto MP, said, "My constituents have been very clear. They do not think we should go to war without a UN sanction and even then, they have serious reservations about this war," she said.

"We're a sovereign country and we make our own judgment. We're not on autopilot. Nobody should count us automatically in for anything," Godfrey said.

Those examples were reported by Anne Dawson and Sheldon Alberts in the *National Post* of January 14, 2003, in a story speculating on whether a split had appeared in the prime minister's party over the issue of Canadian participation in the war. In the same dispatch, the reporters also reported on a movement to withhold neighborly cooperation even if the U.N.'s requirements were designed to be impossible for the United States to meet, which would place Canada's decisions in the hands of a widely disparate group of other nations. Would Canada really throw in with Syria (a Security Council nonpermanent member implacably opposed to a war in Iraq), or stick with its old friend, the giant next door? David Pratt, a Liberal MP and chairman of the Commons defense committee, said: "I would not want to see us get into a situation in the future where every potential action that Canada might be involved in must have the sanction of the U.N."

But other members of parliament upped the ante on the antiwar side, insisting that Canada should not join in the war *even if the United Nations approved it,* which took Canadian *paxpolitic* to an entirely new level of relations with the United States: total opposition, no matter how just the cause. As odious as that may have been to sensible Canadians who were opposed to national self-immolation, anti-Americanism had become the de facto Canadian position.

To iron out the apparent discrepancy wrinkle, the defense minister was forced to claim that there was no dispute in the government over its policy toward the impending war. But he refused to make clear exactly what that policy was, other than to say "we're keeping all our options open." For the Canadian government, it was all wait and see, mixed in with hope-against-hope that the United States would eventually cave. Convinced that its neighbor must be too big, and too powerful, to be threatened by a tin-pot dictator in the desert, Canada was willing to approve war only if the Security Council said there was no other way. Since the United Nations hadn't been asked for a final decision, Canada was left without a position of its own.

So it was that fence-sitting became Canada's policy toward Iraq— at least officially. In truth, through the fog of "maybe-maybe not" from the Canadian political leaders, Canada's reluctance to go to war was quite clear. But in his 2002 year-end speech, Prime Minister Jean Chretien seemed eager to muddy the waters, articulating his policy in classic French-Canadian Stengelese: "If the United Nations says there shouldn't be a war, we in Canada never went to war without the authorization of the United Nations." He wasn't even close to correct: Canada had joined the 1999 NATO bombing campaign in Kosovo even though the United Nations had been bypassed and never gave its approval to the campaign.

By mid-February, apparently trying to hedge their bets, the Canadians dispatched two dozen army officers to Qtar to work with General Tommy Franks's Centcom staff. But it was largely a courtesy delegation; by now it was clear which direction Canada was heading. And there was no love lost on either side: public statements out of the White House and the Pentagon suggested that George W. Bush and his administration had not forgotten the series of anti-American remarks made by Chretien's government (and the prime minister himself) in the preceding months—or Chretien's open support for Al Gore during the 2000 campaign.

Jean Chretien's visceral dislike for George W. Bush—and all things American—coupled with Bush's evident profound distrust for Chretien—undoubtedly made it impossible for Canada to wind up in the American coalition of the willing.

"I am a real liberal," Chretien told the *Financial Times.* "In the U.S., a real liberal would be considered almost a Communist."

Bush gets along with one prominent communist, Vladimir Putin. But Jean Chretien was unwilling to say precisely why he does not get along with President Bush—assuming he really understands the true reasons. And the consequences of these foul relations seemed to be of no matter to Chretien. The prime minister, whose relationship with the U.S. president is characterized as "distant" by the *National Post,* "did not appear concerned that Canada's stand could alienate Mr. Bush, suggesting that Republican leadership in the White House is too right-wing."

Meanwhile, however, while Canadians were dividing their time between debating the war and passing judgment on the Americans, their own military experts stepped forward with an unpleasant surprise of their own. Even if the government should actually break down and order the Canadian military to join the American troops in Iraq, it turned out, the Canadian armed forces might just to have sit it out anyway—because of its diminished readiness and insufficient equipment.

The day after the defense minister seemed to suggest that Canada might join the Americans before the United Nations gave its approval, defense experts warned that the Americans and British probably wouldn't want the Canadians in Iraqi airspace with them even if they were available: the few Canadian fighter jets in service had outdated radios that could be overheard by Iraqi monitoring stations. There were similar problems with ships, with ground troops, reconnaissance units—in short, with much of the Canadian military.

As the *Montreal Gazette* reported in late January 2003, Martin Shadwick, a York University defense analyst, believed there would be no way for Canada to match the contribution it made during the Gulf War, when Canada sent a field hospital, two infantry companies, three ships, and two dozen fighter jets.

"The cupboard is not completely bare, but the options are limited," Shadwick said. "Even under UN auspices, I don't think we could get numbers that high."

Rob Huebert, associate director of the Center for Military and Strategic Studies at the University of Calgary, told the *Edmonton Journal* that Canadian soldiers, who had served with Americans in Afghanistan and suffered grievously in a friendly fire incident, were exhausted. Besides, he said, there were political reasons they could not be deployed: "How's Prime Minister Jean Chretien going to respond if Canadian troops are killed and there is a public outcry against it?" asked Huebert.

There had already been considerable public outcry when Canadian participation in the war in Afghanistan went badly. The friendly fire incident occurred when American pilots in the area of Khandahar mistook a Canadian unit on the ground in live fire exercises for enemy Taliban fighters engaged in hostile fire. Under the impression that they were being shot at, the Americans dropped a 500-pound bomb, killing four Canadian soldiers and wounding twelve more. The American pilots were court martialed, but Canadians were only barely mollified. They saw American negligence and swagger throughout the incident. Scandal surmounted tragedy when it was revealed that the pilots were taking amphetamines to stay alert. As proud as Canadians might have been to see their forces helping the Americans rout the Taliban and al

Qaeda forces in Afghanistan, the tragic spectacle of Canadian soldiers being killed by Americans was enough to dissuade the Canadians from taking similar risks the following year. "I can't see him [Chretien] making that type of decision," concluded Huebert.

By the end of January 2003, the *National Post* was publishing polls that showed that more than 50 percent of Canadian respondents believed that George W. Bush poses the greatest threat to world peace. Even if Americans had tended in the past to ignore what Canadians really thought about America, now we were finally starting to catch on.

Some in the media recognized how counterproductive the growing rift could be for Canada. The *National Post*'s Ottawa Bureau Chief, Sheldon Alberts, reminded Canadians that there were consequences to their anti-Americanism: "Almost every issue affecting Canada's well-being, prosperity, and sovereignty—from trade to border security to continental defense—is tied to a strong and friendly relationship with the United States."

But for Jean Chretien, being uninvited to the Bush ranch in Texas was a badge of courage and disliking the Texan was as natural as liking the French.

Despite years of close military ties, when the United States established Northern Command (NORTHCOM) in October 2002 with an eye to protecting North America, Ottawa passed on the chance to participate. "If they come to believe that we can't maintain adequate surveillance of the sea approaches to our end of North America, then they are going to have to do it themselves," said Douglas Bland, chairman of defense management studies at Queen's University in Kingston, Ontario. "If the security of Canada depends on the willingness of the United States to defend us, then we ought to do as much as we can to reinforce their willingness to do that."

For all their military limitations, the Canadians could still have made a valuable contribution to the American war effort in 2003 simply by demonstrating solidarity with their longtime ally. Being refused support from each of its two neighbors, Mexico and Canada, was an unnecessary and unwelcome insult to a nation that had assumed the burden of protecting North America for most of the twentieth century. But Canada had taken up residence on the fence and would not be easily moved.

Central Command in Florida waited patiently for months. In November, the Pentagon asked Canada to provide Coyote armored reconnaissance vehicles and a small number of JTF-2 commandos, as well as warships and surveillance aircraft, for the war against Iraq. Canada waited more than a month before it informed the United States it would not contribute its military to the war effort until and unless the United Nations approved military action. By early January 2003, the Centcom commanders in Florida had to ask their Canadian colleagues to stop attending confidential war-planning meetings to which they had previously been invited.

Soon it was apparent to everyone that the United Nations' delays had for all practical and logistical purposes put Canada out of the running. As an unnamed senior Canadian officer who'd participated in the war in Afghanistan told Reuters: "We can't possibly get anything into position on time." Even Canadian military officers who were eager to assist in the American-led war were forced to watch time slip away until it was simply too late. "We have almost no airlift capability and it takes weeks for ships to reach the Middle East, so a decision on whether or not to move troops to the Persian Gulf must be made immediately. It should have been made last month," said one Canadian military official in February 2002. Princess Patricia's Battle Group, which had served in Afghanistan, had no way to get to battle on its own: In Afghanistan it had been moved onto the battlefield by American military transport aircraft.

As the diplomatic and military stalemate dragged out, the *National Post* reminded Canadians of exactly who they were being so disagreeable with, using data from an economic summit. The American economy, it noted, may be strong enough to rebound from great blows, but it also accounts for 13 percent of the world's economic growth, and imports one-fifth of the entire planet's goods and services—a staggering $1.4 trillion out of a world total of $7 trillion. As its largest trading partner, Canada had every economic reason in the world to want to see America do well—not to mention to avoid getting into a fight with its southern neighbor.

So how did this happen? How did Canada go from being one of America's most reliable friends, and principal beneficiary of America's neighbor economy, to an emboldened choir of almost hysterical naysayers and wanton purveyors of condemnation? Of Canada's five major political parties, four were either dead set against helping the Americans or willing to go along only if the United Nations approved. Only one party, the Canadian Alliance, advocated supporting the United States unconditionally. Standing at America's northern gate, Canada had begun to look like a crowd at the moat, farmers and townsfolk with torches and pitchforks demanding to know what horrible plans Dr. Frankenstein was cooking up.

The malevolence between Bush and Chretien certainly had something to do with it. More deeply, though, a huge wave of suspicion and rank anti-Americanism had finally been given occasion to rise to the surface in Canada, and this time America paid attention.

"As individuals, Americans are legendary for being as open, generous and friendly as a golden retriever (albeit one with an occasionally itchy trigger paw)," wrote Jack Knox in the Can West News Service on February 19, 2003. "And right now, that golden retriever is prancing by the door with a leash in its mouth, urging us to take it for a walk—to Iraq."

And what was the Canadian attitude toward the American retriever with the itchy trigger paw? "Sit, boy, sit," Knox said softly.

As many Canadians do when pushed on the issue, Knox acknowledged that Canada was deeply mired in a visceral and primal anti-Americanism. "America-bashing is as Canadian as hockey, rye, and ginger, or cheating on the GST. We tsk-tsk at America's gun laws, rage against its trade practices, sneer at its mawkish, bellicose version of patriotism, chortle at its ignorance of the world beyond its borders. Let's not even mention their beer. In short, we treat the Americans the way the French treat—well, everybody."

If the debate over the Iraq war had one benefit for Canadian-American relations, it was shining the spotlight on the disturbing growth of anti-Americanism in the Canadian consciousness. As David Bercuson and Barry Cooper wrote the *Windsor Star* on January 20, 2003: "In Canada and around the world, George Bush has unfairly become the target for some of the most vitriolic invective ever hurled at an American president." They added, "Characterized as everything from a moron to a war criminal, Bush's latest fan—NDP leadership hopeful Bill Blaikie—told the world last week that George Bush just pines to kill Iraqi children."

The *Star* properly chastised Blaikie, but his attitude was the norm. In a culture quietly embarrassed by its economic and military dependence on the behemoth to its south, the discussion only grew more hysterical, personal, and vicious once the Canadians smelled blood in the American water.

After publishing a column supporting America's position on Iraq, Connie Woodcock of the *Toronto Sun* was astonished enough by her mail from readers to devote a second column to it. She reported, surprisingly, that only a minority of opinion actually opposed the American policy. But what shocked her was "the depth and breadth of its anti-Americanism."

The anti-American letters were only one in eight, by her estimate. But "it was obvious that for most of these people, anti-Americanism is not something new but a deeply held belief that simmers away in them even at the best of times. At the worst of times—now, for instance—it boils over."

Woodcock laid out a few highlights of a history of rocky relationships with America, but still seemed stunned by what the readers' letters revealed. "It appears anti-Americanism is alive and well in Canada, perhaps stronger and more widespread than it has ever been."

She mentioned one reader who thought Canada could get along without American defense, "because we have no enemies except those that we might create by allying ourselves with them."

Another writer suggested boycotting American goods, which Woodcock noted would be quite a trick given how much Canada imports from America. "It will be difficult, of course," the writer had conceded. "But trade sanctions and embargoes against the United States may be the world's only means of controlling someone with an ego the size of its army."

Americans slowly came to the conclusion that the Canadians were not with us, even though they'd been there for us so many times before. From the beaches of Normandy to Afghanistan, the Canadians may not have been the mightiest force in pure numbers, but they were friends, they showed up for the fight, and they fought heroically and helped us carry the day. This time, Canadian worries about the angry, hostile, truculent Americans overcame that long and proud tradition.

The Canadian newspaper columnist Mark Steyn (who lives in New Hampshire, and regularly defends America to his own homefolks as well as the world) was asked about the American backlash against Europeans who had been a bit too prominently giddy in their America bashing before and during the Iraq war. "They don't get it. They insulted America decade in, decade out, and no one cared because no one noticed. After 9/11, Americans started noticing." The same could be said about his fellow countrymen: Americans had begun to notice.

What has become clear through the course of this nasty and all-too-public debate is that, like most of the rest of the world, Canada had believed that it truly understood America. In fact, Canada (like France, Germany, Belgium, and parts of Britain) profoundly missed the point, and much to its detriment. Canadians simply failed to recognize how much 9/11 had changed Americans: they failed to understand how alert America has become to the terrorist threat, and how little Americans will take before lashing back.

"For us, the threat is real; Al Qa'ida wants to hit us again," U.S. Ambassador Paul Cellucci told Hubert Bauch of the *Montreal Gazette,* assessing Canada-American relations in early June 2003. "Some in Canada just don't have that same sense." "*Some*" was a diplomatic understatement. Many, if not most, Canadians feel very removed from any such threat—and they believe their complacency is completely sensible and should be adopted by the Americans.

Last, many Canadians don't appear to have given much thought to what an America backlash might mean. Canada has no advantage in this fight, except the self-satisfied sense of national goodness, the smug superiority Canadians cling to as if it were life itself.

Perhaps it has to do with being a small guy wearing big pants. Canada is a huge place, an enormous land mass, but a breathtakingly small number of people. In the last census, Canada tipped the scales at 31 million people. In America's last census, the United States *grew* by 40 million people, for a total of 281 million, and projections for the last few years put us at 288 million. The number of Hispanics in the United States exceeds the entire Canadian population. The United States may be on track to lapping the Dominion every second time Canada counts its people (Canada conducts a census every five years, the United States once a decade). The disparity in population is now nine to one, and accelerating.

Some people think that Canadian anti-Americanism is a function of this disparity in size; some believe it's because Canadians live so close, absorb so much American media, that they assume they know America as well as they know their own people.

But the anti-Americanism of the Canadian people wasn't a matter of blue-collar prejudice alone. Among intellectuals and academics, the America-hating may have been more thoughtful, but it was certainly no less apocalyptic. Historian Robert Bothwell of the University of Toronto, for instance, told the *Toronto Sun:* "Instead of consensual alliances, there will be the U.S. and a coalition of the bribed and the bullied, and the sullenly acquiescent, which will be us."

In Bothwell's glowering view, the new U.S. policy of preemption, articulated in the September 2002 National Security Strategy, amounted to "America, King of the World." He predicted: "It will be, 'Sign on or face retribution,' and that will mean a leeching effect on other countries, including us. We won't be allies, we'll be vassals paying tribute."

"I believe anti-Americanism is now at a fifteen-year high," respected historian Jack Granatstein observed in testimony before a parliamentary committee in the weeks before Canada's antiwar position was finally settled. "We seem to believe the Americans, especially the Bush administration, are bullies, beating up on their friends and enemies alike."

Granatstein called Canadian anti-Americanism "stupid and unworthy," and he predicted that if the United States decided to go to war without U.N. approval, Canada would join in. It was an optimistic assessment, and it was very much wrong.

But in his testimony he also explained why he and so many other Canadians were disappointed and angry at the actions of their own government. "The only answer [to American power] many Europeans offer is to constrain and contain American power. By default, they end up on the side of Saddam, in an intellectually corrupt position," said

Granatstein. "That, in my view, precisely sums up the Canadian position today."

Granatstein dismissed the United Nations as weak and ineffective—a bad bargain if the trade was losing the United States. Granatstein saw the pragmatic reasons to support the United States, based on the fact that Canada has no substitute for the United States as a trading partner, a force to keep the vulnerable Canadian economy full and afloat. In Granatstein's view, the politics of George W. Bush are almost irrelevant. "Mr. Bush is not my favourite leader either. The coming war on Iraq is not a war I would fight if I had a choice." However, he continued, "As much as I hate to say it, he just might be right."

And some Canadians began to notice the effect of their anti-Americanism, which often seemed to bubble over into sheer hatred. In late February 2003, Peter Shawn Taylor reported in the *National Post* that Australian Prime Minister John Howard was trying to offer Australia to replace Canada as the former British colony the Americans could most count on. "Those footsteps you hear could be kangaroos," Taylor wrote, judging that the Australian leader had greatly inflated his country's importance to the White House. "Need it be mentioned that the reputation of another Western-style democracy with a colonial British past and close ties to the United States (and a slightly more convenient location)," Taylor asked, "is heading in the exact opposite direction?"

But Taylor also quoted David Bercuson, director of the Center for Military and Strategic Studies at the University of Calgary: "Australia's star is clearly rising in Washington. And when you are in good favor with Congress, that can have a significant effect on your economic and security prospects."

As Taylor perceived, "While Australia is busy earning brownie points in Washington . . . Prime Minister Jean Chretien's famous preference for avoiding decisions has left Canada suspended on the white picket fence of the world's longest undefended border."

Some Canadians recognized that the folly of Chretien's refusal to decide in favor of the United States was a horrible economic mistake, compounded by shouts from Parliament that the Americans surely would not ignore. "The PM refuses to explain which side Canada will take if the UN is unable to act, and has not pledged any real support to the Coalition of the Willing. In the meantime, members of his Liberal backbench eagerly praise Iraq and heap scorn on Bush," Taylor wrote disapprovingly. "Yet the areas Australia is targeting for increased trade with the United States—car parts, information technology, agriculture and movies—are much the same things that Canada specializes in. Talk of increased border restrictions and inspections by the United States for security reasons could substantially reduce the important transportation advantage Canada currently enjoys."

Nothing about the run-up to the war in Iraq could be called a win for Canada, except the aforementioned daubing of salve on the national conscience.

What did Canada get in return? Well, improved relations with France, which has been relegated by the United States to observer status on the world stage. Not to mention a gaping wound in Canadian relations with the United States—a mistake for any country, and a disaster for one that shares a continent-wide border with America. The same might be said about Mexico, except that the Mexican press and officialdom were not nearly as scathing and insulting as some in Canada, and George W. Bush didn't find himself quite so angry with Vicente Fox, Mexico's president.

Jean Chretien was quite another story. Chretien and Bush have managed only the slightest possible bit of civil relations in the months since the debacle. Bush, of course, remembered what Chretien had said about him during the 2000 election, and he couldn't ignore the role Chretien and Canada took in making certain the United Nations would never issue an approval for a war in Iraq. But there were other reasons as well.

While matters of war and peace were driving a wedge between America and Canada, Ottawa decided to take up a list of other social agenda items certain to annoy and anger the American government: legalizing pot, setting up heroin injection centers, and legalizing gay marriage. It was as if Canada were on mission to alienate America.

On most social matters, the U.S. government cannot take an official position. The confusion thrown into American marital law by legalizing gay marriage was just something the courts would have to deal with. But drugs was another thing entirely.

The American drug czar, in an exercise that seemed more resigned than impassioned, flew to parliamentary hearings to tell Canada that the United States would be forced to respond if marijuana were legalized along the long, unprotected, and essentially open border.

Vancouver Mayor Larry Campbell told the same parliamentarians that the United States was simply wrong—not to mention arrogant to have come north with such an empty argument. "In the coming years, the U.S. will probably want to emulate us."

Mayor Campbell's statement hints at another shading of the Canadians' particular brand of anti-Americanism: a sense that Americans have been temporarily seized by a misbegotten political spasm (known as George W. Bush) that will soon pass, like a bad storm or a kidney stone. Soon, the Canadians think wishfully, the Americans will wake up, recognize that the advice they'd been ignoring from their European and Canadian friends was in fact solid wisdom, and start following it.

American national pride is little understood in other countries; people outside the United States are frightened by the combined feelings of nationalism and vulnerability that have been unleashed in Americans. It's exactly this kind of concern that leads George W. Bush to be named in international polls as a bigger threat to world peace than al Qaeda. Mingled with the traditional bitterness and envy about the United States is a clear recognition that America-bashing is subject to a powerful backlash: Bush and America are angry, and they have immeasurable power to strike out.

In the end, of course, Canada abstained from the war in Iraq, and America went to war on its own—that is, with the help of the Brits and a number of other countries, but not the United Nations, or the Security Council, nor America's old friends in Europe.

And after the war, the Canadians who had opposed it went on a "we-were-right" campaign.

The chiseled visage of Canadian television news, the virtually sainted Peter Mansbridge, captured the triumphal snottiness of Canadian antiwar types in a piece for *McLean*'s in June 2003. "So much—at least so far—for the much-heralded reason for the war," Mansbridge wrote, referring to the unresolved search for weapons of mass destruction. "And what about the plan for postwar Iraq? At least you can say that the United States didn't wait long to send in a new civil administrator when it became clear that the looting was working better than the electricity."

Mansbridge then went on to repeat a series of rumors and theories emanating from antiwar Europe, and antiwar Russia, and antiwar Arabia, and anti-American Iran (though no doubt the Iranians were pro-war) that had the Pentagon cutting deals with Iraqi generals and Saddam himself to prevent any disastrous house-to-house fighting for Baghdad. All of which raised in turn the delicious possibility that America was lying about everything: the reasons we went to war, the way the war was fought, the reasons it was won. Mansbridge even cast doubt and aspersions on the rescue of Private Jessica Lynch, demeaning her as a simple "maintenance" worker whose convoy "misread maps, took a wrong turn, and were either killed or captured after a quick firefight."

Unwilling to wait for the facts to be revealed, Mansbridge was all wrong. Private Lynch's convoy didn't misread maps; it was not informed (by radio) of a change in plans to take an alternate route. Mansbridge wants to call it a quick firefight, but the facts say otherwise: Lynch's company ran in and out of Al Nasiriya twice through a withering wall of fire; one of the big rigs ahead of her Humvee jackknifed; the driver of her vehicle smashed into it, and she was the only one in her vehicle to survive, albeit with massive compression fractures of her legs and arms and spine. "In Canada, we would have had a year-long, multimillion-dollar royal commission studying the blunder; in the U.S., the players become national icons, and the myths become legend."

In his snide and condescending description of events that were still unclear at the time he wrote, Mansbridge reinvigorated and reempowered those Canadians who love to wallow in their anti-Americanism, encouraging them to take yet another nice long soak in the America-hating mud.

Worse, he dragged up a series of bogus "investigations" by a Canadian newspaper and the BBC that cast doubt on the circumstances of the Lynch rescue. "The 'rescue' of Pvt. Lynch (who holds her silence) was actually a pickup from an Iraqi hospital from where officials had been trying unsuccessfully to turn her over to the Americans for days." Perhaps the sainted Mansbridge—no field commander he—was golfing the day his class in military tactics covered the dangers of assuming that enemy "officials" who were "inviting" Americans to come pick up their injured Private Lynch would be honest—not setting up an ambush or a trap. Pity the poor commander who followed the Mansbridge Doctrine (when at war, accept invitations; no point in being rude), and managed to get more of his soldiers killed.

What rankled, of course, wasn't the fact that a single daft television anchor would go on this way about those damn Americans. The real trouble is that this kind of anti-American drivel is what passes itself off as intellectualism up north, bringing huzzahs from the Canadian gallery.

Mansbridge and his fellow Canadians appear to be having a hard time reconciling themselves to the fact that their nation is so heavily dependent on its neighbor—a neighbor they feel compelled to kick at every turn.

Some make peace with the contrast by changing their spots. Canadian singers and television anchors and business executives and authors come to America every year, and of course they blend in better than any other nationals would. With their North American accent, they look and sound like Americans, and they pass without trouble. Seven hundred thousand Canadians are living and working in America today. Some come because they can't stand their own countrymen and they believe America is right. Some come for the money, refusing to abandon their deep-seated hatred for America—merely keeping it under their hat while they reap the benefits of our robust economy.

They are here among us, and they are lurking over the border, in their *kanata* villages along the American line (Toronto, Montreal, and the rest). And the Canadian anti-Americans are determined to proclaim their independence by turning their nose up at America at every turn—no matter the cost.

If Canada is so determined to remain France's *mini-moi,* though, why doesn't it reconcile itself to enjoying the good life *France* bestows on its subjects? Let the Canadians go to France the next time they want a vacation—or a job.

America is on to them, these three unworthies: Belgium, Canada, and South Korea. Three brothers in anti-Americanism: one sullen, one self-consciously outraged, the third looking a whole lot more like Kim Jong-Il's new province every day.

Beware the Axis of Envy.

ALL THE WORLD
DESPISES
GEORGE W. BUSH*

*(Including a Few American Democrats)

The [latest stage in the] Bush Presidency began this week with
President George W. Bush heading for Europe to assure the lead-
ers of the Old World that, in the words of one of his own men,
"He is not a shallow, arrogant, gun-loving, abortion-hating,
Christian fundamentalist Texas buffoon."

> —Richard Reeves, Universal Press Syndicate, June 15, 2001

F ORTY-EIGHT HOURS BEFORE THE United States of America
launched its war to remove the regime of Saddam Hussein in
Iraq, President George W. Bush addressed the nation. In Great
Britain, opponents of the war watched closely and passed judgment.

"The tone was one of cold menace in the style favored by Hollywood scriptwriters. It was an exercise in Dirty Harry diplomacy—'Go on, punk, make my day'—and it is hardly surprising, therefore, that it seems to have done its job of rallying domestic opinion. The impact abroad was less favorable, and amongst Europeans in particular, Bush's glassy-eyed earnestness and simple reasoning will have confirmed the prejudices of those who see him as a dangerous simpleton in charge of a rogue state. But then Bush wasn't speaking for their benefit."

This was the judgment of David Clark, a special advisor to former British foreign secretary Robin Cook, as the Iraq war grew closer.

In truth, it was nothing we hadn't heard before. Such characterizations of Bush have been *de rigeur* from the day the world began sizing up George H. W. Bush's son as he considered running for his father's former job.

The world decided in fairly short order what it thinks of George W. Bush.

And the verdict was ugly. George W. Bush appears to personify what the world detests about America; he is accused of leading America astray, of deceiving, even tricking his fellow Americans into policies that defy the wisdom of international judgment.

As usual, the world has it wrong. George W. Bush reflects the views of Americans coast to coast to a much greater degree than the world realizes, even among that sizeable group of Americans who did not vote for him—and who, as the 2004 election approaches, profess to detest him as much as their European counterparts do.

Even Bush's strongest American opponents understand him far better than his detractors and opponents in the world beyond America's shores.

For the one-worlders—the Europeans who view international law and the U.N. Security Council as holy writ and shrine—Bush commits the worst of all crimes in the international community: He is American and nothing else.

After a June 3, 2002, cover story asking whether Europe really hates America, *Newsweek* received this letter from Willem Oltmans, who lives in Amsterdam: "Most people here not only despise George W. Bush and his collaborators, they consider him a more unpredictable disaster than his father and totally unworthy to occupy the White House or lead the free world. Some see him as a global terrorist. . . . Many of us hope he will disappear after one term, as his father did."

Even for those who might argue that the world doesn't really hate America (despite massive evidence to the contrary), it's impossible to look at the body of world comment—from television to newspaper editorials to the man on the street—and not conclude that the world despises George W. Bush, the president and the person. Precious few opinions appear to be held so universally among both intellectuals and ordinary people as this: They despise Bush from head to toe, from his boots to his roots. They hate his cowboy hats, the state (Texas) where he was raised and later served as governor, and the fact that he found his way to the White House becoming the most powerful individual man on the face of the earth.

It is astonishing: From his policies to the very way he walks, no single thing about George W. Bush is overlooked. Opinion makers worldwide are threatened by his unilateralism, his disregard for the strictures of so-called international law—and, perhaps most of all, his absolute indifference toward world opinion. They have a personal, visceral reaction to the man as well as his ideas.

And they express their reaction in the harshest of words. When George W. Bush speaks, he is "arrogant," "dictatorial," a "cowboy." When he walks into a room or onto Air Force One, he "struts" and "swaggers." When he takes action in defense of the United States, he is a "rogue," a "renegade," a "loose cannon," a "danger."

"One day last week, I awoke to discover that George W. Bush had replaced Ariel Sharon as the most hated man on earth," wrote Shmuley Boteach in the *Jerusalem Post* on April 3, 2003.

For Americans this has been a startling revelation because it has seemed so overblown and disconnected from reality. From a hodge-podge of disconnected television images, free-associating Europeans seem to have created an American president who only slightly resembles the one Americans see every day in their White House. Bush is hardly perfect (a category of weakness called "Eating Pretzels Without Nearly Asphyxiating" comes to mind), but the internal debate within the United States has a much different tone than the one raging throughout the rest of the world. Americans recognize his faults, as polling at the conclusion of the Iraq war demonstrated: His approval ratings were still in the high seventies, but his father's ratings had reached the low nineties by the end of the Gulf War more than a decade earlier.

When Americans examine their president, they accept his flaws. He is not history's best leader (he's up against stiff competition in American history alone), but Americans recognize him as distinctly one of their own, a man who takes his job seriously, does it well, and is focused on what he and much of the country believe must be done. Even Democrats who voted against him and opposed his war policies supported him in the Iraq war and approved of his performance. After the war, as his domestic opponents grew more venomous—even as a *Time* magazine cover asked "Bush: Love Him or Hate Him?"—the criticism was different in tone and content from that of the anti-Bush lobby around the world.

By 2003, it appeared that much of the world—including much of Britain, as well as France, Germany, Russia, Belgium, Spain, Italy, China, Canada, Japan, Scandanavia, India, Pakistan, and all of the Middle East (with the exception of Israel)—had arrived at a curiously irrational consensus on Bush, a fevered hysteria that found Bush-haters gorging themselves on any new evidence of Bush's flaws and comparing him with the worst the world has ever produced.

Writing in the *New Statesman* in February 2003, John Lloyd described how the antiwar *Daily Mirror* had goosed its circulation with

TV advertising that merged the images of Saddam Hussein and George W. Bush into one. He noted *Guardian* columnist Madeleine Bunting's description of Saddam and Bush as "two erratic, angry men, both of whom control quantities of lethal weapons and both of whom are making a mockery of the UN and any concept of international law."

"It says much about the [British] left's state of mind—and how it has been seduced by far-left strategies," Lloyd wrote, "that it equates the leader of a state that has an elective democracy, free media, an exceptionally lively civil society and a history of anti-imperialism with a dictator who has murdered thousands of his own people, who rules by fear and who seeks weapons of mass destruction in order to dominate neighbouring states."

In the *Australian Financial Review* of April 2, 2003, Andrew Burrell titled his report "Why Bush Is Enemy No.1 In Indonesia" and quoted Amien Rais, a prominent Muslim politician in Indonesia and potential future president, as characterizing Bush as a "crazed cowboy," and calling for the leaders of the United States and its allies to be put on trial for war crimes over their military campaign against Iraq.

But it wasn't just the war. One of Europe's worst-kept secrets is that Europeans think they too should be able to vote for the American president—that it is a responsibility too weighty to be left to the ignorant American voters.

As K. B. Van der Poel of Sorgues, France, wrote to the editor of *Newsweek,* Europeans did not hate Bush—they were simply "disappointed" in him. That might seem downright civilized, had Van der Poel not revealed his true contempt in the very next sentence: "We see him as a puppet with strings controlled by the energy, steel and defense industries, the Jewish lobby and the Israeli government, the Christian right." He continued: "Responsible Europeans feel let down after the dubious outcome of the 2000 election—still considered by many here as stolen. The Bush administration is seen as the return of the Ugly American: the only remaining superpower refuses to cooperate with the rest of the world or to sign existing international treaties like Kyoto, the International Criminal court and ABM."

Does that really sound like simple "disappointment"? The argument about Bush's rejection of those three treaties is a strawman: Most Americans recognized these treaties as international attempts to restrain America's economic and military strength. The Kyoto Environmental Accord would have penalized the American economy and driven the world economy down. The International Criminal Court was an explicit attempt to give the Belgians a mandate to drag American war planners and individual soldiers before a kangaroo court. The Anti-Ballistic Missile treaty with Russia (the former Soviet Union) was proven to be an antique when, shortly after Bush pulled out, the North Koreans were shown to be developing a missile capable of reaching Los Angeles. (Even the Hollywood liberals didn't make much of a fuss over that one; the thought of Kim's missiles reaching their backyard must have scared some sense into them.)

But Europe and the rest of the world like to keep a good thing going—and the fact that Bush's actions on those three treaties, and others, were proven right by events was ignored in the rising tide of anti-American arguments.

Every now and then, expatriate Americans reported in to confirm that everybody hates America—including, in some cases, the expat himself. Gregory Smith, living comfortably in Stockholm, Sweden, blasted his native country on everything from incompatible electric plugs on hair dryers to "America's near-total cultural isolation from the World Cup, an event that brings the entire world together." That's right: In the European view, America's defiance of the world is so complete it actually insists on its own brand of football and refuses to accept the global passion for another kind. This most willful refusal to admit the primacy of a foot-eye game over a hand-eye game seems to seal the argument for Smith and the rest of the world.

Smith went on: "What really bugs all of us is [America's] violence, simple-mindedness, provincialism, arrogance, ignorance and unilateralism. So, to answer your question, no, it's not Europe alone that hates [Bush]; we all really hate him." Mr. Smith's implication—that a significant number of Americans hate Bush with the same vehemence as the rest of the world—suggests that he's suffering from his own variant of the Stockholm syndrome. Polling confirms that Americans have consistently supported Bush and his policies, even more so as the war came to a successful conclusion.

The hatred of George W. Bush was seeded around the time he assumed the presidency. In Australia, the *Canberra Times* called him "the village idiot," and tried to dissect the kind of "dumb" it saw in George W. Bush: "Dumb, in the way George W. Bush comes across as dumb—a sinister mix of incurious apathy about the world, a homespun platitudinousness about the needy, and sheer, piggy-eyed bloodthirstiness when it comes to the death penalty—is not the kind of dumb anyone should wish to inhabit the U.S. presidency." The Australians are obviously among those who feel that choosing the U.S. president might be better left to themselves.

In the Arab world, of course, the hatred for George W. Bush is as nearly unanimous as possible. The venom that pours off the pages of the Arab press and out of the millions of televisions tuned to the Arabic satellite networks, is what news people call "wall to wall": full coverage, 24/7.

Dr. Mohammad T. Al-Rasheed, writing in the April 2003 *Arab News:* "Watching George W. Bush deliver his speeches is becoming more alarming as his diction and body language become ever so transparently arrogant. The President issues statements that polarize and divide: 'You are either with us or with them' is the most obvious. There are plenty of such declarations that an elected official is not supposed to contemplate, let alone utter. This diction is the linguistic realm of the dictator who has to answer to no one."

In the same *Arab News,* Nourah Abdul Aziz Al-Khereiji addressed Bush directly: "As for your allegation that Iraq threatens U.S. security, what about you? You threaten the whole world." Al-Khereiji asked: "Has conceit made you believe that Americans are made of something better than all other humans?"

All this vitriol did not come from out of nowhere. In embryonic form, it could be found in the world media coverage of George W. Bush—the candidate for president. But within weeks after 9/11, the world's whispers about George W. Bush turned to shouts, and by the time of the Afghanistan War, which engendered much world suspicion, the international skepticism toward Bush was edging inexorably into passionate disgust.

When the run-up to the Iraq war eventually took the shape of a standoff between Bush and the United Nations, the world decided that the president had abandoned all pretense of caring about world opinion, and reacted with the shock of imagined betrayal.

The image and presidency of George W. Bush have become the universal emblem, the war cry, of the anti-Americanism that is sweeping the world—with a few exceptions, such as Iraq itself and about half of the British public. And before long, in their eagerness to have their way, the voices of world opinion began talking as if they actually *could* somehow participate in the American electoral process. As of this writing, the nations of the world are pinning their hopes on the American people to come to their senses and fire George W. Bush.

Writing from Paris in the *International Herald Tribune,* John Vinocur put it this way: "If the Americans would only get rid of George W. Bush, their doubters in Europe say, then ready hands would reach out to lead them tiptoeing back into the halls of International Respectability."

According to Vinocur, even as it was racing to keep up with Bush's military planning, Europe held firm to "this idea of saving

America from its president." This despite the fact that if the United Nations managed to dissuade Bush from acting, the horrors of the Saddam regime would have been carried on the battered heads and flailed backs of 23 million Iraqis long into the future.

As Vinocur summarized it, the European attitude went like this: "If the American people had been cruelly misled and misguided"— citing a *Los Angeles Times* poll showing 74 percent approval for the war, including 68 percent from Democrats—the American people "were recuperable. Not George Bush."

George W. Bush was one American too far, the single American among 280 million who could be neither rehabilitated nor accepted. No doubt his cronies would also have to go, of course; but the only way to the demise of that cabal was simply to encourage the Americans to wake up and elect someone else.

Vinocur cited a wide range of European published opinion on the subject. From the Germans: "It was time to get back in good with the United States, because in the post-Iraq new world order, it will be an America without Bush." The French daily *Le Monde* even appeared ready to endorse Bush's opponent in 2004, regardless of who it might be: "In 18 months the United States in rejecting George W. Bush would turn its back on a policy that isolates it from the world."

In February 2004, Canada's *McLean's* magazine reported that 85 percent of Canadians would vote against George W. Bush—and wished they could. The magazine cover read: "Canadians To Bush: Hope You Lose, Eh."

Among all the motivations for this deep-seated anger toward Bush, perhaps the strongest is that he has reminded the world that America has the power to act alone—and that Europeans are powerless to do anything about it.

The British, for instance, believe they know the empire business so well that they can spot a president with imperial ambitions—

particularly one they felt was so obviously over his head. Writing in the leftist *Guardian* in the early days of the war, Jonathan Freedland said, "George Bush has cast off the restraint which held back America's 42 previous presidents—including his father. Now he is seeking, as an unashamed objective, to get into the empire business, aiming to rule a post-Saddam Iraq directly through an American governor-general . . . this is a form of foreign rule so direct we have not seen its like since the last days of the British empire. It represents a break with everything America has long believed in."

Evidently Freedland had forgotten America's governor-general in postwar Japan, General Douglas MacArthur—and the prosperous, democratic, and successful Japan that was born during his tenure.

Freedland's assessment willfully ignored the stated objectives of the United States and George W. Bush. But then the Euros actually have a rich history of this kind of self-deception—as in the case of Reagan's Pershing missile deployments in Europe, a decision that all parties now agree broke the Soviet threat to the east. The success of that policy is undeniable—and yet to most Europeans it was lost forever in the outrage over Reagan's own brand of "cowboy mentality."

Of course a dictatorial empire-builder should be constrained, rejected, perhaps even despised: After all, that's why Bush's father had thrown Saddam out of Kuwait. But Freedland and the world must have known that imperialism wasn't on George W. Bush's agenda. What the president had in mind was eliminating a state that would offer safe harbor, money, travel documents, training facilities, and wherewithal to the otherwise insidious and slippery soldiers of terrorism, whose avowed goal is to attack America. In doing so, we would also be liberating a population from a murderous and despised dictator—and yet that fact was not even grudgingly accepted by peaceniks, who should have been ashamed to side with the warrior Saddam against the forces of American liberation.

Oddly, the same Jonathan Freedland had appeared to understand, just a year earlier, exactly why Americans supported George W. Bush. Watching Bush give a speech in Cincinnati during the midterm election campaign, Freedland was forced to admit that Bush is in touch with his American audience—and that he gives a good speech. "For one thing, he delivers it well," Freedland wrote in the *Guardian*. "It's a surprise, given the satirists' depiction of him as a linguistically challenged dunce, to see him speak fluently and without so much as a glance at any notes. And hearing him at length is different from seeing a soundbite on the news. It will break liberal hearts to admit it, *but he's good*" [emphasis added].

Even as this simple observation was sinking in for the leftist *Guardian* readers, no doubt clashing with their prejudices, Freedland drove the point home: "In marked contrast to his dad, who always came across as an East Coast aristocrat, Junior has mastered the common touch.

"The language is folksy and accessible throughout," he continued, "even on the most grave, international questions. The war on terror is explained like this: 'See, it's a different kind of war we face. In the old days, you could destroy tanks or airplanes or boats and know you're making progress. [But] these are the kind of people who hide in caves and send youngsters to their suicidal deaths. They don't care.' Europeans may baulk at the simplicity of that," Freedland concluded, "but it's potent and effective."

Could Freedland have been any clearer? Americans will support Bush because Bush supports Americans.

Freedland's warning of only a year earlier was ignored by Europe and the world. When it came time for the Iraq war, Europe and the world were holding out hope against reality, and they seemed surprised that George W. Bush acted precisely as they should have expected.

And when Bush did lead America into the military campaign, Europeans gave in to their periodic taste for conspiracy over fact.

According to a wartime Pew poll that appeared in *Time,* 76 percent of Russians, 75 percent of French, 54 percent of Germans, and 44 percent of British respondents believed that the desire to control Iraq's oil was behind Bush's "bellicosity." Only 22 percent of Americans held that view.

The world thought the war was for free oil. Americans were well aware it was not—that we have always paid for oil and always will, to the tune of billions and billions of dollars. But what does it mean when nearly three quarters of Europeans conclude that the president of the United States is using his vast armies as a thief, an outright armed robber stealing the riches of the Iraqi people?

This suggests more than mere dislike. This is a matter of hatred.

Time magazine has reported that a former minister in the British Conservative Party—the *pro*-American wing of U.K. politics, mind you—recently described Bush as "terrifying," "ignorant," "a prisoner of the religious right who believes God tells him what to do." Bush, in this man's opinion, was "like a child running around with a grenade with the pin pulled out."

Writing in the *New York Times* from London in the days before Baghdad fell, Sarah Lyall reported, "there is a deep unease here about the way the war is being waged, with what many regard as a bluster and swagger both dangerously inappropriate and all too American."

Particularly offensive to Europeans, *Time*'s J. F. O. McAllister reported, "are Bush's swagger, tough talk and invocations of God and right and wrong, part of his born-again tradition that is attuned to the U.S. mood after Sept. 11."

"It's nonsense to say, 'We're the force of good,'" Pierre Hassner, an expert on trans-Atlantic relations at the Center for International Studies and Research in Paris, says in McAllister's report. "We're living through the battle of the born-agains: Bush the born-again Christian, bin Laden the born-again Muslim."

McAllister also cited the standard European claim of superiority over America, quoting the claim of Dominique Chagnollaud, a professor of constitutional studies at the Sorbonne, that the United States "is astonishingly ignorant about other cultures," while at the same time "it is always telling everyone else what to do."

McAllister recognized the broad consensus of European, Asian, and Arab discussion: that George W. Bush is at least as bad as Saddam Hussein or Osama bin Laden, if not worse, and that Americans don't understand the world enough to deserve the authority they clearly possess.

Both claims are patently absurd—the contemptuous condescension of a world of America-haters.

To claim that George W. Bush and bin Laden are comparable is more than simply a "point of view." It is a lie, a slander, a calumny that reveals the mindless hatred of those making the claim. Ultimately, it's not the Americans who fail to understand the world: it's the world that doesn't have a clue about America.

In some ways, perhaps this is to be expected. The world sees America through McDonald's golden arches—through tough-guy action movies, violent or overtly sexual music videos. If the people who make those American contributions to the world were America in its entirety, Al Gore might be president.

What's surprising—and shameful—is that the supposed intellectual giants of Europe have chosen to interpret the American character through its popular culture alone. They are hothouse commentators, unable to divorce serious matters of terrorism and international security from their snobbish contempt for the American entertainment exports they consume at the cost of billions of dollars every year.

The Europeans cling to the notion that all this would change, of course, if Bush were to be removed from office. As Vinocur observes, "Important segments of Europe seem to want to believe that Bush's approach to the world would vanish from American instinct with a successful Democratic presidential candidacy." Yet Vinocur cautions Europe and the world: "It is doubtful that with a victory in Iraq, an electable Democrat could run on a platform of American regret and contrition. The United States may listen better, refine its diplomacy, and talk less coarsely on the international stage in the future, but the idea of depending on the world to make up its mind is one removed from the mainstream of American history."

Despite such clear warnings—and there have been many offered up to public opinion—the world still treats George W. Bush as if he is a lone gunman acting without support from the American public, as if some secretive cabal had foisted Bush onto the American people. If that is so, the American pollsters ought to be put out of business: Their results consistently demonstrate the opposite.

During the war, when Europeans were opposing it by 80 percent margins, Americans supported it by similar margins. On April 7, the day U.S. commanders ordered a massive bombing on a Baghdad restaurant Saddam Hussein was seen entering, a *Washington Post-ABCNews* poll showed that 77 percent of Americans supported the war; self-described conservative Republicans supported it at a startling 99 percent; self-described moderate Republicans at 92 percent; men supported it at 82 percent; women at 72 percent. Even Democrats supported the war at 65 percent.

Europe persisted in its antiwar crusade. In an article on the annual Davos meeting in Switzerland early in 2003, Frederick Kempe of the *Wall Street Journal* quoted Andrei Piontkovsky of the Moscow-based Center for Strategic Studies: "The French and German political elite are quite hysterical, but they don't have any solutions. Their problem is how to accommodate themselves to this huge preponderance of American power. Iraq is a pretext for exploding this frustration."

The frustration Piontkovsky described had been simmering since the Cold War, when Europe and the rest of the world lived comfortably in the shadow of two threatening and menacing superpowers. When one of them suddenly disappeared in 1989, the people in the shadows succumbed to irrational fears about the motives of the victors. As America kept up its military spending at a rate that outpaced any other power on the planet, Europeans grew suspicious that America would eventually go spoiling for war.

The terrorist attack on 9/11, to Europeans, was merely the opening America's military machine had been looking for all along. And to Europe's horror, it found George W. Bush in charge; they imagined him scanning the horizon for enemies, and scrambled to their newspaper desks to try to stop him.

Hating George W. Bush has become its own wildly popular sport, throughout Europe especially. It is best described as a sport rather than a political movement, for it bears the hallmark of wild-eyed sports events. It is fanatical, based on blind emotion rather than reason; it is passionate, gaining strength even in the face of repeated losses; and it offers a chance for average citizens of all kinds to belong to a team and shout down the enemy.

Among the more startling aspects of this anti–Bush hatred is the extent to which it is fed by religion. Whenever George W. Bush refers to his religion, God, Jesus, faith, or prayer, he is characterized by the dons of Europe as frightening, appalling, out of bounds, a crusader, a fundamentalist on the order of Osama bin Laden.

In an April 2003 dispatch, Reuters reporter Tom Hennigan quoted Hans Kueng, the controversial Swiss Catholic theologian, who said Bush "feels he was called by God to the presidency. He practices his foreign policy with the authority of God behind him. He is strengthened in this by Christian fundamentalists, to whom he owes his electoral victory to a large extent. I think you have to call him a fundamentalist in this political way."

Further, Hennigan reported, Cardinal Karl Lehmann, head of the German Bishop's Conference, told the Catholic weekly *Rheinischer*

Merkur that "this careless way of using religious language is not acceptable anymore in today's world."

Is there anybody who seriously believes that George W. Bush is "careless" in his references to religion? Quite the contrary. As Guy Lawson reported in a serious summer 2003 profile for *GQ,* Bush is quite purposeful in his use of religious language. His beliefs and faith are genuine, Lawson observed—and in that way he represents a huge number of Americans.

In Sweden, invoking God in politics is so unusual that parliamentarian Hans Lindqvist told Reuters: "I've never seen anything like this before." Perhaps Lindqvist should keep a better eye on the American public, where religious references are quite common. He might take note of the proclamation "In God We Trust" on U.S. currency, for example, or listen to any opening of the sessions of the U.S. Congress, in which the house chaplain asks for God's guidance. For that matter, he might tune in to American news coverage of the families of soldiers who have served, been captured as prisoners of war, or actually been killed or wounded in the war. Rarely do family members interviewed fail to mention their prayers to God to help and preserve their loved one as he or she faces danger in defense of their country.

In France, the prestigious and influential *Le Monde* reacted sharply to the news that the U.S. House of Representatives had called for a day of national prayer and fasting to secure divine blessings for U.S. troops in Iraq. "This bizarre approach shocks Europeans," it said in an editorial.

"One is tempted to say the destiny of America is in the hands of a small group of Protestant bigots," Henri Tincq wrote in *Le Monde.* Tincq should look a little more closely at American demographics. He would find a vast majority express faith in God.

These and other statements confirm that Europeans are unaware of the deep seam of religion that runs through American society—

either unaware, or so uncomfortable with it that they refuse to recognize it. It wasn't just George W. Bush who spoke about God's guidance in his prosecution of the war. So did a large number of lesser political leaders, reflecting the views of their constituents. Religion in American life is not the exception; it is the rule.

Just as Europeans hate the death penalty, guns, and anti-abortion politicians, they are deeply contemptuous of public figures who display their religious beliefs in the open. George W. Bush, the former Texas governor, is pro-death penalty, pro-gun ownership, and anti-abortion; he is also pro-tax cuts, anti-big government, and emphatically Christian. He is everything they scorn, disapprove, and hate.

No wonder the world has convinced itself that the presidency of George W. Bush must be an aberration, a one-term abomination, a fundamentalist Christian regime in the hands of right-wing conservative bigots—in short, a peculiarly misguided decision by the American people, who just happen to do stupid things quite often.

When the world looks upon George W. Bush's America, it gazes downward from a lofty height of self-described superiority. It is wiser than America, more intellectual, more progressive, more aware of everything. It views Americans as willfully ignorant of the truths of the world, unable to speak anything but American English, unwilling to learn anything at all about other people, an island of self-imposed mediocrity drifting in a sea of knowledge, refusing the help of those with the brainpower and experience to lend a hand.

And all of this is laid at the feet of George W. Bush, who embodies America's darkest urges.

This absolutely stunning hatred for the American president and the country that elected him (including that sizeable part that did not choose him, but has come to support him) is no mere American paranoid fantasy. It is available to anyone who cares to career around the www.world reading the international press, and the transcribed electronic media.

Writing in *Time* in September 2003, Charles Krauthammer wondered "What Makes the Bush Haters So Mad?"

First of all, he observes, Bush-haters at home and abroad branded him from the start as entirely illegitimate, based on the mythology of the "stolen" 2000 election. "Bush's great crime is that he is the illegitimate President who became consequential—revolutionizing American foreign policy, reshaping economic policy and dominating the political scene ever since his emergence as the post 9/11 war President."

The broken crockery of failed international treaties only added to the picture, says Krauthammer. "The President's unilateral assertion of U.S. Power has redefined America's role in the world. Here was Bush breaking every liberal idol: the ABM Treaty, the Kyoto Protocol, deference to U.N., subservience to the 'international community.' It was an astonishing performance that left the world reeling."

It is wrong to conclude that all this focused hate is the result of America's Iraq war. The world viewed that war as illegal, even though it had its benefits. Even those who grudgingly admitted that Saddam was best gone—and this remains a contested point in some quarters—saw dark, foreboding figures in the American Marines and U.S. Army tank divisions, an occupying force that intended to stay, to colonize Iraq and use it as a forward base of operations against the rest of the Arab world. And the world blamed Bush, even more than it had blamed previous presidents for American actions.

Make no mistake: There is a rich history of opposing, even hating, American presidents; such rhetoric has long been a part of the anti-American perspective. Indeed, some parts of the world actively attacked Bill Clinton and bitterly opposed the policies of George H. W. Bush and Ronald Reagan. Anti-Americanism has a storied history in Europe, although the Europeans like to keep it under the radar if possible. In the Arab/Muslim world, hating America rages unabated on the new satellite news networks, from the traditional and Internet press, and from the mosques and *madrassas*. In Asia, anti-Americanism is a voice rising from the streets and shops, dutifully papered over by skittish governments.

But the attacks on George W. Bush have set a new standard for vitriol and disgust. They are eye-popping in their depth and audacity. And what they fail to recognize is this: It's not America that's on a train wreck course with history, it's the rest of the world.

THEY'RE WRONG.
WE'RE RIGHT.
GET USED TO IT.

When I left office, there was a substantial amount of biological and chemical material unaccounted for. That is, at the end of the first Gulf war, we knew what he had. We knew what was destroyed in all the inspection processes and that was a lot. And then we bombed with the British for four days in 1998. We might have gotten it all; we might have gotten half of it; we might have gotten none of it. But we didn't know.

—former president Bill Clinton, in an interview
with Larry King, July 22, 2003

I N THE SUBTITLE OF the book—as in my comments about the world's opinion of George W. Bush—I've referred to hating America as a "new world sport." Perhaps I should be clearer about what I mean. Calling hate a "sport" might imply that the behavior in question is merely frivolous, light, not serious or worthy of thoughtful consideration. Sport, after all, is supposed to be fun.

In fact, fun *is* a major element of anti-Americanism around the world. People *love* hating America. It makes them feel better about themselves; it gives them a villain to root against.

Hatred and sport also bear other strong similarities. Hatred is inherently illogical, in the same way a fan's dedication to his team defies logic. Arab and Muslim America-haters fail even the simplest history test, as Barry Rubin pointed out in a December 2002 *Foreign Affairs* commentary: "Over the years, the United States has spent blood and treasure saving Muslims in Afghanistan from the Soviets; in Kuwait and Saudi Arabia from Iraq; and in Bosnia and Kosovo from Yugoslavia. It has supported Muslim Pakistan against India and Muslim Turkey against Greece."

Defying logic is the specialty of a sports fan. Even losers have fans, and in some cases in greater numbers than winners. In sports, the fan isn't necessarily from the city where the team is located. The fan may simply be drawn to the team colors, or the team emblem, or the team mascot. When you go to the roulette table, do you play red or black? The accident of the choice is usually long forgotten in the fervor of the cheering.

Hating America fulfills a variety of needs that will sound familiar to the general manager of any major sports franchise. Fans are devoted despite reason, despite hardship, despite plenty of incentives to think or believe differently. Sport fans are endlessly susceptible to defenses of their side, just as America haters are everywhere in the world. Who, after all, thinks the *fatwas* and sermons of Osama bin Laden made any sense at all, except those who were already disposed to hate America, and join the bin Laden "team"?

Like sport, phony reasoning is often accepted as clear thinking in the effort to buttress the devotion of the fans. Among America-haters, the reasons for hate are all over the map: America has caused so many thousands of deaths; America is an exploiter of the world's poor; America countenances the oppression of certain groups (the Palestinians, for example); America is a force for evil. These arguments can be easily defeated by readily available facts—except in the minds of the people devoted to holding these views.

Regardless of what team they're rooting for, their opponent is always America—and their opponent will always be wrong.

So let's check the scores.

America, for the moment, is close to losing Britain. The British are essentially pro-American, but the anti-American minority is large and loud. The British are angry because as America's best friend they think their advice ought to be heeded, and when it wasn't on the question of Iraq they were deeply embarrassed. The Brits deeply resented being dragged along in America's singled-minded fight, and they have punished Tony Blair for his alignment with George W. Bush.

France, on the other hand, has lost America. The French behaved—and continue to behave—so badly that they've lost touch with the real world. In the postwar period, Jacques Chirac has traveled far and wide, pointing to the challenges of peacekeeping on the ground in Iraq and saying, "I was right." In their quest to retrieve *l'ancien glorie,* the French have decided that their role in the world is to be the un-America, the opposing force in the world. The French had plans to disarm Saddam but leave him in place, having spent years trying to clean up Saddam's image enough that they could openly do business with him. They had visions that a big and expensive military action could be rendered unnecessary by their "soft power" skills at negotiations, diplomacy, government-granted economic incentives, and a veto at the United Nations. Their plans were thwarted.

In Germany, on the other hand, there is some good news: The Germans are still afraid of war. Having donned the mantle of pacifist to the world, the Germans have now gone looking for someone to play the role of the Nazi. America was perfect. It was big, pushy, and when it actually initiated a war, the Germans could hardly resist asking, "Okay, who's home to Hitler *now*?"

To pick on Belgium is tantamount to swatting fruit flies with sledgehammers. With the Iraq war largely behind us, the Belgians are back where they started, playing Napoleon in their hometown of Waterloo.

The South Koreans? Ingrates. They're fortunate that America has the good grace not to turn them over to the North.

Canada is America's *France-Next-Door*. The Canadians can't help themselves. They know the United States isn't going to invade them, so they feel empowered—if not entitled—to act as self-consciously superior as possible. Canada's most important paycheck comes from the United States; its national defense is provided *gratis* by the United States; its young people run to the United States to find opportunity; its elderly flock to Florida for sun. Canada's relationship with America is highly beneficial, perhaps essential, and yet the Canadians will persist in criticizing and complaining about America until the last maple tree is tapped dry. If Canada wants to be aligned with France, perhaps we should let them.

What all these nations share is a high percentage of their populations who have come to despise America—because of the war in Iraq, because of America's economic and cultural domination (the new governor of California is as recognizable in Amman, Jordan, as he is in Los Angeles) and because the United States has grown so powerful that no nation has the power to restrain it when it has determined to act.

When the world claimed that America should not invade Iraq, America looked toward the oppressed Iraqi people—and the Middle East threatened by Saddam's shadow—and decided otherwise. America made its own decision; it would not be stopped by the legalistic arguments of Europeans who'd chosen to exclude themselves from the war room.

As America's victory in the major combat phase of the war receded from memory, some chose to revive the argument that the war was unwise—that Saddam should have remained "in his box," as the Europeans were fond of saying. Others, disturbed by our failure to find weapons of mass destruction, claimed it was unjustified, illegal, immoral, a complete blunder. Still others, in the questionable question of Al Gore, asked: "Why did we invade Iraq to catch Osama bin Laden?"

Let's take a short train ride and connect the dots.

On November 23, 2003, the Port Authority of New York and New Jersey, owner of the World Trade Center, the Holland and Lincoln Tunnels, LaGuardia, Newark, and JFK airports, the George Washington Bridge, and just about every other major public transportation facility in the New York-New Jersey area, reopened PATH (Port Authority Trans-Hudson) train service from the Exchange Place Station in Jersey City to the World Trade Center Station in New York City. The "tubes" that carried PATH trains beneath the Hudson to and from New Jersey, first opened in 1909, were damaged but not destroyed in the September 11 attacks. But they were located in the deepest part of the World Trade Center basement, and as a consequence the Port Authority Station was one of the last parts of the complex to be dug out in the months-long cleanup operation. The new $323 million station is a temporary structure, which will be replaced by a permanent station when the World Trade Center is rebuilt.

Even though it is temporary, the PATH station and tracks in the now-empty World Trade Center site were the first major steps in the reconstruction of the Center, rebuilt at the base of what will be new towers, a plaza, and a 9/11 memorial. The architects and urban planners whose vision will replace the twin towers will be building on top of the PATH.

For thousands of commuters who cross the Hudson each day into Manhattan—including me—the return of train service after two years and two months has been a relief. The reopening of the tunnel across the Hudson sped up my commute considerably, and evidently did the same for many thousands of others. Ferry service, the most popular alternative while the PATH was unavailable, is colorful and fun, but the train makes direct subway connections, saving a ten-minute outdoor walk from the ferry dock to the nearest subway station.

In these early weeks of restored rail service, though, the train from Jersey into New York has had another special aspect to recommend it.

Where once the PATH ride was like any other subway journey—rumbling through the dark, arriving in a fluorescent-lit station—now the train emerges from the trans-Hudson tunnel into the broad daylight and the startling sight of the absolute ground floor at Ground Zero. An ordinary commuter route has suddenly become something larger: an up-close exploration of the most traumatic and spectacular act of terror ever visited on the United States—the very spot, the hallowed ground, where 2,752 people died. Passengers find themselves struck by the enormity, the heavy sorrow of the place. When the train emerges from the tube under the river into the empty hole in the ground that was the World Trade Center, the temporary tracks tour an oddly bland Dantesque circle of Hell—death and destruction on a world scale, cleaned up now but still twitching and flinching with raw pain.

We have seen the pictures of the ramp at Ground Zero, from the street to the floor of the pit; now we pass beneath it every day. We have seen pictures of the wall of the "bathtub," also known to engineers as "the slurry wall," studded with 1,500 enormous tieback anchors sunk at angles thirty-five feet into bedrock to hold the wall erect and keep the water out. Now we travel through a portal in that wall. We have seen pictures of all these things that make the pit of the World Trade Center familiar, and now we pass through, all of it in full view from the windows of an ordinary commuter train.

You may be caught up in your everyday travels, carried along by the crowds, moving forward toward the office, but you are no longer simply passing by. You are no longer kept back by barricades and national guardsmen and police; you no longer crane your neck for a fraction of a view, a fleeting image of Ground Zero. Instead, you are thrust into a spot where only months before lay a smoldering mass of broken concrete and ripped steel and burning debris—a spot that became known as "the pile." Here was the spot where nearly three thousand people died—and America realized its vulnerabilities.

Eventually, the dramatic and surprising train ride will be taken for granted, like all the wonders of New York City. But in the early days of the resumption of service, I have heard startled passengers gasp at the sight. My friend Roy, whom you met in the introduction to this book, told me he's seen people break down in tears. I have heard people say they "forgot" where exactly the train would be going, only to be cold-cocked by the sight, left agape as the train car suddenly filled with sunlight. Roy's friend J.R.—the one who had a date to ride the 8 A.M. ferry over to the World Trade Center on September 11—had an angry reaction. "Now tourists are going to be riding the commuter train just to gawk at the spot where I lost thirty friends?"

Gawk is a fair description. I am like other passengers on the run from Jersey City to New York. When the train emerges from darkness into the light, I stand and look, absorbing the details—the stubs of the enormous reinforcing rods visible through the concrete wall of the bathtub, the coarse surfaces that give the structure its embattled appearance—and pondering once again how this happened.

Investigators now know that the critical moment was 7:59 A.M., on September 11, 2001, when Mohammed Atta, aboard American Airlines Flight 11, placed a call on his cell phone to Marwan Al-Shehhi, aboard United Airlines Flight 175. Both planes were on the runway waiting to take off from Boston for Los Angeles. Investigators have not revealed if they know what was said in this last phone call between the hijackers, other than the obvious: a simple confirmation that the plot was on.

In the years it took to build the twin 110-story towers, sixty construction workers died. In the half-hour after the first plane struck the South Tower, more than three times that number—approximately 200 people—were either blown out of the windows of the upper stories or jumped to escape the flames.

All of that explains why George W. Bush is the right president for America.

Bill Clinton was the Brits' favorite president of recent times. The British were shocked and appalled when his heir apparent, Al Gore, lost the presidency to George W. Bush.

And yet after the war, when the British began carping about the still-missing weapons of mass destruction, the Brits failed to take account of what former President Clinton had to say about the tricky issue of those weapons.

As the antiwar, anti-Bush rhetoric heated up in the Democratic Party, Bill Clinton felt compelled to say that he did not entirely disagree with George W. Bush that the time might come that the United States would need to act to remove Saddam Hussein from power in Iraq.

Bill Clinton recognized the threat of Iraq. The four-day bombing campaign he launched during his own presidency proves that he foresaw the need to act to solve the Saddam Hussein problem. As Clinton told Larry King in July 2003, "I thought it was prudent for the president to go to the U.N. and for the U.N. to say you got to let those inspectors in, and this time if you don't cooperate the penalty could be regime change, not just continued sanctions. I mean, we're all more sensitive to any possible stocks of chemical and biological weapons."

Clinton was watching from sidelines as the leading Democratic candidates for president headed for the same rhetorical cliff the

Europeans had already thrown themselves over: that it was unjustified to put Saddam Hussein out of power. What was the logical alternative? That we were better off with Saddam *in* power?

"People can quarrel with whether we should have more troops in Afghanistan or internationalize Iraq or whatever," Clinton said, "but it is incontestable that on the day I left office, there were unaccounted-for stocks of biological and chemical weapons [in Iraq]. We might have destroyed them in '98. We tried to, but we sure as heck didn't know because we never got back in there."

In retrospect, it's interesting to wonder whether President Clinton—whose swagger was of a different order entirely—might have had an easier time of it with the British and European public if he had acted to overthrow Saddam. In any event, it seems delusional to think that after September 11 any American president would be able to live with the threat posed by Saddam Hussein retaining power in Iraq, free to play cat-and-mouse games with inspectors while making side deals with terrorists.

And that leads to the second question: What about proof of a Saddam—al Qaeda connection? Europeans and American Democrats have been trying to pick a fight with President Bush on that score at least since he made his Axis of Evil speech. But when it comes to a terror threat—and the possibility of deaths in the thousands—how much proof is required? The fact is that Saddam Hussein—whose own behavior qualifies him in every meaningful way as a terrorist—had a history of consorting with terrorists in the past, and there is no reason to believe that as soon as our back was turned he would not do so again.

What the Europeans fail to understand—in such overwhelming poll numbers that it appeared they simply *refused* to understand—is that the president of the United States must use his *own* judgment in defending his country, not that of our allies. When a foreign power such as Iraq or al Qaeda poses a threat, as President Bush and his administration judged, we should not be forced to prove the case beyond a reasonable doubt before acting, as if the defense of a nation were akin to the tawdry O.J. Simpson trial. When thousands, perhaps millions, of American lives are at stake, we must require not a *higher* standard of proof, but a much *lower* threshold—a subjective judgment based on the best available estimates of motive, means, and probabilities.

Otherwise, our national security—and the security of the world—could be hamstrung by a legalistic "dream team" like the one the anti-Americans cobbled together on Saddam Hussein's behalf—Dominique de Villepin, Jacques Chirac, Joschka Fischer, Jean Chretien—holding our foreign policy hostage as they litigate and obfuscate every last point to a stalemate in the United Nations, or some phony courtroom in Belgium, or wherever else they see fit.

And it is in the hollowed-out basement structure of the World Trade Center—the very spot where nearly three thousand people died by immolation, by leaping from great heights, or by having the enormous structures collapse on top of them—that proof of the connection between the September 11 attackers and Saddam Hussein can be found. It is here, if we open our eyes, that we can answer Al Gore's question—yes, we invaded Iraq to get Osama bin Laden.

Among the people who died when the twin towers collapsed was the chief of security for the Port Authority of New York and New Jersey, the former head of the FBI's terror fighting counter-intelligence unit: a man named John P. O'Neill.

O'Neill had left the FBI and started his new job less than two weeks before the attacks. On the morning of September 11, at the moment the first plane hit the North Tower, he was in his office there. "He immediately left his office and headed to the lobby of the [North] Tower to determine what had happened, and to assess the damage. A command post was set up in the lobby of the [North] Tower from where he was able to direct the rescue efforts of the first responders. When the second plane hit the [South] Tower, he returned there to coordinate the rescue efforts in that building, and was killed when that building collapsed." So noted the lawsuit filed by O'Neill's wife and children—against al Qaeda, Iraq, and various terrorist entities for the wrongful death of O'Neill. The O'Neills are seeking a billion dollars in damages.

The litigants know it is unlikely that they will ever recover money from the suit. But it provides an effective vehicle to present evidence of the joint terror operations of Saddam Hussein and Osama bin Laden, and to prove the connection forever in the public mind.

There is no way to know for certain what John O'Neill's thoughts were in the time between the first plane's impact on the North Tower and his death in the collapse of the South Tower. Given O'Neill's long and tumultuous career in the FBI, however, he must have known that it was a terrorist attack, and he must have suspected that it was the work of Osama bin Laden and his silent partner Saddam Hussein.

Everything in O'Neill's professional life supports that conclusion. He had been chasing bin Laden and his organization's involvement with Iraq for years. His was one of a few lonely voices trying to warn America of bin Laden's 1998 *fatwa* against the United States. He knew that Saddam Hussein was seeking revenge for the 1991 Gulf War. He had seen proof that bin Laden and his deputy Ayman Al-Zawahiri were in contact with Saddam Hussein for key resources like training in bomb-making and assistance with all-important travel documents. On September 11, 2001, he should still have been engaged in that fight, but his bullheaded determination to press the investigation forward (along with O'Neill's penchant for the high life) led to trouble with his FBI bosses, which culminated in his retirement in the late summer of 2001. Forced out of his FBI counter-intelligence job, he was off the Osama hunt. But in his new job at the World Trade Center, in a supreme coincidence, Osama found him.

John O'Neill was a handsome man, striking and gregarious, given to well-tailored dark suits and crisp white shirts. He was a regular at New York night spots, where he mixed easily with the literary and entertainment crowds, and where he might have been mistaken for just another expense account corporate executive.

But the details in his family's lawsuit—supported by information from his own files and from his professional colleagues in the intelligence community—indicate that O'Neill was no ordinary man. He was one of the few Americans who was keenly aware of the threat that Saddam Hussein and Osama bin Laden posed jointly to America. They shared a common goal—to attack the United States by whatever means could be devised.

O'Neill's lawyers say that they can prove the following assertions:

- Bin Laden's al Qaeda first engaged in contacts with Iraqi intelligence in 1992, the same year Al-Zawahiri's Egyptian Islamic Jihad group spent several days in Baghdad meeting with Iraqi intelligence. Bin Laden and Al-Zawahiri merged their terror groups in 1998, and Al-Zawahiri became bin Laden's deputy.
- The 1993 World Trade Center bombing was planned by Mahmud Abouhalima (later convicted in the bombing) with his uncle Kadri Abu Bakr, who lived in Iraq and was a member of a PLO faction allied with Saddam Hussein.
- Ramzi Ahmed Yousef, "an Iraqi Intelligence agent," traveled to the United States "using travel documents forged in Kuwait during the Iraqi occupation of that country in 1991." Yousef was later convicted as the "mastermind" of the bombing.
- Abdul Rahman Yasin, a U.S. citizen born here to Iraqi parents, but raised in Iraq, was questioned in the 1993 WTC bombing, but before he could be taken into custody he fled to Iraq, where he lived under the protection of Saddam Hussein in defiance of U.S. demands that he return to face trial.

- Al Qaeda terrorists met and conspired in November 1995 with Iraqi intelligence and Iranian Hezbollah members to bomb the Khobar Towers in Dhahran, Saudi Arabia, an event in which nineteen American service people were killed.

- In February 1997, bin Laden publicly merged Iraqi and al Qaeda interests, declaring that "The hearts of the Muslims are filled with hatred toward the United States of America and the American President for American conduct toward Iraq."

- Saddam Hussein, on the advice of his sons—intelligence chief Qusay and fedayeen chief Uday—"concluded that a campaign of terror attacks against the United States, under the banner of bin Laden and al Qaeda, was the most effective means of both deflecting U.S. attempts to topple his regime and obtain[ing] Iraqi revenge."

- In the 1998 *fatwa* ordering Muslims to kill Americans, bin Laden cited among his reasons "the Americans' continuing aggression against the Iraqi people."

- In March 1998, al Qaeda and Baghdad cemented formal relations based on their mutual hatred for America and Saudi Arabia. Bin Laden was invited to Baghdad, where he was spotted by an Italian businessman in the five-star Al Rashid Hotel.

- In the spring of 1998, two of bin Laden's senior commanders spent a week in Baghdad in meetings with Qusay Hussein, the czar of Iraqi intelligence, and got commitments from Iraq to provide training, intelligence, clandestine Saudi border crossings, financial support, and weapons and explosives for al Qaeda.

- During a July 1998 visit, Al-Zawahiri toured a potential site for a new headquarters for bin Laden and al Qaeda, and went to an Iraqi military base and nuclear and chemical weapons facility near Fallujah. "In recognition of bin Laden's and al Qaeda's leadership role in the terrorist war against the United States, Iraqi officials allowed Zawahiri to assume formal command over the al-Nasiyirah training camp."

- To demonstrate its commitment to Iraq and its anti-U.S. policies, in the spring of 1998, al Qaeda planned terrorist bombing attacks on the U.S. embassies in Nairobi, Kenya, and Dar Es Salaam, Tanzania. The bombings were carried out on August 7, 1998, killing 224 people and injuring thousands.

- Following Bill Clinton's four-day airstrike campaign in December 1998, Iraqi trade minister Muhammed Madhi Salah said that he expected terror activity against the United States to increase, and the Arabic newspaper *Al-Quds Al-Arabi* said in an editorial: "President Saddam Hussein . . . will look for support in taking revenge on the United States and Britain by cooperating with Saudi . . . Osama bin Laden, whom the United States considers to be the most wanted man in the world."

  The newspaper added that bin Laden was planning to move to Iraq before the American bombing.

- Iraq offered bin Laden and al Qaeda an open-ended commitment to conduct joint operations against the United States and its "moderate" Arab allies in exchange for an absolute guarantee that bin Laden, al Qaeda, and their allies would not attempt to overthrow Saddam Hussein.

- The October 12, 2000, bombing of the American warship USS *Cole* was a joint Iraqi intelligence–al Qaeda operation.

- On January 22, 2001, the Arabic newspaper *Al Watan Al-Arabi* reported that Saddam Hussein and his sons had called for an Arab alliance to "launch a global terrorist war against the United States and its allies." Hussein called for a "scorched earth" policy.

On the hotly contested matter of whether the Iraqis were involved with the September 11 attacks themselves, President Bush has stopped short of claiming any direct connection.

The family of John O'Neill thought otherwise.

In their lawsuit, they say that Iraq knew in advance that al Qaeda was planning to attack U.S. landmarks and civilians in Washington and New York in September 2001, and that Saddam's regime supported the attacks.

Iraqi newspaper columnist Naeem Abd Mulhalhal, who has been connected with Iraqi intelligence for two decades, wrote in his July 21, 2001 column that bin Laden was making plans to "demolish the Pentagon after he destroys the White House," and that bin Laden would strike America "on the arm that is already hurting," referring to the World Trade Center.

Evidence of Iraqi contributions to the 9/11 attacks included:

- A meeting between Iraqi intelligence agents and September 11 hijackers Zaid Jarrah and Marwan Al-Shehhi in Dubai, UAE; not long after the meeting, both hijackers entered the United States.
- The claim by Czech intelligence sources that on June 2, 2000, Mohammed Atta traveled to Prague to meet other co-conspirators—the day before he flew to Newark International Airport in the United States.

One of the most hotly debated pieces of information throughout the entire 9/11 investigation has to be the purported meeting between Mohammed Atta and Iraqi intelligence agent Al-Ani in Prague from April 8 to April 11, 2001. O'Neill's lawsuit contends that the meeting did in fact take place, asserting that the information has been confirmed by Czech interior minister Stanislav Gross. This claim is still vehemently denied by official U.S. intelligence sources, though the vice president of the United States, Dick Cheney, appears to remain unconvinced that the report is in error.

In addition, O'Neill's suit claims that a general in the Iraqi secret service, Habib Al-Mamouri, was stationed in Rome as an "instructor" for children of Iraqi diplomats, and that during his time there he met with Atta in Rome, Hamburg, and Prague. "Al-Mamouri has not been seen in Rome since July 2001," the lawsuit points out, "shortly after he last met with Atta."

Much of this evidence of cooperation between Iraq and al Qaeda was reported in the *Weekly Standard* in late 2003. The magazine had obtained a copy of a secret document prepared by the staff of Deputy Secretary of Defense Douglas Feith, which compiled and interpreted all known intelligence from U.S. and foreign services on al Qaeda contacts with Iraq. But most of it was left out of official arguments for the war, except for vague references to "cooperation" between al Qaeda and Iraq.

Why this evidence has been omitted from America's official case is open to speculation. It's possible that the administration simply wanted to avoid having to submit every detail of its case to the ever-suspicious court of world opinion—as they are now, alas, under increasing pressure to do. But they must also have known that, after September 11, Americans had no reason to doubt the American government and intelligence community's belief that Iraq, like al Qaeda, was a hostile power that posed a threat to the stability of the Middle East—and thus to America and the world.

Others, of course, saw things differently. But their offense was not that they saw the same facts and came to a different conclusion. It was that the rest of the world refused to concede that America, as the injured party, had the right to decide on its own course of action in preserving international security.

America heard their arguments and rejected them. Instead it acted, with only a few friends and allies—and against strong public opinion—on its own judgment. And today nearly everyone, including most of Bush's strongest critics, concede that the world is better off with Saddam Hussein in American custody.

True, there are good and important arguments in favor of internationalism. In a case like Afghanistan, certainly, the cooperation of a broad coalition could not be underestimated in deposing the brutal Taliban. But America has come to recognize that internationalism may not always be in our best interest—not when it leaves open the possibility that adversarial countries might suddenly be able to stop the United States from taking whatever steps it believes are necessary to protect its people.

With the war long over, and the postwar occupation offering both the long-delayed promise of Iraqi democracy and a daily reminder of the bloody sacrifices of war (for U.S. and coalition troops and civilian workers), President Bush made an official visit to Britain in November 2003. In a major speech at Banqueting Hall in Westminster, he told his world audience: "we did not charge . . . only to retreat."

The next day, the left-wing *Independent* grudgingly admitted that its frequent characterization of Mr. Bush as a tongue-tied moron was probably wrong. "Mr. Bush offered his audience a forceful restatement of his already known views, delivered with a degree of verve, eloquence and even humor that defied his reputation as the least articulate American President since the silent Calvin Coolidge."

The *Independent* and other Bush critics cited "unilateralism"—the crime of acting without international permission—as America's sin. They insisted that America was wrong no matter what reasons it gave. And then, to their frustration, they found themselves left out of the decisions about Iraq—because, to put it simply, they are not Americans. They don't get a vote.

It has been startling to see just how completely our foreign friends have failed to realize that they were *spectators* to the disaster in which Americans were victims. When it comes to September 11 and its aftermath, Americans have the only true claim on ownership. Thanks for the sympathetic sounds, Mr. Chirac, but it was not for France to decide how America should respond to such an attack; nor was it for the British. Their counsel may be welcome, but no one holds a veto over America's actions but Americans themselves.

This fact has led to an oddity of international relations: the growing number of international observers who have taken a passionate interest in the upcoming American presidential elections. The BBC Washington correspondent Katty Kay described the phenomenon on *Meet the Press* in mid-November 2003: "I think actually people do know the other Democratic candidates. We are fascinated in the American elections. We are particularly fascinated this time around, I think, because so many Brits are opposed to George Bush and don't want him to be re-elected, and so they're looking at all the alternatives. I think that, you know, somebody like Wes Clark is playing very well in Britain. People would like to see him win the nomination."

Pity Wes Clark can't count his British votes.

"There's a lot of animosity toward President Bush in Britain," Kay continued. "Sometimes I'm concerned that that animosity toward the administration slipped into a more general anti-Americanism. It's almost as if it's really not cool to like America at the moment. It's become an intellectually lazy trend thing that you can't like anything about America. But at its root is President Bush."

And what is it that the British find so scary about President Bush? The same old message: "They are frightened by policies like the doctrine of preemptive action. They don't like it. But there's also a style thing. There's a sense that he is a unilateralist who has this sort of swagger, who doesn't really appreciate his allies, who hasn't made much effort to bring allies on board."

With their purblind insistence that "appreciating one's allies" is more important than defending one's country—not to mention their infantile focus on issues like *style* and *swagger*—it was clear that our so-called allies had failed to appreciate the dual motivating forces all Americans shared after 9/11: *anger* and *fear*.

It's fear, in my opinion, that has been the more powerful of the two forces. September 11 underscored, in the most dramatic way possible, the vulnerabilities of the United States to the hatred and resentment of others around the world. This hate is so widely and commonly discussed overseas it's usually dismissed, in the euphemistic shorthand, as "anti-Americanism." As many Americans realized for the first time on that morning in 2001, however, this was no mere political position. It was hatred, and it was real.

On one level, it was a hatred that many Americans found essentially inexplicable. If they hate us so much, we could be forgiven for wondering, why does this great tide of immigration—this flood of brothers and sisters and uncles and aunts, mothers, fathers, cousins, friends and neighbors—land on our shores every year? Never mind the Brits and Canadians who flock to American jobs, what about the 1.2 million Arabs in America, a figure that has doubled in the past twenty years?

Even after the immigration clampdown of the post-9/11 era, the number of foreign-born residents in the United States has jumped by three million. How many more would have come had the pipeline not been restricted by security concerns?

And how strong would the chances of further hatred-inspired attacks against America be, if September 11 had not given rise to the inevitable and decisive American military response? Sadly enough, though American forces have liberated the Iraqi people from brutal dictatorship, their gratitude shows little sign of spreading to the wider world. Had there never been an American military campaign in Iraq, the worldwide hatred for America might not have felt like a "blast furnace," as Tim Russert described it on *Meet the Press* one Sunday in late 2003. But it would have been there, the same red-eyed monster we see today. Hating America was an international tradition long before September 11.

We must let the events of September 11 show us the way. The world would like us to forget 9/11, just as they would prefer to forget it, too. They'd like us to forget that those who hate us may eventually try to kill us—because they now know that we will never allow that to happen without exacting a price on those who would attempt it.

The war in Iraq put the world on notice.

America will fight.

ACKNOWLEDGMENTS

Thanks to Judith Regan for signing on; to Cal Morgan for shepherding this book and lending his peerless editing skills; to my son, Jake Gibson, whose research efforts were invaluable; and to Mel Berger of the William Morris Agency for great patience.

Special thanks to those websites and search engines that provide English translations of all the talk going on elsewhere in the world.

INDEX